Managing Conflict at Organizational Interfaces

L. DAVID BROWN
Boston University

Managing Conflict at Organizational Interfaces

ADDISON-WESLEY PUBLISHING COMPANY

Reading, Massachusetts · Menlo Park, California
London · Amsterdam · Don Mills, Ontario · Sydney

THE ADDISON-WESLEY SERIES ON MANAGING HUMAN RESOURCES

Series Editor: John P. Wanous, Michigan State University

Fairness in Selecting Employees
Richard D. Arvey, University of Houston

Organizational Entry: Recruitment, Selection, and Socialization of Newcomers
John P. Wanous, Michigan State University

Increasing Productivity through Performance Appraisal
Gary P. Latham, University of Washington, and Kenneth N. Wexley,
Michigan State University

Managing Conflict at Organizational Interfaces
David Brown, Boston University

Employee Turnover: Causes, Consequences and Control
William H. Mobley, Texas A & M University

Managing Careers
Manuel London, AT&T and Stephen A. Stumpf,
N.Y. University

Library of Congress Cataloging in Publication Data

Brown, L. David (L. Dave)
    Managing conflict at organizational interfaces

    (The Addison-Wesley series on managing human resources)
    Bibliography: p.
    Includes indexes.
    1. Organizational behavior.   2. Organizational change.
3. Social conflict.   I. Title.   II. Series.
HD58.7.B756   658.3'145   82-6762
ISBN 0-201-00884-X   AACR2

ISBN 0-201-00884-X
ABCDEFGHIJ-AL-898765432

Series Foreword

Widespread attention given to the effective management of human resources came of age in the 1970s. As we enter the 1980s, the importance placed on it continues to grow. Personnel departments, which used to be little more than the keepers of employee files, are now moving to the forefront in corporate visibility.

The difficulties encountered in effective human resource management are without parallel. Surveys of managers and top level executives consistently show "human problems" at the top of most lists. The influx of the behavioral sciences into business school programs is further testimony to the active concern now placed on human resources as a crucial element in organizational effectiveness.

The primary objective of this Addison-Wesley series is to articulate new solutions to chronic human resource problems; for example, the selection and entry of newcomers, performance appraisal, leadership, conflict management, career management, and employee turnover. The aim is to communicate with a variety of audiences, including present managers, students as future managers, and fellow professionals in business, government, and academia.

John P. Wanous
Series Editor

To

Jane Covey Brown

with whom I first learned
the reality of constructive conflict

Preface

The ideas in this book have grown out of my work as an organization and community researcher and consultant over the last two decades. I have been particularly interested in social and organizational change, and I have pursued that interest in industrial, educational, governmental, and voluntary organizations; in rural, suburban, and urban communities; and in developed and developing countries. I have been especially concerned with developmental change—and have found that change is often closely tied to conflict. Sometimes change breeds conflict; sometimes conflict breeds change. Effective conflict management is often critical to constructive change processes.

A word about underlying values: I was initially trained in a conceptual and ideological perspective that emphasizes societal consensus, the importance of social order and stability, and the pathological character of conflict. This perspective is particularly congenial to the "haves" of the world—managers, Republicans, Americans—who understandably appreciate present social arrangements. Conceptual perspectives emphasizing societal conflicts of interest, the importance of social change, and the value of conflict are more congenial to "have-nots"—union organizers, Socialists, poor citizens of Third World countries. I am convinced by my experience—particularly my experience in conflict between unequally powerful parties—that the contest perspective

v

is as valuable as the consensus perspective. Long-term organizational effectiveness, democratic values, and social justice can all be enhanced by conflict management activities that recognize fundamental conflicts of interest as well as common goals, the importance of change as well as the need for order, and the value of conflict as well as its problems.

This book differs in several ways from many others about conflict management. First, the concept of interfaces between social subunits is central. While problems of conflict and change are common, they are particularly difficult to understand and manage at social interfaces. Most treatments of conflict focus on the parties rather than on the interface within which they interact. I have tried to develop a general framework that illuminates linkage problems across social systems.

Second, I have tried to deal with both the positive and negative sides of conflict, rather than assume that conflict resolution is always desirable. Too much conflict is usually a more visible problem than too little conflict. However, constructive change often requires productive debate as well as cooperative effort, so I have emphasized strategies and tactics for promoting constructive conflict as well as interventions for reducing destructive fighting.

Third, I have also sought to develop a framework that is applicable to many forms of conflict in many organizational settings, rather than to focus on a narrowly defined conflict situation. I have written chapters on departmental relations, relations between hierarchical levels, relations across cultural differences, relations between different organizations, and relations between combinations of these differences. I have used examples drawn from industrial, public, community, and health organizations. The resulting framework offers analysis and intervention options relevant to many diverse situations.

I owe many people for their support and stimulation as this book has taken shape. I wrote an initial draft while I was teaching at the Case Western Reserve School of Management during 1978, and students in my graduate seminar struggled through that draft and offered many helpful comments. Many people involved in the case studies were generous with their time and thought to improve those chapters; among them Alvin Butler, David Berg, Howard Bowens, Corty Cammann, Hugh Johnston, Bob Kaplan, Bill Pasmore, Tom Wells, and Kathy Wilt. Darlene Malonek Wolfe performed prodigies of emergency typing to prepare the manuscript for the seminar that spring.

I spent the following year on sabbatical at the Public Enterprises Centre for Continuing Education in New Delhi, learning about conflict and change in Indian public enterprises, trade unions, and rural villages, and revising the manuscript in spare moments. I am grateful to my colleagues at the Centre—particularly Rajesh Tandon, Prem Chadha, and Nitish De—for many stimulating conversations about and opportunities to understand conflict and change in India. I am also grateful to the Centre's secretarial staff—Manju Chhabra, R. Chitra, Ravi Gupta, Gracy John, and Sushil Kumar—who puzzled out my handwriting and my American spelling to type another draft of the manuscript.

I have revised the manuscript further since returning to the United States. I am particularly grateful to the hardy souls who plowed through the entire manuscript at various stages. Clay Alderfer, Rosabeth Kanter, Ray Payne, Lou Pondy, and Ken Thomas all offered penetrating comments on the manuscript as a whole. I have not always followed their suggestions, but I have always been stimulated by them. John Wanous, indefatigable series editor, read and commented in detail on no less than four drafts, and enhanced the readability of the book immeasurably by his commitment to clear exposition. Ruth Anderson cheerfully typed the last two drafts, and asked clarifying questions when my prose became more impenetrable than usual. Vince Mahler and Maurice Isserman of the Boston University School of Management Word Processing Center typed the last revision in extraordinarily short order.

My ideas owe much to continuing work with several close colleagues. Clay Alderfer, Alvin Butler, Jane Covey Brown, Barbara Gray Gricar, Bob Kaplan, Rajesh Tandon, and Kathy Wilt have all struggled with me to understand and influence the world. Finally, my family—Jane, Rachel, and Nathan—has put up with "the book," rejoiced at its completion, and continues to teach me about constructive and destructive engagement with other human beings.

Brookline, Massachusetts   L.D.B.
January 1982

Contents

Introduction

1

Organizational interfaces? Good grief! Should they be lubricated with graphite? injected with penicillin? polished with Turtlewax? I inflict this term on the reader because I cannot dream up an adequate alternative. It simply means the meeting grounds where social units come face to face and parties interact. These social units may be groups, departments, or whole organizations, and their contact may be recurrent and well-established or fleeting and episodic. But there is always some kind of interaction between the parties.

Conflict and its management are critical at organizational interfaces. Conflict affects virtually all kinds of organizations—businesses, government agencies, schools, hospitals, law firms, unions, armies, volunteer organizations—but conflict dynamics are more visible in some than in others. Consider the following drama, in which the conflict dynamics are particularly visible:

> On December 15, 1978, the City of Cleveland defaulted on payment of $15.5 million in short-term notes held by six local banks. The city thus achieved the dubious distinction of being the first major American city to default on its notes since the Depression, though others—notably New York—had only missed that title by a whisker. Observers suggested that the consequences of Cleveland's default might include

state control over the city's finances, seriously restricted access to municipal bond markets (at a time when the city was in dire need of capital for rebuilding its deteriorating physical plants), layoffs of public employees and reductions of already inadequate municipal services, and wholesale exodus of the city's remaining business and industrial firms. Default was not seen as a desirable event by anyone.

Cleveland's financial crisis sprang from many sources. Long-term out-migration of upper- and middle-income families left a central city populated by poor ethnic whites on the West Side and poor blacks on the East Side. Deteriorating city services, strong unions, and obsolete technical installations encouraged business and industry departures that further eroded the city's tax base. Voter resistance to income tax increases led to discrepancies between tax revenues and the city's operating expenses. To cover operating costs, city administrations surreptitiously dipped into capital improvement funds to meet current expenses. Shortly before the crisis, the incumbent Administration revealed that the capital investment funds were short $40 million because of these invasions.

In the shorter term, the city's gloomy financial picture was complicated by several other factors. The incumbent Administration had negotiated a settlement with public employee unions characterized by some City Councilmen as a "budget-buster." The city's Municipal Light Plant could not compete with private suppliers of power, and required heavy subsidies from the city. Opinions differed as to the potential future profitability of the Plant, but the Mayor had taken a strong stand against an agreement to sell the Plant negotiated by his predecessor.

The Mayor had been a City Councilman from a white ethnic ward, and he challenged "Big Business" interests vociferously in his campaign. He campaigned vigorously against tax increases and the sale of the Municipal Light Plant, a transaction he described as a deal to benefit business interests at the expense of the poor. The Mayor's staff and close associates were on the whole young and inexperienced in municipal management.

The Cleveland City Council was roughly half black and half white. The President of the Council was a black councilman who had opposed the new Mayor on a variety of issues for years. The Council President favored the sale of the Municipal Light Plant.

Publicity about the missing capital improvement funds and charges of financial mismanagement at City Hall contributed to lowered ratings of the city's bonds on national markets. The six local banks holding the city's notes informed the Administration that they could not responsibly renew the city's notes without evidence of improved financial control over the city's funds.

Several days before the notes were due, the Mayor made a dramatic televised appeal for a tax increase (whose burden, he argued, would be largely borne by Big Business and suburban residents) and for retention of the Municipal Light Plant. The banks avoided public reference to the Plant, but some observers suggested that "fiscal responsibility" required its sale. Conferences between the Mayor, the Council President, and bank representatives were spotlighted by intense media interest as the deadline drew nigh. Credible response to the banks required agreement by both Mayor and Council. A few hours before midnight the Council President pushed a resolution through the Council supporting a tax increase referendum and the sale of the Light Plant. The Mayor rejected the resolution. A counter-resolution for the tax referendum without selling the Light Plant was killed in the Council shortly before midnight. The Council adjourned at midnight. Cleveland was in default.

What can we learn from Cleveland's experience? Although this description does not tell the whole story (different parties have different perspectives), it can help us answer three questions: (1) What is conflict and conflict management? (2) What types of organizational interfaces are critical? (3) Why is conflict at organizational interfaces important?

CONFLICT AND CONFLICT MANAGEMENT

The phenomenon of conflict has drawn much attention from social scientists. The relevant literature is virtually endless and proposes many different definitions. Some definitions of conflict emphasize the conditions that breed disagreement, such as scarce resources or divergent interests; others emphasize the perceptions and feelings arising in conflict, such as stereotypes, hostility, and antagonism; still others focus on the behavior, such as covert resistance or overt aggression (see Pondy, 1967; Schmidt and Kochan, 1972; Katz and Kahn, 1978). The definition used here emphasizes both behavior and interests: *Conflict is incompatible behavior between parties whose interests differ.* In the following paragraphs I discuss interests and behavior in detail, before turning to their interaction.

The concept of interests is complex and widely discussed in the literature. For our purposes, *interests refer to recognized and unrecognized stakes that are affected by the interaction of parties.* Interests may be common when both parties stand to gain from their interaction, or interests may conflict, so that one party gains only at the expense of the other. At organizational interfaces, the parties are in some degree interdependent—and so share some common interests. The Cleveland banks and the City Government, for example, have a general common interest in the continued financial viability of the city and more specific common interests in continued relations as creditor and debtor. Conflicts of interest among parties at organization interfaces are also frequent. The fiscal responsibility desired by the Cleveland banks and the "power to the people" advocated by the Mayor were not easily reconciled. Conflict at organizational interfaces, in short, often involves a mix of conflicting and common interests among the parties, and the kind of interaction may depend on the balance of interests, as perceived by the parties.

It is important to note that parties do not always perceive their own interests accurately. They may not recognize their own immediate interests; they may recognize immediate but not long-term interests; they may confuse their interests with the interests of others (Tilly, 1978). The real interests of the parties are often difficult to establish, and their perceptions of their own and others' interests may be very different from the perceptions of neutral outside observers.

The other element in the definition of conflict is incompatible behavior. *Incompatible behavior refers to actions by one party intended to oppose or frustrate the other party.* This means intentional behavior; accidental frustration of the other party is not included, though continuing "accidents" may be. Incompatible behavior has many levels of intensity: passive lack of support, explicit disagreement and debate, sabotage, violence, and outright warfare. Interests are often obscure, but behavior is relatively easy to see. In the Cleveland situation, for example, actions by the Mayor and the bank presidents escalated from private disagreement to public name-calling and personal attack, duly reported in detail by the media.

When we treat conflicting interest and incompatible behavior as separate dimensions (see Table 1.1), the four possibilities become clear (Deutsch, 1973). *Conflict* is the result of both conflicting interests and incompatible behavior. The Cleveland banks and the Mayor defined their interests differently and behaved accordingly, and so engaged in conflict. If neither conflicting interests nor incompatible behaviors had existed, the result would have been *no conflict.* The six bank creditors, ordinarily competitors, defined their interests as common vis-à-vis the city and acted in harmony. For the conflict and no conflict cells of Table 1.1, interests and behavior are consistent. *Latent conflict* is found when conflicting interests are accompanied by compatible behavior. Some observers charged the Mayor with excessive cooperation with Cleveland's public employee unions, when conflicts of interest required more hard-nosed bargaining. *False conflict* involves common interests but incompatible behavior, so that parties disagree in spite of similar needs. Some observers of Cleveland argued that the struggle between the Mayor and the Council President was based on "misunderstanding of their real interests" or on "personality clashes," since they had a shared interest in the welfare of their common constituencies. Pressures to redefine interests or alter behavior may emerge when major inconsistencies between them become apparent.

TABLE 1.1
Interests and behavior as elements of conflict

		Interests	
		CONFLICTING	COMMON
Behavior	INCOMPATIBLE	CONFLICT (e.g., Cleveland banks and Mayor)	FALSE CONFLICT (e.g., between Mayor and Council President)
	COMPATIBLE	LATENT CONFLICT (e.g., Cleveland Mayor and unions)	NO CONFLICT (e.g., among Cleveland banks)

Organizational interfaces bring together parties with common and conflicting interests, and with potential for compatible or incompatible behavior. In this book the focus is on conflict, the cell at the upper left of Table 1.1; however, the problems presented by latent conflict and false conflict are also considered since they may easily evolve into conflict.

Conflict management requires consideration of the situation, kinds of intervention, and the desired outcomes. Interventions can be designed to promote a variety of values. Some emphasize organizational effectiveness and efficiency (e.g., Filley, 1975; Robbins, 1974); others are concerned with values like learning and creativity (e.g., Argyris and Schon, 1978); still others put social justice and influence by all organizational stakeholders at the center (e.g., Crowfoot and Chesler, 1974; Ackoff, 1974; Laue and Cormick, 1978). The point to be emphasized here is that *conflict management is based on the choice of values, whether those choices are recognized or not.*

Is conflict in itself bad? good? neutral? Much of the social science literature can be divided into two perspectives on conflict. In one tradition, in which social integration and stability are emphasized, conflict is seen as disruptive, dangerous, and indicative of underlying social pathologies. This tradition has been influential in American management circles, and many American managers regard conflict as a problem to be defused or suppressed as quickly as possible. Conflict management strategies from this perspective focus particularly on conflict resolution (e.g., Deutsch, 1973; Filley, 1975). In another important social science tradition, in which social diversity and development are emphasized, conflict is seen as energizing, creative, and evidence of social dynamism. In this tradition conflict management strategies emphasize differentiation and conflict stimulation (Walton, 1969; Robbins, 1974). The assumption in this book is that *conflict may be either good or bad, depending on the circumstances and the values of the observer.* Many of Cleveland's poorer residents were delighted when their Mayor challenged the banks, but the business world verged on apoplexy at the mention of his name. The bank–city confrontation held the seeds of better city management and a more responsive business community, though such constructive outcomes were not visible in the actual events of the default.

Conflict at social interfaces can also be seen in terms of outcomes—the long-term consequences of events at an interface. These outcomes can affect several aspects of the situation: distribution of resources, flow of information, quality of decisions, or future relations among participants. *Positive outcomes* of conflict include expanded understanding of the issues, mobilization of party resources and energies, clarification of competing solutions and creative searches for alternatives, and enhanced ability to work together in the future. In the engagement between the banks and the City of Cleveland were several potentially positive outcomes: expanding the city's financial management resources while improving bank loan security; setting precedents for bank–city cooperation in the face of rapid social change; and promoting better business–government relations in general. Unfortunately, the escalation of the conflict undercut such positive outcomes.

Two forms of *negative outcomes* of conflict are important. In some situations, escalating conflict behavior washes out positive outcomes in a flood of antagonism and hostility. *Too much conflict* produces high energy coupled with antagonistic attitudes,

restricted and distorted flows of information, low-quality decisions based on poor information and one-sided commitments,
and continuing tensions that undercut future relations among
the parties. Conflict between the Mayor and bank presidents in
Cleveland, for example, produced antagonistic mobilizations,
encouraged personal animosities and deadlocked negotiations,
and eventually eroded the city's financial and political credibility.

In other situations, the parties avoid or suppress their differences and so fail to utilize potentially constructive differences
and complementary resources. *Too little conflict* mobilizes little
energy within parties, prevents disagreement and sharing of
controversial information, promotes decision based on inadequate information, perpetuates unchallenged traditions or
myths, and generates fragile relations that cannot face the rigors
of changing circumstances. Negotiations between Cleveland's
Mayor and public employees, for example, produced low-
intensity conflict and a resulting agreement that threatened the
job security of both in the long run.

Conflict outcomes and conflict intensity are the axes of the
graph in Figure 1.1. The curve in the figure represents an
hypothesized relationship between conflict intensity (behavior)
and conflict outcomes for parties with interdependent but different interests. The vertical dashed lines roughly indicate the
ranges of too little, too much, and appropriate intensities of
conflict. The horizontal dashed line indicates the shifting balance

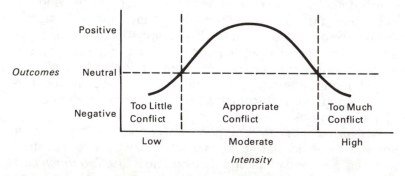

Fig. 1.1. *Conflict intensity and conflict outcomes.*

of positive and negative outcomes. The point where conflict intensity becomes excessive in either direction depends on the specific situation. *Conflict management can require intervention to reduce conflict if there is too much, or intervention to promote conflict if there is too little.* Relations between the Mayor and the City Council, for example, might have been improved by interventions that reduced conflict intensity before it escalated to the point of deadlock. Relations between the Mayor and the public employees, in contrast, might have benefited from interventions to promote more debate of the alternatives facing them. Conflict management activities, in short, should encourage conflict intensity appropriate to the differences and interdependencies of the parties.

TYPES OF INTERFACE

Emphasis on interfaces as the center of attention is uncommon, though not unprecedented (e.g., Chin, 1961; Baker and O'Brien, 1971). It draws attention to several aspects of behavior in organizations that are sometimes ignored. First, interface analysis focuses on the *linkage between parties* rather than on the parties themselves. It is the relationship between the Mayor's Office and the City Council that is critical, not their characteristics as social units. Second, interface analysis highlights the *evolution over time* of linkages between parties rather than a single static snapshot of their relations. Relations between Cleveland City Government and local banks were rooted in a history of interaction, and events surrounding the default were greatly influenced by perceptions of the past and expectations for the future. Finally, interface analysis encourages attention on forces for *interface integration and disintegration.* Interface characteristics are the result of differences and similarities, conflicts and interdependencies. In Cleveland rich and poor, blacks and whites are at once bound together by common fates and separated by conflicting interests. Choosing interfaces as a central concept commits us to examining linkages, relations over time, and forces for disintegration as well as integration. If we consider the Cleveland City Government as an organization, what interfaces played a role in the city's financial crisis?

The last-minute deadlock that preceded the default cast the
Mayor and the Council President as major antagonists. Each
represented a branch of the City Government: The Mayor spoke
for his Administration, and the Council President represented the
Council (or at least the Council majority). Credible response to
the financial crisis by the City Government required interdependent action by both Administration and Council. Thus, contact
between the Mayor's Administration and City Council is a *department interface.* Department interfaces bring together subunits that need each other to achieve organizational goals. Conflict at department interfaces affects task performance—the
Mayor/Council deadlock produced a default neither wanted. In
other settings department interfaces bring together maintenance and production, or hospital laboratory and operating
room. Figure 1.2 depicts a department interface in general terms.
Representatives (smaller circles) interact with each other on behalf of their parties (larger circles) within a more or less well-
defined interface (oval). The parties and their interface are embedded in an organization (triangle), and that organization is
itself embedded within a larger context (rectangle) that may
influence events. In the Cleveland situation, Mayor and Council
President were representatives; Council and Administration

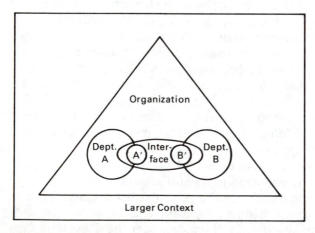

Fig. 1.2. *Department interface.*

were parties; their relationship was an evolving department interface; the City Government was the surrounding organization; city, state, and national environments were the larger context.

The rise of operating costs over revenues set the stage for Cleveland's financial crisis. The rising costs resulted in part from skyrocketing wages paid to public employees. Elected officials (e.g., the Mayor) formally have more organizational power than lower level public employees (e.g., police officers), but in practice the employees had been extremely successful in influencing their financial standing. One important contributor to the financial crisis was the "budget-busting" agreement to increase public employees' wages negotiated by the new Mayor—an event described by some observers as mayoral capitulation to employees at the expense of the taxpayers. The interface between public employees and city officials is an example of a *level interface.* Level interfaces bring together parties with different ranks in the organizational hierarchy. Conflict at level interfaces may result in debilitating power struggles, abdication of leadership responsibilities, or escalating exploitation of the weak by the strong. Other examples of level interfaces are headquarters/ branch relations in large corporations or relations between doctors and nurses in health care organizations. Figure 1.3 portrays in general terms a level interface. As in the previous figure, representatives (small circles) speak for parties (larger circles) at an interface (oval) within a larger organization (triangle) embedded in a context (rectangle). In Figure 1.3, however, the parties and representatives are positioned vertically within the organizational context—reflecting their hierarchical position. In Cleveland, police union officials negotiated with the Mayor at a collective bargaining interface, influenced by events in the City Government and in the larger world of Cleveland, Ohio, and the United States.

The events in Cleveland were also influenced by forces rooted in the larger context. The Mayor campaigned as a representative of "the poor," fighting exploitation by "Big Business." Much discussion was devoted to the effect of the financial crisis on the "rich" and the "poor," and class-related tensions in the

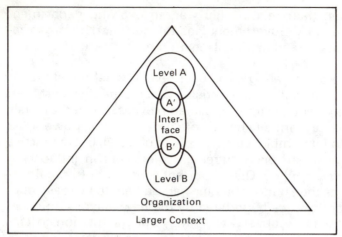

Fig. 1.3. *Level interface.*

larger society colored much of the political maneuvering before the default. The local history of race relations also influenced, albeit less overtly, events leading to the default. The City Council was split on racial dimensions and on postures vis-à-vis the poor, and the eventual midnight deadlock split the Council between blacks and business sympathizers on the one hand and ethnic whites and populists on the other. Organizational contacts between rich and poor and between black and white are examples of *culture interfaces,* whose characteristics are defined by the history of the larger social context. Roles and stereotypes imported from the external culture may produce misunderstanding, bias, or institutionalized discrimination that harm both individuals and organizations. Culture interfaces bring together people defined as different within a shared culture (e.g., men and women, young and old). They may also join representatives of different cultures (e.g., Japanese, North Americans, East Indians) or representatives of different subcultures within a larger society (e.g., blacks and whites in the U.S., Catholics and Protestants in Ireland). Figure 1.4 depicts a culture interface in general terms. Note that the basis for culture differences within the organization is in the larger context (shaded areas), and that representatives of

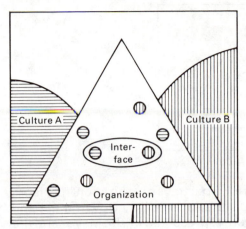

Fig. 1.4. *Culture interface.*

the cultures (shaded small circles) are dispersed in the organization rather than lumped in organizationally-defined parties. Both
City Council and Administration in Cleveland had white and black
members, though they tended to coalesce into culturally defined
parties as the crisis mounted.

The possibility of a default was first raised by six Cleveland
banks holding the city's notes. They argued that responsibility to
their shareholders and to federal regulatory agencies required
they confront financial mismanagement at City Hall. The Mayor,
in contrast, claimed the banks were forcing sale of the Light Plant
to benefit business interests. The banks and the City Government
are separate organizations, and contact between them occurs at
an *organization interface.* Organization interfaces bring together
organizations whose goals and assumptions may be very diverse, though they depend on each other for critical information
or resources. The survival of one or both organizations may be at
stake at their interface—critical resources or information may or
may not be exchanged as a result of their interaction. Thus,
Cleveland failed to satisfy the banks, and the banks refused to
renew the city's notes. Other examples of organization interfaces
include relations between manufacturing firms and their
suppliers of raw materials, or between hospitals and health in-

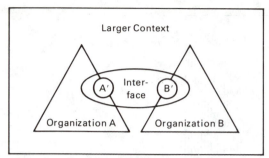

Fig. 1.5. *Organization interface.*

surance corporations. Figure 1.5 portrays organization interfaces in general. In the Cleveland situation, the City Government and six local banks (triangles) were represented by the Mayor and the bank president (small circles) at interface meetings (oval) which were greatly influenced by events in the larger context of city, state, and nation (rectangle).

Each of these interfaces is an abstraction—each emphasizes some aspects of the chaos of charges and countercharges, coalitions and splits, that was Cleveland in late 1978. The reality was far more complex than my description. Many interfaces include elements of several types. The deadlock between the Council President and the Mayor, for example, involved the balance of power among several contending groups as well as two departments: the Mayor and the President embodied different approaches to class differences and represented different ethnic subcultures. In short, the Mayor and the President met at a *complex interface,* where forces associated with several simple interfaces operated together. This book treats simple interfaces first, on the theory that understanding and managing conflict at simple interfaces is good preparation for the more complicated challenges posed by complex interfaces.

THE IMPORTANCE OF CONFLICT AT INTERFACES

So what? Why should you care about interfaces—department, level, culture, organization, complex, or pink with purple spots? How is conflict at an interface different from, and often more important than, a personal argument with a chance acquaintance?

Answer: If you don't manage interface conflicts, interface conflicts will manage you. Persuasive evidence indicates that the importance of managing conflict at the social junctions I call interfaces is increasing rapidly. Consider the following trends.

First, there seems to be a general tendency for organizations to become larger and more internally complex over time (Blau, 1974; Mintzberg, 1979), creating more levels and specialized departments as they grow. *The more numerous and diverse the levels and specialized divisions within an organization, the more opportunities for conflict at their interfaces.* A City Council and a Mayor's Office that represent and respond to different sectors of Cleveland's population, for example, may be expected to have interface conflict. As the City Government expands its services (e.g., fire protection, police services, garbage collection), more coordination problems among subunits are likely. An organization's increasing size and complexity expand the stakes at its internal interfaces.

Second, there is a trend toward increasing interdependence within and between organizations. Organizational performance is affected by the coordination of diverse departments (Galbraith, 1973), and linkages among diverse organizations are important to their performance (e.g., Trist, 1977; Pfeffer and Salancik, 1978). *The more interdependence between parties, the higher the cost of poorly managed conflict at their interface.* The Mayor and the City Council President in Cleveland did not depend on each other for reelection. But coherent policy for the city was impossible unless the two parties could manage their differences. As the city became increasingly dependent on outside sources of funding (e.g., the municipal bond market, the local banks, federal funds), the cost of fragmented decision making became exorbitantly high (e.g., the default). Interdependence increases the stakes of interface conflict.

Third, the rate of social and technological change affecting organizations and societies may still be accelerating. Change is inevitably associated with conflict, as old arrangements become obsolete and new responses must be introduced (Thomas and

Bennis, 1972; Deutsch, 1973). *Social and technological change processes produce conflict at old and new organizational interfaces.* Cleveland's financial crisis emerged from increased costs of services, the decline of the city as an industrial center, and the flight of high- and middle-income populations to the suburbs. The decline of the inner city increased demands for old services (e.g., police and fire protection), reduced resources for providing them, and added previously unknown problems (e.g., the development of a permanently unemployed "underclass"). Change processes alter issues and dynamics at interfaces, and so render old methods of managing conflict obsolete.

Finally, conflict is particularly important at interfaces because, since interfaces are *between social units,* authority, responsibility, and appropriate behavior are often unclear. Within units, lines of authority and shared formal and informal mechanisms regulate the expression of differences. Bowers, Franklin, and Pecorella (1977) suggest that unit boundaries are the "first lines of defense," and so are more valuable to conflict and change. *Interfaces are inherently susceptible to conflict because of their position between social units.* Thus, the shared informal norms and formal structures that constrain behavior within the banking community and within the political world did not operate at the interface between Mayor and bank presidents in Cleveland. Moreover, the Mayor explicitly identified with "the poor," and banks were easily linked to "Big Business," so tensions between rich and poor in Cleveland could easily infect their interface. Interfaces are very vulnerable to the expression of conflicts suppressed in other parts of the social system.

These factors—organizational size and complexity, increasing interdependence, rapid social and technological change, and interface vulnerability to conflict—all contribute to raising the stakes of conflict at organizational interfaces. Managers and administrators of many organizations—public agencies, industrial firms, voluntary organizations, school systems, health organizations—inevitably face conflict at organizational interfaces. This book proposes strategies and tactics for analyzing and managing these conflicts.

THE ORGANIZATION OF THIS BOOK

The next two chapters develop a general framework for analyzing and managing conflict at organizational interfaces. Chapter 2 proposes a framework for analyzing interfaces in terms of the parties, their representatives, the organization of the interface itself, the larger context within which it is embedded, and the dynamics of representative interaction and interface development. This framework provides an analytical outline which is applied to different interfaces in subsequent chapters. Chapter 3 focuses on conflict management, dealing first with the decision to intervene and then with intervention strategies and tactics. The chapter considers alternative intervention targets and strategies for influencing interface events.

Chapters 4, 5, 6, and 7 examine four simple forms of interface, and illustrate interface analysis and conflict management in cases drawn from my experience and that of my colleagues. Chapter 4 deals with department interfaces at which organization subunits interact. Analysis and intervention at department interfaces is described in the case of the Riverview Chemical Works. Chapter 5 examines level interfaces which bring together formally unequal parties. Analysis and intervention at level interfaces is illustrated in the case of the College City Transit Authority. Chapter 6 deals with culture interfaces which bring together representatives of cultural subgroups in the larger society. Conflict analysis and intervention is described in multicultural relations in the South Side Hospital. Chapter 7 focuses on organization interfaces at which interorganizational relations are worked out. The case of the Ghetto Development Corporation describes conflict analysis and management at organization interfaces.

Chapters 8 and 9 are integrative chapters, from two different perspectives. Chapter 8 focuses on complex interfaces compounded of several simple interfaces. Analysis and intervention at complex interfaces are illustrated with cases from earlier chapters. Chapter 9 examines the interventions in the earlier cases— to clarify advantages and disadvantages of different strategies, and to examine the options available to differently positioned conflict managers. This chapter considers intervenor and intervention choices for different situations.

I have chosen the cases in a conscious effort to span a variety of contexts—manufacturing, public service, hospital, and community development organizations—for interface management challenges all kinds of organizations. The chapters are also intended to be cumulative. The first three chapters provide a theoretical base for analysis in the next four. Chapters 4, 5, 6, and 7 focus on dynamics and problems characteristic of particular interfaces, but they also assume the reader's knowledge of earlier chapters. Chapters 8 and 9 integrate all chapters, both theoretical and analytical, to formulate an understanding of conflict management at organizational interfaces that is more generally applicable. The combination of diverse examples and cumulative analysis is designed to provide readers with a framework both sufficiently general and sufficiently complex for application to a variety of real-life organizational problems.

Analyzing Interfaces

2

In this chapter I propose a framework for analyzing conflict at organizational interfaces. The analytic framework and the management strategies described in Chapter 3 are basic to specific forms of interface conflict considered in succeeding chapters.

The chapter begins with an overview of the framework for analysis. The next section covers the elements of that framework in more detail. Then, the interaction of those elements in conflict—the interface dynamics—are analyzed. A summary follows.

A warning: This chapter is necessarily abstract and general. The framework is intended to be general enough to apply to a variety of interfaces and organizational settings—but the price of such generality is abstractness. Readers should not be surprised if this chapter takes them far above the nitty-gritty of real-life struggles. But fear not! There will be more flesh on these abstract bones in later chapters.

A SIMPLE FRAMEWORK

This framework is founded on a simple observation: *Continued interactions between interdependent social units produce interfaces that are social units themselves.* Continued contact encourages the development of boundaries and shared expectations that regulate the interaction of interface participants—the interface itself becomes an organized entity. The United Auto Workers and General Motors, for example, have evolved an interface that persists over time. The same individuals repeatedly participate in negotiations; they negotiate according to shared rules and procedures; and they have stable attitudes toward, and expectations of, each other. Other interfaces are not so well organized. Union organizers and the J.P. Stevens management, for example, shared relatively few expectations and adhered to few formal rules during the company's die-hard resistance to unionization. Interfaces vary substantially in *how much* they are organized, but previous interaction and future interdependence encourage the evolution of an interface as an autonomous linking system.

Conflict at organizational interfaces may involve a bewildering array of people, organizational units, public and private events, visible and invisible forces, and stable and changing relations. In the framework proposed here there are four elements to be analyzed in order to comprehend interface conflicts: *(1) the interface itself, (2) the parties to that interface, (3) the party representatives, and (4) the larger context.* These elements are at different levels of analysis. Representatives are individuals; parties are social units like groups and organizations; the larger context may include organizations or societies; interfaces are intermediate between the parties and the larger context. These different levels of analysis suggest that the causes and effects of conflict itself occur at multiple levels.

Figure 2.1 depicts these four elements at a given moment. Parties (large circles) are social units, such as a GM plant management and a UAW local. Their representatives (small circles), such as union stewards and management negotiators, operate within the interface (oval). Parties and interface are both embedded in a larger context (surrounding rectangle), whose components (e.g., GM Headquarters, UAW International, economic situation) may influence one or several interface elements. This framework is similar to other efforts to analyze conflicts (e.g., Adams, 1976; Thomas, 1976; Katz and Kahn, 1978), though it focuses more than others on interface organization.

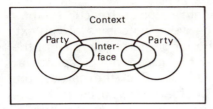

Fig. 2.1. *Interface elements.*

Events at the interface are the result of the interplay of the four elements over time. Some interplays are relatively visible and quick; others move slowly and invisibly. *Interface events involve two dynamics: (1) the long-term interplay of parties, interface context, and interaction outcomes that alter interface definition and organization; and (2) the short-term interaction of representatives' perceptions, communications, and actions within the interface.* In Figure 2.2 arrows are added to Figure 2.1 to demonstrate these two dynamics. The solid arrows between

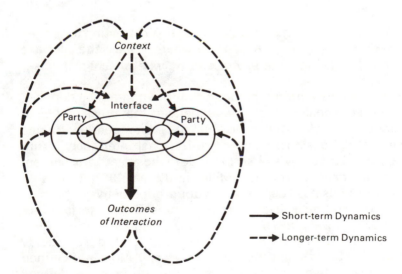

Fig. 2.2. *Dynamics at interfaces.*

representatives depict the immediate action and reaction of their negotiations. The dotted lines between outcomes of context, parties, and interface indicate the longer-term interplay at the larger level of analysis. The two dynamics are not independent: Negotiations between representatives affect the parties, the interface, and even the context—but for the sake of clarity Figure 2.2 illustrates the two dynamics but not all possible interactions.

This framework, in short, has both dynamic and static aspects (see Thomas, 1976). In the next section I deal with interface elements from a static perspective; the section after that is focused on interface dynamics.

INTERFACE ELEMENTS

This section is focused on aspects of interfaces, parties, representatives, and larger contexts relevant to understanding and managing conflict at the interface. The analysis is general, so the concepts can be applied to many different situations.

Interfaces

Two attributes of interfaces are particularly interesting to conflict managers: (1) To what extent and by what criteria is the interface defined? and (2) To what extent and by what mechanisms is it organized?

Interface definition. The definition of an interface depends on the shared goals and interdependencies that press parties to continue to interact. The parties may be interdependent on one or several dimensions. Many organizational interfaces, for instance, are defined by *shared tasks,* for whose accomplishment the parties need each other (Miller and Rice, 1967; Galbraith, 1973). GM's business depends on cooperation between production and marketing divisions, among others. Other interfaces are based on *common social identifications* (e.g., Miller and Rice, 1967; Alderfer, 1976). "Old boy networks" (and more recently women and black support groups) in organizations are defined by shared loyalties and kinship ties. Some interfaces are defined by acceptance of *common authorities* (e.g., Pfeffer and Salancik,

1978). Professional commitments link doctors from different hospitals or specialties even in the face of strong pressures. Still other interfaces are defined by *physical space* (Steele, 1973). Units interact because they are near each other.

These different goals may imply different interface boundaries and composition. In the first, shared tasks, it is tasks that define boundaries and the individuals and resources that are relevant to task accomplishment. Coordinating GM marketing and production may require senior representatives and important resources from both divisions. Interfaces defined by social identification, on the other hand, include individuals and resources on social grounds. "Old boy networks" are full of "old boys": "new boys," "old girls," and others need not apply. At interfaces defined by a common authority, members are expected to meet and live up to standards. Backsliders may be disbarred or defrocked. Interfaces defined by physical space are based on proximity. Neighbors interact, for example.

Interface definitions are not always clear. Strong shared interests can produce clear boundaries, and so can multiple converging criteria. For example, representatives can share tasks, or have common social identifications, or recognize similar authorities, or work in proximity. Subunits with very clear boundaries sometimes evolve such independent identities that parent parties are outraged by their representatives' disloyalty.

Interface organization. Interface organization reflects its capacity to constrain or guide events within it, through varying boundary permeability or regulation of internal activity. In *tightly organized* interfaces external boundaries are comparatively closed and regulation of internal activity is tight; this limits the discretion and flexibility of the representatives. In *loosely organized* interfaces, boundaries are relatively open and regulation is relatively loose. Representatives are free to interact at their own discretion.

All social units depend on inputs from and outputs to their environments for survival, but units vary in how permeable their boundaries are to information, people, or raw materials. Some organizations are relatively closed; information and people are not easily transported across the boundaries of private schools and monasteries, for example (Alderfer and Brown, 1975). Other organizations are relatively open; Unitarian congregations and public high schools, for example, are relatively open to information and people (Alderfer, 1979). Figure 2.3 depicts a continuum of boundary permeability and locates some sample organizations on it.

A variety of mechanisms influence transactions at social boundaries. Organizations create procedures, roles, and even departments to control inputs and outputs of critical information, personnel, and materials. On the input side, procurement departments and procedures control material inputs; research units gather information; legal departments prevent invasions; personnel recruitment, selection, and orientation procedures control the inflow of personnel (e.g., Wanous, 1980). On the output side, quality control and sales departments handle outgoing products; public relations departments and rules about proprietary information control information export; outplacement services and retirement packages regulate outgoing personnel. Such mechanisms control the degree to which organizational boundaries are open to inputs and outputs.

Social units must also provide some internal regulation over the interaction of their subunits if subunits are to continue to perform tasks and solve problems efficiently. For social units that face well-understood problems, stable environments, or situations demanding rapid and well-coordinated responses, relatively tight regulation may be desirable. For example, military organizations emphasize hierarchical control, and assembly lines require well-defined operator activities. On the other hand, units that face novel problems, or have low influence over their

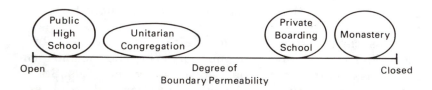

Fig. 2.3. *A continuum of boundary permeability.*

participants, may require relatively loose regulation of activity. Close control over research and development departments, for example, has often reduced rather than improved effectiveness, and imposing ideological discipline on American political parties may undercut their appeal to diverse voters. Figure 2.4 represents a continuum of internal regulation and locates sample organizations on it.

How is internal regulation accomplished? Several mechanisms are frequently used (Brown, 1980). Leaders, for example, regulate activities of their followers: Unit members do what formal (e.g., the military "chain of command") or informal authorities suggest. Formal structures constrain behavior: Unit members follow rules and policies, role and job definitions, incentives or reward systems, and patterns established by "standard operating procedures." Cultural elements also shape behavior: Unit members obey unwritten standards and norms (e.g., "a fair day's work for a fair day's pay"), shared values, and theories and beliefs about appropriate behavior. Technologies and physical arrangements also constrain activity: Unit members act within limits set by space and technical requirements (e.g., the pace and operations of the assembly line). These regulatory mechanisms may work together or at cross-purposes to define acceptable activity for social unit members.

Boundary permeability and internal activity regulation, the factors underlying the *organization* of a social unit, tend to reinforce each other. Closed external boundaries protect tight internal regulation from disruption by external forces; tight regulation supports control of boundary transactions. Open external boundaries permit unexpected inputs and outputs that loosen

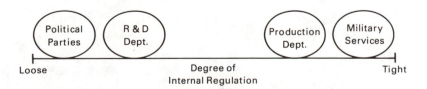

Fig. 2.4. *A continuum of internal regulation.*

internal regulation; loose internal regulation allows open exchanges of inputs and outputs. Figure 2.5 plots the continua of Figures 2.3 and 2.4 against each other to illustrate this link. Note that social units with closed boundaries (private boarding schools, monasteries) tend to be tightly regulated, and units with tight internal regulations (production departments, military organizations) tend to have closed boundaries. In contrast, social units with open boundaries (public schools, Unitarian congregations) are often loosely regulated, and units with loose internal

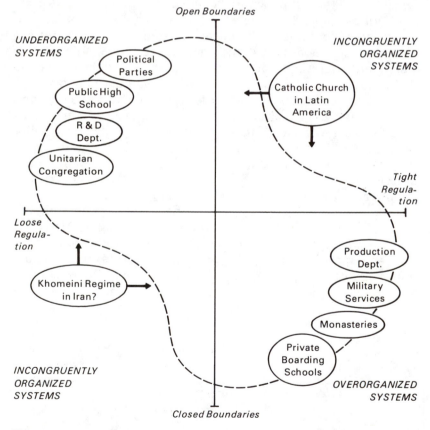

Fig. 2.5. *A continuum of organization.*

regulations (research and development departments, political parties) often have open boundaries.

What of the other quadrants in Figure 2.5? Is it possible to have closed boundaries and loose internal regulation; or open boundaries and tight internal regulation? Incongruent organization seems theoretically possible, but empirically unstable. The Khomeini Regime in Iran, for example, has been relatively closed to the external world, but it also appears loosely regulated internally, as different factions struggle for power. In time that regime might be expected to move either toward more open boundaries or toward tighter internal controls, as indicated by the arrows in Figure 2.5. The Catholic Church, in contrast, has a long history of tight regulation of its priesthood, but many priests in Latin America have been radicalized by the plight of their parishioners. Institutional boundaries open to information and influence at lower levels have embroiled the Church in political quandaries that may produce efforts to close those boundaries, or efforts to loosen internal regulation, or both.

The dashed line in Figure 2.5 represents the area of viable social unit organization. What is optimal depends on the tasks facing the unit, the people within it, and the context in which it is embedded. For some units tight organization is appropriate; for others loose organization is desirable; for still others incongruent organization may be necessary. Interface organizations that fall *outside* the dashed line are likely to display problems associated with being overorganized, underorganized, or incongruently organized.

But what of interfaces? This discussion has focused more on organizational systems than interfaces. But the concept of "organization" defined in the preceding paragraphs is central for understanding interfaces and interface conflict. How do the characteristic problems in underorganized or overorganized social units (Alderfer, 1976, 1979; Brown, 1980) affect interfaces?

Underorganized interfaces typically have ill-defined and excessively open external boundaries. New information from parties or context cannot be filtered to extract relevant or nondisruptive inputs, and information outputs cannot be controlled to prevent inappropriate "leaks." Entry and exit of representatives cannot be easily regulated, so late arrivals, inappropriate recruits, early departures, and loss of critical personnel are constant problems. Desirable resources are difficult to keep in and disruptive invasions are difficult to keep out. When boundaries are sufficiently permeable to outside invasion the interface becomes indistinguishable from the chaotic context it was created to manage.

The internal regulation of underorganized interfaces is excessively loose. There is little agreement about who has authority, and interface goals are undefined or conflicting. Formal regulatory mechanisms are not well-developed: Representative roles are fragmented, conflicted, or undefined, and procedures for handling issues are unclear or ineffectual. Informal mechanisms provide few clear constraints: Theories and values about the interface are not shared; representatives believe that chaos is imminent, so fighting or fleeing are appropriate; cultural differences based in the invading environment are more important than task differences.

The combination of open external boundaries and loose internal regulation provides little direction or guidance for representatives. Several problems are characteristic within underorganized interfaces. Resources are typically in short supply; the interface lacks personnel, information, energy, and time. Available energy is diffused by the lack of clear focus and the ever-present potential for leaving the system. Finally, differences easily lead to two forms of negative conflict permitted by loose organization: (1) *withdrawal* from differences and (2) *escalation* of conflict.

Overorganized interfaces, in contrast, have boundaries that are clearly defined and excessively closed. Information is not easily imported or exported, and interface mechanisms hamper entry and exit of representatives. Sufficiently impermeable boundaries may slow interface response to a crawl—representatives and activities gradually become pickled in their own slowly curdling juices.

The internal regulation of overorganized interfaces is correspondingly tight. Leadership is centralized and unquestioned. Interface goals are well-defined, unambiguous, and conservative. Formal mechanisms clearly constrain activity: Roles are well-defined and enforced, and rules are detailed, well-understood, and seldom violated. Informal expectations also

guide behavior: Theories and values are shared among all representatives; beliefs in the continuation of the interface and the
dependability of leadership prevail; task differences related to
dominant interface goals supersede culture differences.

The combination of closed boundaries and tight regulation
severely restrict the representatives' discretion at overorganized
interfaces, and activity is largely predictable. Several problems
are characteristic of overorganized interfaces. Innovations are in
short supply, which presents serious problems when contexts
and parties face rapid change. Representatives' energies are
well-directed within traditional paths, but suppressed if they
move in other directions. Overt conflict tends to be suppressed
by tight organization and closed boundaries, often resulting in
little productive examination of differences.

The characteristics of underorganized and overorganized interfaces are compared in Table 2.1, which summarizes attributes
drawn from discussions by Alderfer (1979) and Brown (1980).
Appropriately organized interfaces lie somewhere between the
two extremes.

TABLE 2.1*
Characteristics of underorganized and overorganized interfaces

ATTRIBUTE	UNDERORGANIZED INTERFACE	OVERORGANIZED INTERFACE
Boundary permeability		
• Inputs	Open to disruptive inputs of information, resources, people	Closed to necessary inputs of information, resources, people
• Outputs	Open to "leaks" of critical energy, information, people	Closed to export of problem energy, information, people
Interface organization		
• Leadership	No clear authority; competing authorities	Centralized, unquestioned authority
• Goals	No clear goals; multiple conflicting goals	Goals clear but conservative and not subject to challenge

TABLE 2.1 (continued)

Characteristics of underorganized and overorganized interfaces

ATTRIBUTE	UNDERORGANIZED INTERFACE	OVERORGANIZED INTERFACE
• Formal structure	Fragmented, conflicted, isolated, or undefined roles	Well-defined and clearly enforced roles
	Poorly defined ineffectual rules and procedures	Rules and procedures defined and enforced in detail
• Informal culture	Values and theories not articulated or conflicting	Values and theories coherent, shared, and conservative
	Feeling that chaos is imminent and fight/flight is appropriate	Feelings that interface will continue and conformity is required
• Technology	Not routine; artistic; poorly understood work procedures	Routine; assembly-line; well-understood work procedures
• Relevant differences	Culture differences are critical; environment dominates	Task differences are critical; interface goals dominate
Critical problems		
• Resources	Interface is resource-poor, and needs more to survive	Interface is innovation-poor, and needs more to survive
• Energy	Energy is diffused, leaked, poorly channeled	Energy is directed but restricted and constrained
• Conflict	Differences produce withdrawal or escalation that threaten interface continuation	Differences produce suppression or harmonizing that prevent exploration or constructive conflict

This table is based on Alderfer (1979) and Brown (1980).

Parties

Parties are social units with different interests but an interdependent fate that compels them to interact. Parties in this analysis are usually groups or organizations rather than individuals. Although organizational conflict ordinarily involves individuals, many of the most problematic conflicts in organizations involve *individuals acting for groups.* This section deals with characteristics of groups; the following section focuses on the individuals who represent the groups.

What attributes of parties are relevant to conflict at their interfaces? The attributes that are relevant vary according to the situation, but at least two questions should be asked: (1) What are the interests of the parties? and (2) What internal party characteristics influence interface events?

The *interests* of the parties theoretically range from the wholly conflicting, so that gain by one is reflected in loss to the other, to the wholly common, so that gains by one party automatically confer gains on the other. In practice most interface situations involve *mixed interests.* The parties have some common and some conflicting interests (Deutsch, 1973). Interface parties are by definition interdependent, and so share some common interests. The United States and Russia have many conflicting interests, but they have a common interest in limiting conflict that threatens the world ecosystem—neither wants sole control of a global slag heap. Analyzing the mix of common and conflicting interests between the parties is critical to understanding interface conflicts and their outcome possibilities.

The interests visible to an outside observer are often different from those visible to party members and representatives. Parties sometimes overemphasize differences and fail to recognize common interests—"better dead than Red" polarizes the options and encourages conflict escalation without recognizing common ground. Parties also sometimes overemphasize similarities and fail to recognize important differences—"We're all the same under the skin" emphasizes common interests without taking significant differences into account, and so paves the way for avoiding or suppressing conflict. The *perceived* mix of common and conflicting interests is crucial to explaining party behavior; the *possible* mix is equally important for altering that behavior.

Analysis of parties' interests includes how *important* interdependencies are to them. Some interfaces are important to both, so each will commit resources and power to representatives. Other interfaces are important only to one party, and so the other may not invest resources in representatives and interface management.

The relevant *internal characteristics* of parties depend on the situation. Party definition and organization, for example, influence events at the interface. Parties mobilized for conflict display clearly relevant internal characteristics: high internal cohesion, concern with tasks, relatively autocratic leadership, tight structure, and member conformity and loyalty to present a "united front" (Schein, 1970). Such tightly organized social units are more prone to participate in or even provoke interface conflict (Deutsch, 1973). Parties with low cohesion, high concern for people, relatively democratic leadership, loose structure, and a "fragmented front" may be more prone to avoiding differences at interfaces.

Also important are a party's *attitudes* and feelings about itself and other parties. Research on intergroup relations suggests that parties in conflict develop unrealistically positive perceptions of themselves and unrealistically negative perceptions of the other party (Schein, 1970; Blake and Mouton, 1961). These stereotypes justify provocative actions that are blamed on the other—"We attacked them in self-defense!" In contrast, overly positive stereotypes of the other parties ("We can always trust them to look after our interests") or overly negative self-perceptions ("We don't know enough about the situation to question them") may promote withdrawal from or suppression of conflict.

Parties' organization, interests, internal characteristics, and attitudes do not represent an exhaustive list of attributes relevant to interface conflict. These attributes are often relevant, but others may be critical to specific cases.

Representatives

Actual negotiations at organizational interfaces are carried out by individuals who represent the parties. Events at the interface are influenced by the roles individuals occupy and their personal skills and characteristics.

Representatives at organizational interfaces occupy *boundary roles,* so they must represent their parties to the external world. Such roles inevitably create conflict and ambiguity, for individuals must respond both to expectations of their own parties and to expectations of representatives of other parties (Kahn et al., 1964; Adams, 1976). Boundary roles vary widely in the discretion and power they provide their occupants. At one pole, representatives may have much discretion to deal with unforeseen interface problems, and considerable influence within their parties because they deal with issues critical to party survival. Representatives in such roles may be accorded considerable formal or informal power within their parties; top managers are frequently involved in negotiations with powerful unions, for example. At the other extreme, roles may be defined that allow relatively little autonomy, power, or discretion to representatives. Where activities at the subunit boundary are relatively routine and unimportant, roles may be defined that provide little autonomy or influence; welfare case workers, for example, have limited discretion and power. Links between representatives and their parties greatly influence the former's effectiveness at the interface. Close party supervision, for example, increases the press for bargaining and "hard tactics" by representatives who must demonstrate their loyalty; distrust between party and representative consequently can breed distrust at the interface (Adams, 1976). Boundary roles offer opportunities for autonomy and power, but those opportunities are counterbalanced by ambiguity, stress, and continual conflict (Miles, 1980).

Personal characteristics—traits and skills—of representatives also play a role in interface events. One review of research on conflict found that some personal traits (e.g., egalitarianism, trust, open-mindedness, tolerance for ambiguity, need for achievement, favorable view of human nature) seem to be associated with cooperation rather than costly conflict (Terhune, 1970). But Terhune also found that situations involving conflicting interests, fear, and competitive behavior reduced the effect of personal characteristics. Under conditions of high threat, people act competitively no matter what their personal characteristics.

The skills of individual representatives also influence events at the interface. Different conflict situations call for different tactics: Walton and McKersie (1965) argue that *bargaining tactics* (in situations dominated by conflicting interests) involve selective misrepresentation, withholding information, commitment to positions that reduce flexible discussion, and threats and other coercive tactics. On the other hand, *problem-solving tactics* (when common interests prevail) require exchanges of accurate information, flexible search for alternative solutions that meet the needs of both parties, and willingness to influence and be influenced on the basis of trust. These tactics are quite different, and representatives are seldom equally skilled at both. Bargaining tactics undermine the preconditions for problem-solving, so that lack of problem-solving skills on the part of one or both representatives may ensure bargaining even in situations where problem-solving is possible.

The kind of representative behavior at interfaces is determined by the joint operation of the elements of formal roles and personal characteristics, though in a given situation some elements will contribute more than others.

Context

The context is the whole field within which both interface and parties are embedded. The *immediate context* includes the larger social unit or units of which the parties are subunits, as well as third parties interested in the interface. The *larger context* includes social, legal, economic, and political forces that create opportunities for and constraints on the interface.

In the immediate context the *larger social unit* may contain one or both parties. When both parties are part of the same social unit, the characteristics of that unit may greatly influence the parties and their interface. Organizational hierarchies often in-fluence interface conflict: Referring a dispute to a common superior is a common way of resolving differences (Galbraith, 1973), and competition among groups encouraged by their bos-ses is also common. Organizational reward systems can em-phasize common or conflicting interests among parties. In gen-eral, membership in a common larger unit establishes some commonalities across parties: They share a common organiza-tional culture and a common fate if the organization does not survive.

Larger unit characteristics also affect parties that come from different units, so that the parties are themselves representatives of larger wholes. Larger unit characteristics in such situations can sharpen the differences between parties, while the moderating influence of common unit membership is lost. In either case, it is important to recognize the position of parties in larger social units, and the effect of that position on their interaction.

Third parties are social units interested in, but not directly involved in, interface events. The adjective "third" implies that they differ from the two primary parties, though the distinction may be blurred as parties recruit allies and supporters. Laue and Cormick (1978) have suggested a typology of third-party roles: Activists are committed to one party; advocates understand both sides but ally with one; mediators are neutral go-betweens who promote communication; researchers seek valid information about the situation; enforcers maintain compliance to accepted ground rules. Third parties can affect events at the interface either directly, by intervening to influence representative be-havior in some fashion; or indirectly, through recognized willingness to intervene under certain circumstances. Thus the federal government influences collective bargaining both by di-rect intervention and by indirect influence, that is, its potential for direct action.

The effects of the *larger context* may be difficult to predict or even recognize in events at the interface. Trends in the larger context—economic cycles, the emergence of OPEC, the swing to political conservatism, consumer preferences for smaller cars—often baffle the most sophisticated analysts, and few social units have the resources to track all the trends that might influence their futures. But studies of social conflict (e.g., Paige, 1975) suggest that understanding large-scale contextual forces may be critical to understanding the problems involved at the interface.

This section is a general discussion of the characteristics of interfaces, parties, representatives, and context relevant to understanding conflict at interfaces. Table 2.2 is a summary in the form of diagnostic questions for analyzing specific interfaces.

TABLE 2.2
Diagnostic questions: interface elements

Interface
How is the interface defined?
• What goals are shared and what interdependencies are important (tasks, social identifications, common authorities, physical space)?
• What is included in the interface (people, resources)?
• How clearly defined (by what criteria) are interface boundaries?
How is the interface organized?
• How open or closed are interface boundaries? by what mechanisms?
• How tight or loose is interface regulation of activity? by what mechanisms?
• What kind of interface organization is created by the combination of boundary permeability and internal regulation? Is it appropriate to interface activity? overorganized? underorganized?

Parties
What interests do the parties bring to the interface?
• What is the mix of conflicting and common interests?
• What interests are perceived and what not perceived?
• How large are the stakes at issue? Are the parties equally interested?
What internal characteristics of the parties are relevant?
• To what extent are parties mobilized or unmobilized for conflict?
• Do parties have unrealistic stereotypes of themselves or others?

TABLE 2.2   (continued)
Diagnostic questions: interface elements

Representatives

How are representative roles defined?
- What responsibilities and expectations are important?
- What resources, discretion, and autonomy are available?

How do personal representative characteristics affect events?
- What are their relevant personal traits and characteristics?
- What are their relevant skills and tactical competencies?

Context

How does the next level of social unit affect interface events?
- If both parties belong to the same unit, how do hierarchies, reward systems, and other unit features affect relations?
- If parties belong to different larger units, how do those memberships affect interface events?

What part do third parties play at the interface?
- What stances do they take vis-à-vis the parties?
- Do they intervene directly or indirectly?

How does the larger context affect interface events?

The questions follow the order of presentation in this section, which is not necessarily the most appropriate order for diagnostic purposes. We shall return later to diagnostic strategies appropriate to specific cases.

INTERFACE DYNAMICS

Two interlinked dynamics affect events at interfaces. Implicit in the term "dynamics" is the notion of *time:* The focus here is on the interaction of interface events and interface elements in a continuing stream of events that constitute a multileveled history of the interface. At one level is the interaction of representatives' perceptions and action that produces immediate conflict outcomes. At a larger level is the interplay of those outcomes with parties and context to produce stable or changing interfaces over time. Three cases of unproductive conflict illustrate the two levels of dynamics.

The first case focuses on union-management relations that escalated into too much conflict:

In 1972 the General Motors Assembly Plant at Lordstown, Ohio, was the newest and fastest assembly line in the country, built to supply the growing demand for smaller cars. In 1970 plant operators were recognized by management for high quality production. In 1971 a new management team from the GM Assembly Division took over the plant and began to reorganize it "to live up to its potential." Management viewed the changes as largely job redesigns for greater efficiency, but workers claimed management laid off workers, speeded up the line, and overwhelmed workers with extra work.

Angry workers complained; grievances soared from 100 before GMAD took over to 5000. Cars began coming off the line with uncommon defects: keys broken off in locks, gearshifts broken off, windshields broken. Dealers filed more complaints about cars from Lordstown than from all other GM assembly plants combined. In February, 1972, the union voted by 97% to strike. By March, with the strike still in effect, plant management estimated the cost of the conflict at about $45 million in lost production alone (Lee, 1974; Lodge, 1975; Miles, 1980).

The second case involves withdrawal from conflict in a consortium of schools:

In the late sixties many theological schools faced serious declines in student applications and support from parent churches. The combination of ecumenical interests, need to share resources, and the possibility of joint educational innovations prompted seven schools in the same geographical area to create a Consortium to share resources and experiment with common courses and projects.

Over the next several years the Consortium hired two full-time professional staff members, and launched a series of joint programs: shared library services, cross-registered courses, special joint educational events, innovative internships, special access to resources available at only one

school, and so on. A Plenary Council composed of adminis-
trators, faculty, and students from each school was nomi-
nally in charge of Consortium affairs, though day-to-day
control was vested in the staff and a smaller Executive Coun-
cil. The largest two schools, who initially proposed the Con-
sortium, believed it sufficiently successful to be worth ex-
panding into a statewide institution. But even as the staff
planned the expansion, participation in projects and Consor-
tium meetings by several smaller schools was declining.
Those schools had expressed some reservations in Plenary
Council meetings, but the larger schools were considerably
shocked when several schools proposed at a Council meet-
ing to withdraw altogether from the Consortium (Brown,
Aram, and Bachner, 1974).

Finally, the third case involves conflict suppression among
upper managers of an industrial firm.

The Mercury Corporation was a multi-billion dollar chemical
company, divided into divisions financially controlled by
central headquarters but otherwise largely autonomous. In
the late sixties management formed a New Business Divi-
sion to generate and commercialize new technologies that
could then be turned over to existing divisions. The New
Business Division was deemed necessary because the di-
visions were conservative about commercially untested
products.

Relations among the "barons" of the different divisions were
fiercely competitive, as each preserved the territory and
resources of his division to meet divisional goals and profit
objectives. Divisional performance and achievements were
matters of intense concern to divisional managers and to top
management. The Corporation continued to grow, in large
part because of some important new products. But those
products did not come from the New Business Division. After
ten years and twenty million dollars, the New Business Divi-
sion had yet to produce new business of any consequence.
Yet it remained in operation, without being criticized by top
management for its failure to produce (Argyris and Schon,
1978).

These three cases present different problems in diverse organizational settings. But in each the problems emerged from the interaction of representatives and the interplay of interface elements over a considerable period of time. In the following pages I examine the two levels of interface dynamics that influence behavior over time.

Dynamics of Representative Behavior

Patterns of interaction between representatives may take either of two forms, depending on how representatives conceive their interests. In the terms of Walton and McKersie (1965), and as referred to above, representatives engage in *bargaining* when they respond primarily to conflicting interests, and in *problem-solving* if they respond primarily to common interests. Bargaining often involves suspicion or distrust, guarded or distorted information exchanges, and "hard-ball" tactics of influence. Some of the sales and production departments studied by Walton, Dutton, and Fitch (1966), for example, were constantly jockeying for advantage over each other. Problem-solving, in contrast, often involves trust and friendliness among representatives, open and accurate exchanges of information, and largely cooperative tactics. Other sales and production departments in the same study displayed more problem-solving behavior. Some situations, where the interests of the parties are clearly common or conflicting, require one mode or the other. But in many more situations representatives have considerable latitude for seeing the conflict in *either* bargaining or problem-solving terms (Deutsch, 1973). Walton, Dutton, and Fitch's (1966) sales and production departments could and did see very similar situations in quite different terms.

Problem-solving and bargaining may both produce appropriate conflict between representatives. But either may also produce negative outcomes. Bargaining particularly is likely to produce problems of too much conflict; problem-solving can produce problems of too little conflict. Either pattern may be relatively stable, maintaining relatively similar levels of conflict over long periods of time. But interplay of representatives' perceptions, communications, and actions may also lead to dramatic escalation or suppression of conflict.

Figure 2.6 depicts five different patterns of perception and interaction between representatives (circles). The first two patterns (A) involve productive conflict. In problem-solving, for example, the arrows representing interactions reflect open and undistorted patterns of exchange. In bargaining, shorter arrows reflect more guarded interaction, but interaction that continues in a common direction within interface constraints.

In interaction patterns characterized by too much conflict (B), representatives' perceptions and actions combine to create increasing distance and escalating tensions. In this pattern the arrows meet head-on and rebound in opposite directions. At Lordstown, for example, managers expanded jobs and sped up the assembly line to reach planned line capacity; workers responded with resistance and grievances; managers increased the pressure for productivity; workers began slowdowns and sabotage; managers shortened hours and pay in retaliation; workers struck. Increasing distrust and antagonism on both sides, decreased and distorted communications, and coercive influence attempts interacted to fuel conflict escalation which each side blamed on the other.

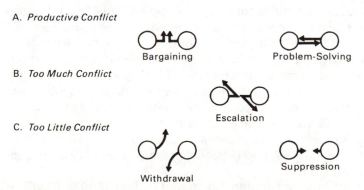

A. *Productive Conflict*

Bargaining

Problem-Solving

B. *Too Much Conflict*

Escalation

C. *Too Little Conflict*

Withdrawal

Suppression

Fig. 2.6. *Dynamics of representatives' interaction.*

Too little conflict between representatives may take two forms (C). Withdrawal involves avoiding problematic differences, portrayed in Figure 2.6 by arrows actively directed away from the other representative. In the Consortium, for example, small school representatives felt unable to challenge large schools' representatives; representatives in general were unwilling to discuss difficulties; representatives who broached problems were reassured or politely ignored; representatives happy with the status quo perpetuated it largely in ignorance of others' dissatisfactions; small school representatives eventually came to believe that total withdrawal was the only answer to their difficulties. Assumed common interests, personal preferences for cooperative interaction (e.g., "turning the other cheek"), and reduced communications all contributed to patterns of avoidance that threatened to become total withdrawal from each other.

Another form of too little conflict is suppression, in which parties deny their differences and act as if their interests were all common. This pattern is represented in Figure 2.6 by arrows that never actually engage the other party. In the Mercury Corporation, for example, the general rule of close top management control over divisional target setting and performance was mysteriously but regularly violated for the New Business Division. Potential challenges were suppressed because of a long history of struggle between top management and divisional "barons" over innovative new products. Challenging the New Business Division performance would take the lid off a series of failures (which no one wanted to discuss), and bring to light the endemic distrust and manipulation in relations between top management and divisional barons. Furthermore, the long-term suppression of information resulted in no one really understanding what was going on—although everyone knew enough to avoid the issue of the Division's performance. Suppression of conflict reduces flows of information, propagates myths and stereotypic perceptions of other parties, and constricts areas for activity and especially innovation.

Perceptions, communications, and actions tend to interlock in patterns of mutually reinforcing interpersonal relations among representatives. Those cycles may promote stable repetitions of recurrent interaction, or rapid change. The cycles may also produce productive conflict, or explosively problematic outcomes.

Dynamics of Interface Evolution

The pattern of representative behavior is easy to see; actual individuals act and react or report perceptions in interpersonal dynamics that are readily observable. But those dynamics are embedded in and constrained by less visible forces that define and organize the interface, and that interface also evolves— although less visibly and less quickly.

Interfaces become more or less defined and organized over time as a consequence of representative interactions, changes in the external context, and developments within one or both parties. Changes at the interface may be the result of direct impacts by other elements. But over time different interface elements also interact to influence one another. Events at the interface feed back to influence the external context or conceptions of party interests and so contribute to looser, or tighter, interface organization in the future.

Figure 2.7 depicts interfaces associated with the patterns of conflict portrayed in Figure 2.6. In productive conflict (A), interfaces typically exhibit moderately open boundaries and moderate internal regulation (the dashed ovals in Figure 2.7). In productive bargaining or problem-solving, there is enough control of boundary permeability to insure exchange of relevant inputs and outputs without permitting disruption or leakage, and enough internal regulation to prevent escalation or withdrawal without suppressing critical differences.

Too much conflict, in contrast, promotes interfaces that are poorly defined and loosely organized (B). As tensions and interpersonal conflict increased at Lordstown, each party became more mobilized against the "intolerable" actions of the other (see heavy boundaries of parties). Each party looked to external allies for support (GMAD to the Corporation, the union to the UAW). Increasingly coercive tactics by representatives contributed to the decline of interface organization to the point where it

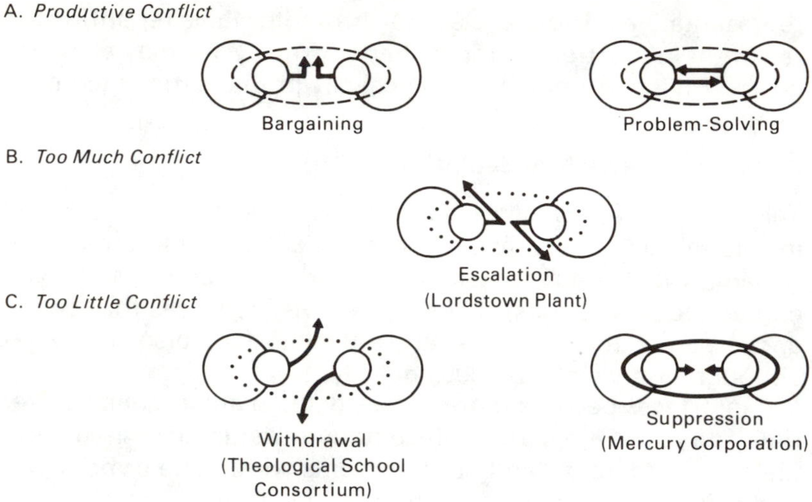

A. *Productive Conflict*

Bargaining   Problem-Solving

B. *Too Much Conflict*

Escalation
(Lordstown Plant)

C. *Too Little Conflict*

Withdrawal   Suppression
(Theological School   (Mercury Corporation)
Consortium)

Fig. 2.7. *Dynamics of interface development.*

became underorganized for the conflict involved (dotted oval in Figure 2.7). The combination of factors all helped to disorganize the interface, and so undermine the possibility of future productive relations.

Too little conflict is associated with two different kinds of interface evolution (C). On the one hand, the interface may become so loosely organized that it permits the withdrawal and loss of critical resources. Failure to confront different interests of smaller schools in the Consortium gradually mobilized some parties against further participation. This trend was reinforced by the doubts of parent churches as a contextual force. Over time the Consortium as an interface became underorganized (dotted oval in Figure 2.7), and so vulnerable to organizational withdrawal as well as representative avoidance of important issues.

On the other hand, the interface may become so tightly organized that it suppresses the expression of differences. The combination of the divisionalized structure of the Mercury Corporation, with the need for parties to avoid association with failure, and the history of representatives' avoidance of New Business Division performance, all contributed to the overorganization of the Division's interface with top management (heavy oval in Figure 2.7). That overorganization suppressed much relevant information and debate.

Events at organizational interfaces are affected by two kinds of dynamics that operate at different levels with different time perspectives: (1) a highly visible, rapid-fire exchange of actions and perceptions between representatives, and (2) a less visible, slowly evolving interplay among context, parties, and outcomes of representative behavior that alters the organization and definition of the interface. Table 2.3 summarizes diagnostic questions for analyzing the dynamics of interface elements at both levels.

TABLE 2.3
Diagnostic questions: interface dynamics

Dynamics of representative behavior

How do representative perceptions, communications, and actions interact?
- bargaining: negative perceptions, guarded communications, coercive tactics?
- problem-solving: positive perceptions, open communications, cooperative tactics?

Is the pattern of interaction stable or changing?

Are the outcomes of interaction positive or negative?
- productive conflict (bargaining or problem-solving)?
- too much conflict (escalation)?
- too little conflict (withdrawal or suppression)?

Dynamics of interface development

How do outcomes of representatives' interaction, contextual forces, and party characteristics interact over time to alter or maintain the interface?
- direct impacts on interfaces?
- mutual influence over time?

Is the interface stable or changing over time?

Is the organization of the interface appropriate?
- underorganization that encourages too much or too little conflict?
- overorganization that encourages too little conflict?
- appropriate organization that encourages productive conflict?

SUMMARY

In this chapter I suggest a framework for analyzing organizational interfaces and conflicts within them. I argue that interfaces may be fruitfully analyzed in terms of four elements: (1) the definition and organization of the interface itself, (2) the interests and characteristics of the parties, (3) the impacts of immediate and larger contexts, and (4) the roles and personal characteristics of the representatives. These four elements combine to produce dynamics at two levels: (1) interpersonal dynamics between representatives, and (2) the interplay between representatives' interaction, context, and parties that alters or maintains the interface. The diagnostic questions in Tables 2.2 and 2.3 summarize this approach to understanding a specific interface.

But analyzing complex social situations is not as simple as this framework implies—the process is more akin to peeling away the layers of an onion, letting loose new levels of understanding and frequent tears, than it is to Socratic question-and-answer analysis. The order of questions appropriate to diagnosing specific situations depends on the situations themselves. In cases of escalated conflicts, for example, it may be fruitful to begin with representatives' behavior and work back to understand the role of contextual factors, the changes in interface organization, and the interests of the parties. In cases of too little conflict, in contrast, the problems are often sins of omission rather than sins of commission. It may be necessary to begin with analysis of various interests and work from there through different elements and their interaction to understand behavior that is significant in its absence.

The point is that this framework is a "sensitizing concept," suggesting areas of interest rather than a specific point by point analytic procedure. In later chapters the framework is used to examine several forms of interface. These chapters offer more concrete illustrations of how it is used to explore specific situations.

Management Strategies

3

This chapter presents strategies for managing conflict at organizational interfaces. As in Chapter 2, presentation is in the form of a general overview rather than a detailed discussion of tactics. More specific approaches are considered in later chapters.

The chapter begins with the choice to intervene—when does the level of conflict require action? Next, four general classes of conflict management intervention are described: redirecting behavior, reallocating resources, reframing perspectives, and realigning underlying forces. The third section considers intervention to alter dynamics of representative interaction and interface evolution. The last section, a summary, is also a prelude to the focus on different interfaces in chapters to follow.

CHOOSING TO INTERVENE

How much conflict is "appropriate"? On what grounds should conflict managers promote more or less conflict? After all, the wrong choice can be costly: Misapplied interventions may reduce appropriate conflict to too little, or escalate appropriate conflict to too much. So, given an initial diagnosis of the situation, how and in what direction should managers intervene?

There are no easy answers to this question. The level of conflict that is "just right" at a given interface depends on unique combinations of interests, personnel, context, and history, and there is no substitute for detailed knowledge of the situation. But there are some indicators associated with too much or too little conflict; those indicators, in conjunction with a sense of desirable outcomes, can provide the basis for choosing to intervene.

Too much conflict produces a variety of consequences. Parties and representatives tend to perceive themselves as innocent victims and their opponents as malignant villains; they regard opponents with antagonism, hostility, and extreme distrust; communications between the parties are reduced in amount and quality by distrust and distortion; coercive tactics of influence are extensively used, including sabotage and violence. These perceptions, communications, and actions tend to interact to reinforce each other in escalating cycles that often produce poor decisions based on distorted information and low commitment, harm to one or both parties, and reduced capacity of the interface to sustain productive conflict in the future. At Lordstown, for example (see Chapter 2), the *escalation* of conflict between union and management was halted by GMAD agreement to reduce assembly-line speed and rehire laid-off workers—but that decision did not repair relations between workers and management, who continued to engage in antagonistic conflict for years after the strike. This conflict cost millions in lost production, more millions in worker losses, enormous amounts of energy, time, and commitment, and substantial declines in the quality of many vehicles sold to unsuspecting consumers.

Too little conflict is more difficult to see, for the absence of productive debate is less visible than escalation. Too little conflict sometimes involves *suppression* of critical differences when discussion would be important. The dynamics of suppressed conflict involve perceptions that deny differences and overemphasize similarities, restricted communications about topics that might generate controversy, and actions that submerge differences and suppress productive disagreement. Top managers in the Mercury Corporation, for example (see Chapter 2), tacitly agreed to suppress challenges of the New Business Division so that other difficult issues could remain undiscussed. Such suppression produces decisions based on inadequate information, poor analysis of options, failure to confront outmoded traditions and myths, and little awareness of critical interdependencies. In the long term, conflict suppression is associated with interface overorganization which encourages inattention to important differences and interdependencies among the parties. Conflict suppression in the Mercury Corporation allowed a continual financial drain for little return, and continuing inattention to relations between top management and divisional barons that undercut future development of new business. Conflict suppression may also have serious long- and short-term costs.

Too little conflict in the form of *withdrawal* also produces problems. In withdrawal, differences may be recognized but not explicitly articulated between parties; communications are reduced as parties avoid potentially controversial interaction; representatives avoid engagement, ignore differences, or leave the field to prevent conflict. In the Theological School Consortium, for example (see Chapter 2), representatives withdrew from discussion of controversial topics and focused their energies elsewhere. In the short run withdrawal can produce low attendance, low commitment to decisions, infrequent participation, and decisions based on little or low-quality information. In the longer term, withdrawal may undercut the continuing existence of the interface as representatives cease to attend or restrict discussion to noncontroversial issues. The Consortium's viability was threatened by member withdrawal, and its viability was important to schools that hoped to achieve accreditation or an alternative base to an overly restrictive parent church.

In their full-blown forms, escalation, suppression, or withdrawal would obviously benefit from interventions that moderate their negative outcomes. But is conflict level a serious problem below such extremes? Too much conflict often presents problems in organizations, and examples of its negative effects are everywhere (e.g., Blake, Shepard, and Mouton, 1964; Katz and Kahn, 1978). Too little conflict less obviously requires intervention, though there is evidence that the impacts of suppression and withdrawal are more widespread than is commonly recognized. Janis (1972), for example, argued that disastrous foreign policy decisions could often be understood as the outcomes of low-conflict "groupthink" among policymakers. Katz (1980) concluded after studying fifty research and development teams that continuing internal conflict was associated with high performance. The problems of too little conflict are often not blatant, but conflict-stimulating interventions are often desirable (e.g., Robbins, 1974).

But intervention toward what end? What is *appropriate conflict?* Chapter 2 identified two kinds of appropriate conflict behavior—problem-solving and bargaining. Each displays characteristic patterns of communication, perception, action, and outcomes associated with productive conflict.

Bargaining situations require parties to negotiate predominantly conflicting interests, so that one party's gain is the other's loss. But productive conflict is often possible within that context. The parties perceive their conflicting interests without losing sight of common underlying interdependencies; communications are guarded and selective, as each party informs the other in ways that safeguard its own interests; bargaining tactics include information management, commitments to positions that are difficult to yield, and threats and promises designed to elicit compliance. There is potential for escalation in these patterns, but the parties remain aware of common interests in the preservation of an interface deemed legitimate by both sides. In the short term, bargaining can produce decisions accepted by both sides in a process that ensures a continuing and relatively stable interface for future negotiations. Collective bargaining at Lordstown, for example, produced mutually accepted outcomes prior to the advent of GMAD: Previous management conferred quality awards on the workers. Productive bargaining at the Mercury Corporation might have clarified expectations and needs of the New Business Division as well as top management and the other divisions. Bargaining at the Theological School Consortium might have clarified the resource problems of various schools and the mix of interests being met by the institution. Productive bargaining conflict can clarify party interests, mobilize their resources and define their boundaries, establish which differences are real and which are imagined, and promote interface organization in which differences can be constructively negotiated over the long term (Coser, 1956; Walton and McKersie, 1965).

Appropriate conflict in *problem-solving* situations involves exploring party differences that are not necessarily in conflict. Problem-solving involves clarifying common interests and differences, developing trust and communicating accurate information between parties, flexibly exploring alternatives and the potential for mutual benefit, and choosing alternatives that maximize gains to both parties. In the short term, problem-solving can generate decisions based on accurate and complete information, joint commitments, and creative new perspectives. Over the longer run, problem-solving also encourages stable relations among the parties, recognition of common interests as well as conflicts, skills for creating jointly acceptable alternatives, and a basis for future relations. Problem-solving relations at Lordstown, for example, might have focused on redesigning assembly-line operation to promote more productivity and higher quality of work life for its operators. At the Mercury Corporation, problem-solving could have focused on employing New Business Division resources without creating threats to the divisional barons. In the Theological Consortium, problem-solving could have been used to formulate projects that would meet small school needs without undercutting Consortium benefits to big schools (Walton and McKersie, 1965; Deutsch, 1973).

So when is intervention needed to manage conflict at interfaces? The answer depends on the specific situation, but there are dimensions for examining specific situations before choosing to intervene. Table 3.1 summarizes conflict characteristics on four dimensions. Perceptions, communications, and actions refer to the dynamics of representative interaction, and so are visible or easy to infer from ongoing behavior. Outcomes are short- and long-term consequences of conflict. Potential intervenors can use this table to evaluate either ongoing interactions or past history to assess the need for conflict-reducing or conflict-promoting intervention.

AN OVERVIEW OF CONFLICT MANAGEMENT STRATEGIES

Conflict management strategies have been developed to deal with many problems—international war, negotiations with terrorists, tensions in communities, arguments between spouses.

TABLE 3.1
Assessing levels of conflict: choosing to intervene

CONFLICT LEVEL	PERCEPTIONS	COMMUNICATIONS	ACTIONS	OUTCOMES
Too much Escalation	Common interests unrecognized Extreme distrust Hostility	Extreme restriction Serious distortion of information	Exaggerate differences Coercive influence Violence and sabotage	Decision on poor information, low commitment Harm to parties Future relations deteriorate
Productive Bargaining	Conflicting interests dominate Common interests known Opponent recognized Distrust	Exchange guarded Selective offer and acceptance of information	Preserve differences Rigid commitments Threats and promises	Decisions distribute fixed resources Accepted process Future relations in bargaining mode

Problem-solving	Common interests dominate Conflicting interests known Friendliness and trust	Open exchanges Accurate information	Explore differences Flexible generation of alternatives Consensus decisions	Decisions provide mutual benefits Creative alternatives Future relations in problem-solving mode
Too little Suppression	Conflicting interests unrecognized Differences denied	Controversial information suppressed Agreement emphasized	Deny differences Suppress disagreement	Decisions based on little information, analysis, or challenge to myths Future relations as parties without differences
Withdrawal	Conflicting interests recognized but avoided Fear of other party and conflict	Controversy avoided Low exchange of information	Avoid differences Reduce investment Decide by default	No decisions, or decision by default Low commitment and participation Future relations in doubt

This section deals with classes of intervention relevant to conflict at organizational interfaces. More specifically, four general categories of conflict management intervention are considered: (1) interventions that *redirect immediate behavior,* (2) interventions that *reallocate relevant resources,* (3) interventions that *reframe perspectives* on the conflict, and (4) interventions that *realign structural forces* that underlie the situation. Each general category is first briefly described and then more specific tactics are outlined.

Redirecting Behavior

Events at the interface are produced by interactions among representatives. *Interventions may redirect behavior by refocusing representatives' attention on new issues or alternatives, by altering flows of information among representatives, or by providing new tactical options for representative action.* Redirecting behavior depends on the intervenor's access to, and influence over, at least one representative. Zaltman and Duncan (1975) have suggested that agents for change employ educative strategies based on information, facilitative strategies based on added resources, persuasive strategies based on presentation or personal impact, and coercive strategies based on control over target outcomes. Each approach may be appropriate to influence immediate representative behavior at the interface. Four interventions may be used to redirect representative behavior: controlling the issues in contention, refocusing on new alternative outcomes, altering patterns of distorted communications, or changing problematic tactics.

Controlling issues. The issues at interfaces range from very small to very large. Fisher (1964) suggested that large issues may be "fractionated" to *reduce* conflict. Big issues associated with too much conflict may be broken up so that (1) parties are small, (2) specific problems are minor, (3) larger principles are not involved, (4) substantive precedents are not set, and (5) procedural precedents are not set. In the Lordstown struggle, for example, the issues could have been broken apart so that: parties were individuals, not the UAW local and GMAD; problems focused on single job definitions, not layoffs of hundreds; "union integrity" and "management prerogatives" were not involved; rehiring one individual did not require rehiring hundreds; and settlements were not believed to encourage future sabotage or speedups. Issue control reduces the size of issues, and enables easier resolution.

Issue control may also be used to *enlarge* issues to promote more productive debate. Withdrawal from conflict in the Theological Consortium, for example, might have been counteracted by emphasizing school investments in an issue, by highlighting the systemic indifference to small schools implied in otherwise minor incidents, by clarifying the relevance of ecumenicism and self-determination to specific issues, and by emphasizing the procedural and substantive implications of continuing avoidance.

Refocusing alternatives. Alternatives posed at interfaces define the outcomes of conflict for parties. Too much conflict frequently produces deadlocks, in which the acceptable alternatives have become restricted to two incompatible positions. Interventions that offer previously unrecognized alternatives may help unfreeze parties who could not otherwise abandon their commitments (Schelling, 1960; Walton and McKersie, 1965). Management and workers at Lordstown, for example, deadlocked over whether workers would be allowed to "double up"—a practice by which some workers did two jobs while others loafed. Refocusing on the question of productivity ("Doubling up is O.K. as long as production quantity and quality are improved") might have unfrozen the deadlock.

In too little conflict, the range of possible alternatives is impoverished by suppression of or withdrawal from controversial alternatives. Interventions that focus on "hard choices" or on "trade-offs" of decisions may expand the vision of the parties. Focusing attention on the development of new business at the Mercury Corporation, for example, revealed a variety of unexplored issues and alternatives. Pressing representatives to the Theological School Consortium to clarify their preferences also illuminated a range of previously unconsidered possibilities.

Altering communications. Too much and too little conflict are both characterized by restricted communications, though the patterns differ. In too much conflict, communications are restricted by representatives' misrepresentations, mutual distrust, and within-party distortions. Approaches to improving communications are legion: Representatives may expand communications and provide information that can be independently validated; mechanisms to insure trustworthy information may be developed; tendencies to distort information within a party to confirm previous stereotypes may be guarded against. Blake, Shepard, and Mouton (1964) reduced conflict escalation by bringing parties together and systematically helping them to share perceptions of each other and of themselves. But expanding communications between parties in escalated conflict can be difficult, for distrust and distortion may undermine the most well-intentioned efforts. At the Lordstown plant, for example, "sensitivity sessions" to improve communications apparently did not reduce continuing distrust and antagonism.

In too little conflict, information is restricted by suppressing or withdrawing from controversy. Representatives may expand communications that have been suppressed by raising the "undiscussable" issues, or by investigating poorly understood performance problems. Third parties may help to clarify communications. Walton (1969) has suggested tactics by which "third-party peacemakers" can help representatives sharpen and then resolve their differences. The problems of the New Business Division of the Mercury Corporation came under scrutiny at the initiative of its own managers, who recruited an external consultant to help them understand the situation. Dealing with withdrawal, on the other hand, involves tracking down information that has been lost or diffused rather than actively suppressed. Interventions that focus attention on and track critical communications may promote productive debate when withdrawal is the problem. Bringing together representatives of the Theological School Consortium and pressing them to discuss controversial issues produced productive conflict and enhanced understanding.

More generally, interventions that encourage the parties to discuss their communications and the ways in which problems are generated can help them understand escalation, withdrawal, or suppression. Once the parties can recognize and explicitly discuss their communications, their control over unintended dynamics may be greatly enhanced (e.g., Bateson et al., 1956; Watzlawick et al., 1967).

Changing tactics.   Representatives' tactics set up chains of interlocking behaviors that can produce either too much or too little conflict. Changing tactics may require training or recruiting representatives to alter initial presentations that establish climates for later interaction, to encourage initiatives to interrupt self-reinforcing cycles, or to counter returns to destructive patterns.

Changing tactics that produce too much conflict may require altering initial competitive stances. Rubin and Brown (1975) found in a review of bargaining studies that an initial cooperative stance and willingness to make concessions promoted trust and mutually beneficial relations, while an initial competitive stance produced mistrust and conflict. Lordstown management, for example, might have encouraged more effective bargaining by adopting a cooperative stance and making some initial concessions to the union. Carefully planned and implemented initiatives may also interrupt conflict escalation. Osgood (1960) proposed and Lindskold and Collins (1978) tested a "graduated reciprocal initiatives" tactic, which combines unilateral "no-strings-attached" cooperative initiatives with announced peaceful intentions and expectations for reciprocation by opponents to reduce conflict. Lordstown union representatives, for example, might have promoted a "high productivity week" as evidence of good will, and invited management to make a comparable initiative to reduce tensions.

Maintaining productive interaction once begun may depend on tactics for countering aggression. Deutsch's (1973) studies of conflict reduction tactics found some to be more effective than others: Altruistic "turn-the-other-cheek" tactics do not reduce conflict, for they are often interpreted as an invitation to exploitation; "deterrent" tactics that punish aggression severely do not produce cooperation, though they may limit aggression; a "non-punitive" response that combines self-defense with willingness to cooperate appeared to be the most effective tactic for creating cooperation from conflict. Lordstown management, for example, could have accepted worker innovations on the assembly line (e.g., "doubling up") provided that quality was maintained, and used its authority to deter changes that undercut production.

Changing tactics may also promote more productive conflict when withdrawal from or suppression of important differences occurs. In their initial presentations representatives can establish positions and climates inconsistent with avoiding conflict or pretending all is harmonious. Formulating clear initial positions and demands, for example, can promote debate; Chesler and Lohman (1971) found that helping high school students clarify their initial bargaining positions promoted more productive conflict with school administrators. School representatives in the Theological Schools Consortium and New Business Division executives at the Mercury Corporation might have taken clear positions on controversial issues early in their negotiations. Such initiatives can also interrupt self-reinforcing cycles of withdrawal and suppression, even after they have been in operation for some time. Actions that increase interaction in place of withdrawal, or that explore rather than deny controversial issues and alternatives, can produce more engagement among representatives. School representatives might have insisted on discussing the outcomes of Consortium participation for different schools, for example, and Mercury Corporation executives might have questioned the failure to discuss New Business Division performance. Representatives can also employ tactics to counter forces that preserve withdrawal or suppression. Actions that allow withdrawal or reinforce denial can be identified, challenged, or undermined. Consortium representatives began to recognize and counter actions by which they ignored or punished representatives who raised controversial topics, and Mercury Corporation executives began to understand and counter the suppression tactics by which they bottled up controversy.

The interventions described in this section are summarized in Table 3.2. Note that these interventions involve action to influ-

TABLE 3.2
Interventions for redirecting behavior

INTERVENTION	FOR TOO MUCH CONFLICT	FOR TOO LITTLE CONFLICT
Control issues	Fractionate issues to reduce size: • smaller parties • smaller problems • principles not involved • no procedural precedent • no substantive precedent	Consolidate issues to enlarge: • larger parties • larger problems • involve principles • set procedural precedents • set substantive precedents
Refocus alternatives	Create alternatives that unfreeze deadlocks and revise commitments	Clarify hard choices and trade-offs in noncontroversial alternatives
Alter communications	Increase believable communications	Raise suppressed or avoided issues
	Build mechanisms that ensure trustworthy information exchange	Encourage investigation and discussion of potential problems
	Guard against within-party distortions of information	Focus attention on lost or ignored information
	Discuss escalation impacts on information flows	Discuss withdrawal and suppression impacts on communications
Change tactics	Initial presentations that permit cooperation; concessions as evidence of peaceful intent	Intial presentations that encourage examining differences; clear positions and demands
	Conflict-reducing initiatives: • minimize risks • clear intentions	Conflict-promoting intiatives: • minimize risks • identify issues

TABLE 3.2   (continued)
Interventions for redirecting behavior

INTERVENTION	FOR TOO MUCH CONFLICT	FOR TOO LITTLE CONFLICT
	• unilateral peaceful step • expected reciprocation Self-defense tactics against escalation: • deterrence for high threat situations • nonpunitive response to encourage cooperation	• explore differences • require interaction Self-defense tactics for withdrawal/suppression • identify withdrawal/suppression maneuvers • confront maneuvers to undercut their impact

ence immediate behavior within the interface, and affect short-term interaction directly.

Reallocating Resources

Conflict at interfaces in part responds to resources available at the interface. *Resource allocation interventions expand or contract the available personnel, information, or other resources relevant to conflict or its management at the interface.* Such interventions assume that the intervenor controls resources relevant to the conflict, and so fall largely under the category of the facilitative strategies for social change identified by Zaltman and Duncan (1975). Resource reallocations can have impacts on either the immediate give-and-take between representatives or on the longer-term dynamics of interface evolution. Two basic approaches for reallocating resources are to alter the nature of the interdependence between the parties or to change the resources available for conflict management.

Altering resource interdependence.   Resource intervention can change the *amount* of critical resources available to the parties. Galbraith (1973) suggests that resource reallocation is often used by default to manage conflict and uncertainty at organizational interfaces: When active efforts to manage conflict problems are not explicitly undertaken, more slack resources are inevitably committed to the interface in the form of reduced performance expectations.

Too much conflict often erupts around the distribution of scarce but critical resources, and expanding supplies of that resource may help to reduce it. At Lordstown, for example, workers and management fought over the appropriate use of worker time and energy, and the resulting tensions might have been substantially reduced by providing more slack in performance expectations.

Resource contractions may also influence conflict levels. Reduced resource allocations may encourage expanded debate over their use. In the Theological School Consortium, for example, limited resources highlighted the Consortium's failure to deliver to some schools, and so encouraged parties to clarify and more vigorously pursue their interests. In other situations, declining resources may highlight party interdependence and reduce conflict between them. Declining company fortunes have sometimes enhanced labor-management cooperation in order to save management's business and workers' jobs.

Interdependence between the parties may also be altered by changing the *sources* of relevant resources. Interdependent parties may become less dependent on each other if new sources of critical resources are introduced. Reduced interdependence in some circumstances may reduce conflict. In a classic study of British coal mining, Trist et al. (1963) found that reducing task interdependence between specialized shifts reduced conflict and eliminated major production bottlenecks. In other situations, reduced interdependence may permit increased conflict. Alternative sources of jobs for workers or of employees for the Lordstown plant might easily have increased union-management conflict there. By the same token, increasing interdependence by consolidating the sources of supply may influence conflict levels as well. If all new business in the Mercury Corporation were funneled through the New Business Division, neither top management nor division barons could afford to allow its performance to go unchallenged.

Altering management resources. Personnel or other critical resources may be redistributed at the interface to promote different conflict management activities. Different quantities or qualities of management resources may be allocated by the parties, and the resources of different parties may be focused to reduce or promote conflict.

More time and energy are commonly invested by primary parties as conflict problems become more serious. Union and management resources invested in the fight at Lordstown were enormous; top managers and divisional barons spent considerable energy suppressing discussion of New Business Division performance; Theological School Consortium representatives wasted time and energy avoiding important differences. Unfortunately, the cyclical quality of conflict dynamics frequently means that increased resources invested by representatives often do as much to preserve the problem as solve it. It is easy for new efforts—more influence attempts at Lordstown, more investigation at Mercury, more issue-raising at the Consortium—to be incorporated into a cycle that supports or escalates the original problem.

As problems become more serious, the involvement of external management resources becomes more likely. Within organizations it is common to refer unresolved conflicts to a common superior, thus bringing to bear higher-level resources. Referral up the hierarchy is particularly common when there is too much conflict. In organizations characterized by much uncertainty and many interdependencies, referrals from lower levels may reach epidemic proportions—threatening to swamp upper management in a sea of trivial decisions (Galbraith, 1973). Upper management is less likely to be drawn into too little conflict, unless performance problems are serious (Robbins, 1974).

Where the parties have no common superior, or upper levels are parties to the dispute, third parties from outside the organization may become critical resources. External third parties may take several roles (see Laue and Cormick, 1978). Enforcers compel obedience to ground rules. The courts and federal administrators enforce labor laws that regulated the interaction between Lordstown workers and managers. Researchers generate improved data about the situation. The consultant to the Mercury Corporation helped managers understand the processes by which new businesses were developed. Activists and advocates mobilize and represent parties. International Union and GM Headquarters representatives offered advice and counsel to union local and plant management. Third-party mediators and consultants promote communications and resolve specific disputes. The Theological School Consortium used consultants to promote more open debate. Since third parties may be relatively neutral, they are in a better position to recognize and interrupt vicious cycles of escalation, suppression, or withdrawal that primary parties may not be able to see or influence.

Table 3.3 summarizes interventions for reallocating resources at the interface. Note that these interventions may influence either short-term or long-term dynamics.

TABLE 3.3
Interventions for reallocating resources

INTERVENTION	FOR TOO MUCH CONFLICT	FOR TOO LITTLE CONFLICT
Alter resource interdependence	Expand resources to reduce conflict over scarcity	Contract resources to emphasize conflicting interests
	Diversify sources to reduce interdependence	Consolidate resources to intensify interdependence
Alter management resources	Increase resources from primary parties	Increase resources from primary parties
	Refer disputes up the hierarchy for resolution	Attract hierarchical attention to lack of conflict
	Third party resources: • enforcers • researchers • consultants/ mediators	Third-party resources: • activists/ advocates • researchers • consultants/ mediators

Reframing Perspectives

Conflict problems are typically intertwined with the ways in which parties and representatives understand the situation. *Reframing interventions alter the perspectives through which parties and representatives understand and assign meaning to events and actions at the interface.* Intervenors who would manage conflict by reframing perspectives must possess relevant information and present that information credibly to parties and representatives. Persuasive and educative change strategies underlie reframing interventions (Zaltman and Duncan, 1975). Reframing depends on the change agent's ability to present information that can be trusted and used by change targets. Four different reframing strategies are discussed here: reformulating party interests, revising unreal stereotypes, reconceptualizing the issues, and recognizing conflict dynamics.

Reformulating party interests. The ways in which parties conceive their interests influence and are influenced by conflict at the interface. Too much conflict encourages overemphasis on differences and underestimates similarities. Interventions that clarify and encourage work toward *superordinate goals,* whose accomplishment is desired by both parties but attainable by neither without the other's cooperation, can reduce conflict (Sherif, 1958). Work with union and management groups at the Lordstown plant to identify common interests in keeping the plant open and operating might have reduced the conflict between them.

In contrast, too little conflict overemphasizes similarities and underestimates differences. Interventions that clarify different interests of the parties and emphasize costs of too little conflict can promote productive debate. Discussions within representative groups of school interests in Theological School Consortium membership provided a base for more active challenge of Consortium policies that conflicted with school priorities.

Revising unrealistic stereotypes. Conflict often gives rise to *unrealistic perceptions*—negative stereotypes of one's opponent and positive stereotypes of oneself. Negative stereotypes of one's opponent may justify coercive and aggressive actions; positive stereotypes of oneself may obscure one's own responsibility for escalation. Interventions that alter unrealistic stereotypes can contribute to reducing conflict based on the stereotyped perspective. Sykes (1966), for example, found that workers' discussions of their foremen's cruelty and brutality led them to recognize that the once-valid stereotype was based on foremen who were no longer present—so the workers revised their perceptions and associated behavior. Not all negative perceptions of opponents or positive perceptions of self are inaccurate, of course. But in the heat of conflict, exaggerations of the villainy of other parties and the virtue of one's own promote escalation. Revision of these unrealistic perceptions may have positive impacts on too much conflict.

Too little conflict encourages other unrealistic perceptions. Suppression of differences permits unrealistic assumptions about similarities; withdrawal enhances unrealistic beliefs in the dangerousness of opponents or in one's own inability to confront differences successfully. Interventions that examine perceptions that underpin too little conflict may promote revisions and more engagement. Diagnostic activities with school representative groups clarified their strengths and contributed to challenge of Theological School Consortium activities. The perceptions that underpin withdrawal and suppression are often unclear, and examination may reveal unrealistic and untested assumptions that inhibit constructive debate.

Reconceptualizing the situation.   Human beings tend to have general theories and assumptions—a sort of "cognitive map"—that explain situations in which they operate, and those theories offer both interpretations of events and guides for action (Argyris and Schon, 1978; Heginbotham, 1975). Interventions can reconceptualize variables or relationships within that theory. Theories may be constructed to bridge what initially appear to be hopelessly incompatible positions. Eiseman (1978) suggests that conflict over interpreting the behavior of a person who walks away from a bully's invitation to fight ("chicken" vs. "brave"), for example, may be resolved by constructing a theory that includes both "physical courage" (to stand up to the bully) and "social courage" (to walk away and so refuse to be drawn into the bully's game). More generally, theoretical orientations that explain the generation of conflict may help to control it. The staff of a professional association were relieved to learn that their internal conflicts were largely generated by their efforts to serve multiple publics rather than their interpersonal differences. Their daily debates did not change in intensity, but their assessment of that debate moved from "too much" to "appropriate."

Situations of too little conflict may also be reconceptualized for more productive debate. Theories that emphasize similarities or harmony-compelling aspects of the situation may be revised to recognize pressures for conflict. In the Mercury Corporation, for example, discussions of new business revealed that tensions among management levels were linked to problems of the New Business Division, and so legitimated more direct debate. A workshop that stressed open negotiation of differences set the stage for more direct debate in the Theological School Consortium. Interventions that alter theoretical contexts may endow conflict behavior with changed meaning and value.

Recognizing conflict dynamics.   Perspectives may also be reframed for better understanding of the self-reinforcing dynamics of too much and too little conflict. Parties and representatives who recognize the vicious cycles that affect them and others are better able to protect themselves against unintended escalation, withdrawal, and suppression.

Educational experiences for learning about conflict dynamics have been devised for various settings. Workshops that bring parties together to examine their own past experience, for example, can provide important insights into conflict dynamics. Blake, Shepard, and Mouton (1964) devised carefully controlled workshops in which party representatives shared perceptions and examined the dynamics of their conflicts. Understanding the links among distorted communications, unrealistic stereotypes, and coercive action allows parties to guard against unintended repetitions by searching for better information, testing stereotypes, and resisting hasty resort to coercion.

By the same token, problems of too little conflict may be controlled by parties and representatives who are sensitive to their own and others' tendencies to stereotype each other, to reduce and distort communications, and to avoid or suppress controversial interaction. Representatives to the Consortium paid more attention to outbursts of disagreement after they became aware of their tendency to avoid disagreements whose discussion would benefit the Consortium as a whole.

Interventions for reframing perspectives are summarized in Table 3.4. These interventions, as previously noted, may influ-

TABLE 3.4
Interventions for reframing perspectives

INTERVENTION	FOR TOO MUCH CONFLICT	FOR TOO LITTLE CONFLICT
Reformulate party interests	Clarify and encourage work for superordinate goals	Clarify and encourage work for diversity of interests
Revise unrealistic stereotypes	Reduce unrealistic stereotypes of opponent's villainy	Reduce unrealistic stereotypes of opponent's similarity or dangerousness
	Reduce unrealistic stereotypes of own innocence and victimization	Reduce unrealistic stereotypes of own similarity or inability to confront
Reconceptualize the situation	Construct theories that include both perspectives	Construct theories that differentiate perspectives
	Clarify forces operating to promote conflict	Clarify forces operating to reduce conflict
Recognize conflict dynamics	Understand escalatory interaction of perceptions, communications, and tactics	Understand withdrawal/suppression interaction of perceptions, communications, and tactics

ence both short- and long-term relations, and they depend on the use of information by credible change agents.

Realigning Underlying Forces

Conflict at interfaces occurs within constraints set by underlying structural forces. *Interventions to realign the pattern of forces that impact on parties and representatives at interfaces may increase or decrease conflict between them.* Realigning interventions are systemically focused rather than individually directed, and operate over a longer term than the immediate impact of interventions that redirect behavior, reframe perspectives, and reallocate resources (see Thomas, 1976). Interventions to realign underlying forces assume that the intervenor has the power to alter present constellations of forces. Realignment interventions create pressures for change similar to Zaltman and Duncan's (1975) coercive change strategies, in which new activities are the result of the change agent's control over the outcomes of change targets. This discussion considers five interventions that realign forces relevant to interface conflict; redefining unit boundaries, altering boundary permeabilities, rewriting rules and procedures, renegotiating norms and values, and refocusing incentives and reward systems. The first approach redefines social units involved; the latter four reorganize social units, and particularly interfaces.

Redefining boundaries. Unit boundaries define the unit and the elements included within it. Interventions may alter the strength of boundary definitions and the criteria by which they are drawn, or they may alter the composition of the unit.

Too much conflict can be moderated by boundary redefinitions that create new or strengthen old interfaces, that change interface composition, or that redefine parties. New interfaces may bring representatives together to work out differences and so reduce conflict. The problems at Lordstown have been managed at other plants through "quality of work life" experiments in which union-management problem-solving activities operate in parallel with collective bargaining interfaces (e.g., Guest, 1979). Recomposing the interface to include new representatives may also reduce conflict. In the now classic "co-optation" of outside pressure groups at the Tennessee Valley Authority, protest representatives were included in policymaking groups and so were made more amenable to influence (Selznick, 1949). More elaborate redefinitions relocate conflict or eliminate interfaces altogether. The introduction of matrix organization, for example, redefines critical conflicts so that the interface becomes an individual, who reports to two bosses (Davis and Lawrence, 1977). Individuals who occupy matrix roles must manage conflicts to avoid being split in half by their roles.

More productive conflict may also be encouraged by redefining relevant boundaries. Withdrawal from differences may be rendered more difficult by clarifying interface boundaries that keep representatives together and engaged. The workshop for the Theological School Consortium, for example, created an arena from which representatives could not easily withdraw. Recomposing the interface may also produce more productive debate. Including consultants in the workshop for the Consortium increased the pressure on representatives to deal with differences more directly.

The suppression of differences may also be altered by redefining boundaries. The New Business Division at the Mercury Corporation redefined their interfaces with top management and other divisions to include an external consultant, and consultant investigations opened discussion of previously suppressed conflicts. That suppression was in part a consequence of divisional boundary definition; organizational redesign would also have altered relations at redefined interfaces.

Altering boundary permeability.   Levels of conflict affect and are affected by the permeabilities of party and interface boundaries to inputs and outputs. Interventions that open or close relevant boundaries to information, personnel, or other critical inputs and outputs can alter levels of conflict at the interface.

Too much conflict is associated with closed party boundaries and open interface boundaries. Interventions may protect interfaces from invasions from or leakage to the outside, or encourage more exchanges of information and personnel across party boundaries, and so reduce conflict. Tensions at the Lordstown plant were enhanced by union and management boundaries closed to information and people from the other camp, and by interface boundaries that were too open to influence by union hotheads and GMAD hard-liners. Party boundaries may be opened to information and personnel exchanges, such as promoting workers into management. Interface boundaries may be closed to external pressures, such as those exerted by extremist party members, and to internal leakages, such as failure to preserve negotiations security.

Too little conflict, in contrast, is associated with interface boundaries that are either so open that they permit withdrawal, or so closed that they require suppression of differences. Closed interface boundaries keep out information and personnel that might compel more attention to differences. In the Mercury Corporation, for example, admitting the external consultant opened up the interface to new ideas that encouraged more open debate. At the Theological School Consortium, in contrast, closing workshop boundaries to losses of critical information and personnel prevented diffusion of energy and withdrawal from differences.

Revising rules and procedures.   Rules and procedures affect conflict levels by setting constraints on representatives' behavior. Intervention can promote or reduce conflict by revising formal rules and procedures in order to loosen or tighten regulation of representatives' interaction. Creating new rules, nullifying old ones, or rewriting procedures all can affect problematic levels of conflict.

Too much conflict is often linked to ill-defined or poorly accepted rules and procedures. In settings where conflict is based on ambiguity and uncertainty, clarifying accepted procedures and standards may be enough to regulate conflict at the interface. In more escalated conflict, fundamental revisions of formal rules may be required. The conflict at Lordstown, for example, undercut the rules that governed worker-manager interaction, and rule violations (reflected in soaring rates of sabotage and grievances) in turn promoted more uncontrolled conflict. Promulgating new rules and procedures is not in itself enough to moderate conflict—the real problem is to create procedures that will be obeyed by both sides.

Too little conflict may be associated with rules that regulate too loosely, and so allow withdrawal, or with rules that regulate too tightly, and so encourage suppression. Rules that are extremely detailed and rigidly obeyed can hamstring efforts to raise important issues. Overreliance on decisions by majority vote, for example, can effectively silence minority oppositions that have valuable points to make. Janis (1972) has suggested a number of dissent-encouraging procedures, such as devil's advocates, multiple subgroup analysis of the same issue, and "second-chance" discussions to reexamine alternatives. In the Mercury Corporation a generally accepted procedure for reviewing new business success and failure would have encouraged more discussion of New Business Division performance. Withdrawal at the Theological School Consortium, in contrast, was encouraged by a lack of procedures to regulate interaction. Procedures for reviewing school activities and examining differences—such as those created for the workshop—could have promoted more direct engagement over problematic issues.

Renegotiating norms and values.   The behavior of representatives is also constrained by informally agreed-upon norms and values. Interventions that alter the regulatory force of shared norms and values at an interface can contribute to reducing or promoting conflict. Shared norms and values emerge from interaction and negotiations among representatives, so altering norms and values involves recognizing and renegotiating agreements that are mutually acceptable (Sherwood and Glidewell, 1973).

Too much conflict is often connected to values and norms that are unclear or conflicting and so offer only loose constraints on representative activity. Assumptions about appropriate behavior brought to Lordstown negotiations by GMAD managers and union representatives were quite different, and the escalating conflict eroded agreement about informal standards as well as formal procedures. Interventions like the carefully managed workshops of Blake, Shepard, and Mouton (1964) develop mutually accepted informal standards to minimize unexpected behavior and "dirty tricks" that might otherwise escalate conflict out of control.

Well-defined but tightly constraining norms and values can suppress disagreement. Diagnosing norms and values that suppress conflict may in itself promote constructive debate. Reconstructing the patterns of new business success and failure at the Mercury Corporation made suppressed tensions between divisional barons and top management explicit. Recognizing norms can undercut their impact: Mercury executives easily conformed to unrecognized constraints, but continued suppression was more difficult after the norm had been made explicit.

Withdrawal is more common when norms and values only loosely regulate behavior, so avoidance does not involve violation of shared assumptions. Ill-defined expectations in the Theological School Consortium enabled representatives to evade controversial questions. When third parties set norms that pressed the primary parties to pursue controversial discussions, the representatives were forced to choose between challenging each other or challenging the consultants—in either case, overt debate could not be avoided.

Refocusing incentives. Implicit and explicit rewards and costs available to parties and representatives often promote and maintain problematic conflict. Interventions that refocus the incentives available at the interface can encourage productive or reduce destructive conflict. Analyzing the incentives offered by the interface, the parties, and the surrounding context can reveal points at which underlying forces may be constructively realigned.

Too much conflict is often rooted in a pattern of incentives for limiting escalation. At Lordstown, for example, as conflict escalated nonaggressive behavior by representatives was interpreted as betrayal by parties and punished accordingly. The larger organization offered no convincing incentives for reducing conflict, though the costs of conflict did deter unlimited escalation after the strike.

Too little conflict is common when conflict costs are clearer than gains, so withdrawal or suppression seems a rational response. Interventions that clarify incentives for constructive conflict or disincentives of withdrawal or suppression can encourage more productive debate. In the Mercury Corporation, the costs of examining relations between divisional barons and top management were tacitly conceded to outweigh those of New Business Division ineffectuality, until more penetrating examination indicated that the long-term costs of the continued suppression might be extremely high. Similarly, the costs of confronting differences in the Theological School Consortium were tacitly assessed as higher than the costs of withdrawal, but uncounted costs of that withdrawal threatened the Consortium's existence.

Table 3.5 summarizes intervention for realigning forces that underlie events at the interfaces. Redefining unit boundaries,

TABLE 3.5
Interventions for realigning underlying forces

INTERVENTION	FOR TOO MUCH CONFLICT	FOR TOO LITTLE CONFLICT SUPPRESSION	WITHDRAWAL
Redefine unit boundaries	Create new interface to manage conflict	Deemphasize to reduce suppression	Clarify boundaries to prevent avoidance
	Include new parties (e.g., co-opt outsiders)	Include assertive representatives	Include trouble makers (e.g., consultants)
	Define parties to cope with conflict (e.g., matrix organization) or to reduce interdependence	Define parties to reduce "fusion" and overlap	Define parties to reduce distance and clarify interdependence

TABLE 3.5   (continued)

Interventions for realigning underlying forces

INTERVENTION	FOR TOO MUCH CONFLICT	FOR TOO LITTLE CONFLICT	
		SUPPRESSION	WITHDRAWAL
Alter boundary permeability	Open party boundaries to new information and personnel rotation	Close party boundaries to establish difference	Open party boundaries to stimulating information and personnel
	Close interface to escalatory inputs, provocative outputs	Open interface to stimulating inputs, ventilating outputs	Close interface to disruptive inputs, outputs that drain critical resources
Revise formal rules and procedures	Define rules and procedures legitimate to both parties	Loosen overly detailed rules and procedures that suppress debate	Tighten rules and procedures that permit withdrawal
Renegotiate shared norms and values	Negotiate shared standards of appropriate behavior and dirty tricks	Loosen shared standards that restrict debate	Negotiate shared standards and values that support debate
Refocus incentives	Clarify incentives for reduced conflict	Clarify incentives for more debate	Clarify incentives for more debate
	Emphasize costs of continued conflict	Clarify costs of continued suppression	Clarify costs of continued withdrawal

altering boundary permeability, revising formal rules and procedures, renegotiating norms and values, and refocusing incentives are all interventions that alter pressures that constrain or
influence interface events. Such interventions are not simple or
inexpensive. Typically they require long-term investments of
time and energy and resources. But they also may be repaid with
long-term alterations in patterns of problematic conflict.

MANAGEMENT STRATEGIES AND CONFLICT DYNAMICS

Chapter 2 described conflict dynamics at two levels—the interaction among representatives' perceptions, communications, and
actions that produces cycles of behavior within the interface, and
the interplay among parties, contextual forces, and conflict outcomes that changes or maintains the definition and organization
of the interface itself. The two dynamics are interrelated, for
outcomes of representatives' interactions impinge on interface
organization, and interface definition and organization constrain
the behavior of representatives. But the two dynamics evolve at
different rates; events move rapidly—even explosively—at the
level of representative behavior, while interface definition and
organization evolve comparatively slowly.

Conflict management interventions become part of the ongoing dynamics at the interface—a stream of events in which
past and present provide the basis for future action and understanding. Perfectly timed and focused interventions may alter
critical aspects of a continuing dynamic, and so catalyze endur-
ing change out of all proportion to the size of the intervention.
Had GMAD chosen to experiment with more participative
strategies for enhancing productivity, for example, dynamics in
the Lordstown plant might have been changed beyond recognition. Much more common than a single incisive stroke that
forever alters interface and representative dynamics, unfortunately, are interventions that are immediately swallowed by ongoing dynamics. Errors in timing or focus produce interventions
that are overwhelmed by conflict dynamics, eroded by lack of
supporting follow-up, or even perverted into making things
worse instead of better. Conflict management activities are sel-

dom easy or simple, and major lasting changes in serious conflict problems usually involve efforts by several actors that produce multiply determined change. So conflict managers need to consider using multiple strategies that influence both the dynamics of representative interaction and the dynamics of interface development.

Intervening in the Dynamics of Representatives' Interaction

Of the four intervention strategies discussed in the last section, the first three are particularly relevant to the immediate give-and-take among representatives. These strategies—redirecting behavior, reframing perspectives, and reallocating resources— impact directly on representatives' perceptions, communications, and actions, and so can interrupt problematic dynamics of escalation, suppression, and withdrawal.

Some interventions directly affect representatives' *actions.* Controlling issues, refocusing alternatives, and changing tactics, for example, enable new behaviors by representatives that can in turn elicit new behavior from their opposite numbers. GMAD managers might have fractionated off some manageable issues and so resolved some conflicts with workers; union officers might have taken unilateral tactical initiatives to demonstrate their willingness to reduce conflict; both parties might have expanded the search for alternatives beyond their entrenched positions. The cycle of escalation and counterescalation might have been controlled at the Lordstown plant if the parties had been able to redirect their representatives' behaviors to reduce tensions.

Other strategies influence *communications* directly. Had managers listened more carefully, or had workers spoken more effectively, about the impact on workers of GMAD efforts to enhance Lordstown productivity, alternative approaches might have been designed without sparking such determined resistance.

Reframing perspectives alters *perceptions* that justify or compel continued problematic dynamics. Had workers and managers at Lordstown been able to emphasize shared superordinate goals, to debunk unrealistic stereotypes, to recognize escalatory dynamics, and to reformulate their conceptualizations of the situation, they might have been more able to control their conflict.

Reallocating resources reduces underlying reasons for tension, or expands resources available for managing it. Ultimately the parties at Lordstown called on massive extra resources to manage their conflict, and earlier reallocation of resources might have prevented much of the escalation that occurred.

It is critical to remember that *the dynamics of representatives' interaction tend to be cyclical and self-reinforcing.* Negative perceptions, distorted communications, and coercive tactics are self-reinforcing in conflict escalation; positive perceptions, restricted communications, and suppression tactics are self-reinforcing in suppression of conflict; unrealistic fear, reduced communication, and avoidance tactics are self-reinforcing in withdrawal. Interventions into one aspect of such cycles influence, and are influenced by, other aspects. Changing one element may lead to changes in others; stability in other elements may over time undercut changes in the initial target. Changed tactics of GMAD managers will not continue if the tactics of workers remain constant, or if managers' perceptions and communications remain inconsistent with new tactics. Successful intervention in the dynamics of representatives' interaction requires combining interventions to establish new cycles of consistent and self-reinforcing actions, perceptions, and communications. Successful initial interventions may not bear long-term fruit if intervenors do not deal with cyclical dynamics that can undermine short-term changes in the longer run.

Intervening in the Dynamics of Interface Development

Interventions in the dynamics of interface development focus on altering characteristics of parties, pressures from the external context, or the definition and organization of the interface itself. Three intervention strategies—reframing perspectives, reallocating resources and realigning underlying forces—provide a catalogue of intervention possibilities.

Reframing interventions reorient the perspectives of parties, contextual elements, or the interface. The schools in the Theological School Consortium, for example, may formulate more compelling superordinate goals; their parent churches may debunk their stereotypes of other denominations; theoretical perspectives that give meaning to action within the interface may be expanded to recognize the value of conflict. Reframing these perspectives would contribute to a better-defined and more tightly organized interface that would permit less withdrawal from constructive debate.

Resource reallocations redefine interdependencies and management capabilities. Resource pressures at several points might have contributed to overt conflict in the Consortium. Tightened resources from parent churches or third-party funders might have compelled closer regulation of representatives' interaction and less withdrawal from hard choices. Investing resources in external consultants and in participation in a workshop on conflict management were Consortium decisions that promoted more debate.

Interventions that realign forces underlying interface organization also affect conflict within it. Redefinition of boundaries and boundary permeability, and changing mechanisms for regulating internal activities, influence interface organization directly. Coming together for a residential workshop defined geographical boundaries around Consortium representatives that made immediate withdrawal from differences more difficult; consultant management of the workshop established formal and informal ground rules oriented to encourage constructive debate. Similar interventions may also reshape pressures from parties or the larger context and so indirectly affect interface development. Discussions in school representative groups produced internal mobilization and commitments to making a clearer case for school needs from the Consortium, and so produced more engagement.

Again at the level of interface development, changes depend on the *interplay* among conflict outcomes, parties, and contextual forces. Several implications of this for changing the dynamics of interfaces are worth noting. The interplay of factors can create major changes in interface definition and organization in response to a relatively tiny intervention. The right combination of intervention and conflict dynamic can strike at the weakest link of the ongoing chain of events—and so produce improvements bordering on the miraculous. Much more common than dramatic change, unfortunately, is dramatic stability. The interlocking stability of parties, context, and conflict outcomes often washes out the effects of intervention—even major intervention—over time. New perceptions among Consortium representatives did not produce major changes in problems of coordination, and old patterns of withdrawal tended to recur. Lasting changes in interface definition and organization often require several interventions to create mutually reinforcing change in several aspects of ongoing dynamics. Reframed perspectives and new behavior by Consortium parties and representatives might have been supported by resource reallocation or realigned underlying forces to produce larger and more stable alterations in withdrawal tendencies.

SUMMARY

This chapter presents an overview of issues and strategies relevant to managing conflict at organizational interfaces. The chapter begins with the choice to intervene in interface conflict, and discusses indicators associated with too much, too little, and appropriate levels of conflict. The choice to intervene always depends on the specific circumstances and the values of intervenors—but several questions relevant to that decision are suggested.

Four general strategies for intervening in interface conflict are considered: redirecting immediate behavior, reallocating resources relevant to the problem, reframing perspectives on the situation, and realigning underlying forces that affect interface events. These strategies involve different currencies (e.g., intervenor credibility with representatives, valid and convincing information, resources relevant to parties and representatives, and authority or legitimacy to redesign underlying forces). They may be applied at several levels of analysis and directed at various targets within the interface framework.

Intervention strategies, like other events, fall into an ongoing stream of events, decisions, and influence efforts. Conflict managers can focus on the dynamics of representatives' interaction, and employ redirecting, reframing, and reallocating strategies to impact the interlocking rounds of representatives' perception, communication, and action inside the interface. Alternatively, conflict managers can alter interface definition and organization that constrain behavior and endow events at the interface with meaning. Reframing, reallocating, and realigning interventions are particularly relevant to the slower but more massive developments at the level of the interface. In the long run, however, successful conflict management involves change at both levels of analysis—productive interaction dynamics occur within interfaces that are organized appropriately for the situation.

The next five chapters apply the ideas of Chapters 2 and 3 in more specific detail to several forms of interface.

Department Interfaces

4

Department interfaces exist where departmental subunits of an organization are interdependent and so must interact. This chapter focuses on too much and too little conflict between interdependent departments, and on strategies for managing these problems.

The chapter moves from the general to the specific and back to the general again. The next section considers department interfaces in general terms, focusing on the characteristics of interfaces, departments, representatives, organizational contexts, and the dynamics of their interaction. The following section discusses in more detail relations between the production and maintenance departments of a chemicals plant. The third section describes and analyzes efforts to manage conflict in the chemicals plant. The fourth section considers more generally strategies and tactics for intervening at department interfaces to reduce or promote conflict. The last section summarizes the chapter and identifies some unique characteristics of department interfaces.

ANALYZING DEPARTMENT INTERFACES

What distinguishes department interfaces from other interfaces? For the purposes here, a department interface is a *simple* interface, whose characteristics are limited by some important simplifying assumptions. These assumptions are not true for many or even most department interfaces—but in order to build from relatively simple to more complex, the department interface is discussed first; Analysis of more complex interfaces is postponed to Chapter 8.

Simple department interfaces are (1) defined by and focused on task interdependencies among (2) relatively equal departments that are (3) largely insulated from most contextual forces by (4) a common larger organization. This definition contains four elements worth elaborating. Department interfaces are *centrally concerned with organizational tasks,* for the parties and their interdependence are defined by task requirements. Hospitals, for example, divide tasks among X-ray departments, operating rooms, and groundskeeping staffs. Manufacturing firms assign different tasks to maintenance, production, and sales departments. Some departments are not highly interdependent. Hospital groundskeepers seldom work with X-ray technicians; maintenance personnel may have little contact with salespeople. But other departments are critically dependent on each other. Operating rooms need diagnostic aid, sometimes quickly, from X-ray departments; production departments cannot function long without maintenance aid. Department interfaces are defined by task interdependencies, and task accomplishment is a central issue in conflict problems.

The definition assumes that the departments have *equal influence* within the organization. In practice, departments frequently have unequal power; examination of the complexities introduced by power differences will be postponed until Chapter 5. The definition also assumes that departments are *not greatly affected by forces outside the organization.* In practice departments are often greatly influenced—even created by—contextual pressures. But this chapter focuses on forces within the organization that influence departmental relations. The issues raised by forces outside the organization will be considered in Chapters 6 and 7. Finally, the definition assumes that departments *share a common organizational context.* This common organization establishes shared goals and a common hierarchy of authority within which both departments operate. Interfaces that involve different organizations will be considered in Chapter 7.

Simple department interfaces may be analyzed in terms of the framework proposed in Chapter 2. That framework focuses attention on the elements of department interfaces and on the dynamics of their interaction.

Elements of Department Interfaces

Elements of department interfaces include the departments, their representatives, the larger organizational context, and, of course, department interfaces themselves. Characteristics of each which contribute to conflict problems will be considered briefly in this section.

Department interface definition and organization.   Department interfaces are typically defined by task interdependencies, and include representatives whose interaction is compelled by those interdependencies. The dominant criterion for defining department interface boundaries is, consequently, task requirements. Creating collegewide policies for a community college with several campuses requires an interface that includes representatives of all its geographic divisions. Coordination of inputs to patient care demands an interface among medical records, physical therapy, and X-ray departments. Coherent marketing strategies necessitate interaction among toothpaste, soap, and mouthwash departments. Available evidence suggests that much organizational conflict is rooted in the need to coordinate across different departments (Pondy, 1967); and research suggests that organizations with specialized departments perform better when they devote resources to well-defined departmental interfaces (Lawrence and Lorsch, 1967; Galbraith, 1973). As department interfaces develop, other boundary criteria may become relevant. Representatives spend time in physical proximity; they develop social bonds; and interface events exert considerable influence over their behavior.

Department interface boundaries vary in permeability to important inputs and outputs. Boundaries that are too closed block critical inputs and outputs of personnel: A closed campus coordinating committee may exclude important information and personnel with valuable perspectives from committee deliberations. Boundaries that are too open permit the interface to be inundated with irrelevant information, or allow loss of critical resources. Control over the flow of information, people, and resources can be accomplished by a variety of mechanisms, ranging from informal rules about confidentiality to formal procedures for acquiring and handling resources.

As department interfaces evolve, they develop internal mechanisms for regulating interaction among representatives, such as formally defined rules, programs, procedures, or roles. Appointing a chairperson and adopting Robert's Rules of Order for the campus coordinating committee meetings are formal regulatory mechanisms. Less formal mechanisms include shared norms, common theories, and shared values and beliefs. Shared assumptions about the respect due to professional colleagues, for example, can moderate behavior in the campus coordinating committee, even when strongly held convictions are at stake. Some department interfaces are loosely organized, and so are vulnerable to withdrawal or conflict escalation. Other department interfaces are so tightly organized that representatives suppress critical differences to preserve superficial harmony at the expense of lower performance.

Between these extremes are moderate degrees of department interface organization that permit appropriate conflict. Walton, Dutton, and Fitch (1966) studied relations between production and sales departments in six plants and found that relatively informal interface organization was associated with problem solving and relatively formal organization was associated with bargaining—but for all the level of conflict was relatively moderate.

Departments as parties.   The most common explicit rationale for specialized departments are gains in organizational productivity from division of labor. Galbraith (1977) suggests that departments can be specialized on three dimensions: geography, inputs, and outputs. *Geographically defined* departments make efficient use of resources when the organization must coordinate across physical distance. Community colleges, for example, often have campuses in different neighborhoods to be close to their students. When departments are geographically defined, department interfaces deal with conflict and coordination problems related to distance. Departments may also be defined by their *inputs to organizational products and services,* such as the medical records, physical therapy, and X-ray departments of a hospital. Department interfaces are needed to coordinate these inputs so that patient care is not fragmented. Departments may also be defined by *direct outputs of organizational products and services.* Manufacturing firms with separate toothpaste, soap, and mouthwash departments need department interfaces to coordinate across outputs so their marketing strategies do not undermine one another. Organizational tasks define departments and department interfaces.

Several dimensions for department definition may be used in a single organization, and large organizations regularly use all three. A multinational corporation might have regional branches in different countries, product (output) divisions within regional branches, and functional (input) departments within product divisions. Department interfaces may have to cope with interregion, interfunction, or interproduct conflict. Some interdependence among departments is inevitable, though its intensity and the issues at stake are influenced by the dimensions on which the departments are defined (Galbraith, 1977).

An important consequence of department definition is that people who share common departments develop shared perceptions, values, and goals as well. Lawrence and Lorsch (1967) found that departments in some business organizations differed in time orientation, interpersonal culture, and formality of structure *in addition* to their diverse task objectives. So division of labor according to task requirements can be associated with other differences. Community college campuses take on ethnic and socioeconomic characteristics of their neighborhoods; medical records, physical therapy, and X-ray departments value different skills and perspectives; toothpaste, soap, and mouthwash departments develop their own informal cultures. Departments with different task interests can also develop internal cultures and structures that contribute to interface problems.

Department representatives.   Department representative roles may be defined differently. In some circumstances, the representative's role is explicit: The dean will represent his or her campus in community college conferences. In other situations, representatives' roles are informally defined: A lab technician may stand up for the laboratory when it is criticized by an X-ray technician in the lunchroom. When relations between departments are critical, formally defined boundary roles and carefully selected representatives are important (Galbraith, 1973). A representative's autonomy and discretion to deal with novel problems must be weighed against a department's need for control and predictability in handling routine issues efficiently (Miles, 1980).

Personal skills and characteristics of department representatives may influence their effectiveness. For example, Strauss (1962) found that purchasing agents used informal influence tactics to deal with multiple department interfaces. Effective agents used a judicious mix of rule-oriented tactics (e.g., appealing to authorities, invoking formal rules, requiring requests in writing), rule evasion (going through the motions, ignoring rules), personal-political pressures (using friendships, using favors, using political allies), educating (direct persuasion, invoking empathy), and organizational tactics (e.g., changing procedures, organizational restructuring). Political savvy, tolerance for ambiguity, and willingness to act in ambiguous and conflict-laden situations are useful characteristics of department representatives.

The organization context. The definition of simple department interface focuses attention on the organization in which the departments are embedded. For most department interfaces, the most important contextual force is the larger organization. Since organizational performance can depend in large part on events at critical department interfaces, conflict problems are often of considerable interest to the rest of the organization.

The impact of a common organizational context on interface conflict can be very direct. Specific issues can be referred up a shared organizational hierarchy for decision by a common superior (Galbraith, 1973). Unresolved interface debates over resource assignments among community college campuses can be referred to the overall college president. Organizational reward systems can reward conflict and so set the stage for escalation, or punish it and so set the stage for withdrawal or suppression (Beer, 1980). If the criteria for assessing the performance of hospital records, X-ray, and physical therapy departments emphasize patient satisfaction, costs of patient care may increase for lack of debate over effective use and coordination of department resources. The structure of the larger organization defines departments and their interdependence, and so shapes interface events. Revising the product-oriented departments of the toothpaste, soap, and mouthwash company into a matrix structure that links product departments with functional divisions can dramatically alter the quantity and quality of interface events (Beer, 1980).

The organizational context can also impinge on events in less formal and direct ways. Sharing an organizational context may provide parties and representatives with common cultural assumptions and shared goals. The joint recognition that "We're all part of the same organization" may moderate tensions between representatives of ethnically different campuses of the community college. So subtle and less visible forces and perspectives from the organizational context can also shape events at the interface.

Dynamics at Department Interfaces

These elements interact in two kinds of dynamics at department interfaces. Representatives' characteristics and expectations interlock in cycles of perception, communication, and action that shape interface events in the short run. The interplay of party characteristics, interface characteristics, and contextual forces define and organize the interface over the longer term.

Department representatives' interaction. Department representatives' behavior revolves around issues and alternatives emerging from department tasks. Appropriate conflict involves relatively stable cycles of bargaining or problem-solving behavior, such as the patterns of representative interaction found in sales and production departments by Walton, Dutton, and Fitch

(1966). Such patterns, once set up, tend to be self-sustaining. New representatives are taught appropriate perceptions and tactics, and so the pattern of bargaining or problem-solving can continue after its initiators have departed.

Patterns of appropriate conflict sometimes shift to more extreme dynamics. Bargaining tactics can escalate into intense conflict, in which compromise and mutually acceptable resolutions are more difficult. Lawrence and Lorsch (1967) identified a "forcing" mode of conflict resolution ("Might overcomes right") associated with relatively lower performance of the larger organization. Excessive conflict between interdependent departments can undermine the accomplishment of organizational goals.

Appropriate conflict can also decline into too little conflict. Problem-solving patterns that generate friendship and trust may be replaced by patterns of suppression or withdrawal from important differences. Alternative solutions to coordination problems may not be critically examined, and important information may be suppressed or avoided to "keep the peace." Too little conflict is similar to the "smoothing" approach to conflict ("Kill your enemies with kindness") that Lawrence and Lorsch (1967) found to be ineffective, and to the dynamics of "groupthink," in which representative diversity is submerged to preserve interface harmony at the cost of poor decisions (Janis, 1972).

Department interface development.   The development of department interfaces influences interaction among representatives, and is itself influenced by parties, contextual forces, and previous representatives' interactions. Departments press representatives to safeguard their interests at the interface, and representatives in turn call on departments for support. Campus representatives to the community college coordinating committee were constrained by the interests and characteristics of their campus constituencies, but they also influenced perceptions and behavior within those constituencies.

The organizational context also influences events at the interface, generally moderating conflict extremes. Escalation produces highly visible departmental fights that draw regulatory attention from upper levels. Extremes of withdrawal and suppression encourage performance deteriorations that are less spectacular but no less problematic in the long term. The larger organization depends on interfaces among interdependent departments for accomplishing its goals, so problematic conflict at those interfaces may draw rapid response. Conflict extremes between X-ray, records, and physical therapy draws attention from doctors or hospital administrators when patient care or costs are affected. The organizational context provides powerful and interested third parties to department interfaces, whose attention limits extremes of immediate interaction.

The department interface can be maintained or changed by the interplay of representative interaction, departmental pressures, and organizational attention. Interface definition and organization can encourage stable cycles of representative interaction. Walton, Dutton, and Fitch (1966) found self-maintaining patterns of interface organization and representative activity. The last two diagrams (C) in Figure 4.1 portray such appropriate conflict, with interaction arrows representing productive problem solving and bargaining, and dashed interface boundaries reflecting moderate organization. Interfaces also may become overorganized, and so encourage problematic suppression of conflict (B). This pattern is represented by the heavy interface boundary linking parties defined by dotted lines, and communication arrows that do not reach the other party. Or the interface may become underorganized, and so permit withdrawal from necessary conflict (B) or escalation of unnecessary warfare (A). These patterns are represented by dotted interface boundaries and arrows that either meet and diverge sharply (escalation) or never meet at all (withdrawal).

A DEPARTMENT INTERFACE AT RIVERVIEW CHEMICAL WORKS

Problems at department interfaces can be illustrated in the relations between the Production and Maintenance Departments in the following case:

The Riverview Chemical Works is a subsidiary of a large international corporation. The Works include three chemical

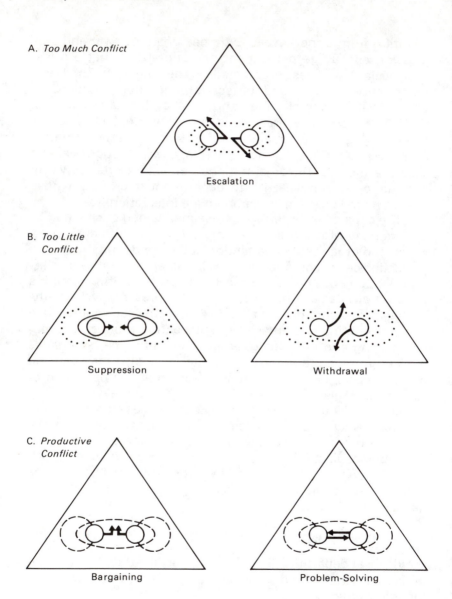

A. *Too Much Conflict*

Escalation

B. *Too Little Conflict*

Suppression   Withdrawal

C. *Productive Conflict*

Bargaining   Problem-Solving

Fig. 4.1. *Conflict at department interfaces.*

plants and several support departments that together employ about a thousand people. The site was built more than twenty years ago, and is now undergoing expansion. Corporate Headquarters wants plant management to produce more "pounds" at lower costs to keep up with market demands.

The three plants are large and technologically sophisticated installations, for the most part manned round-the-clock by 12-hour shifts of Production operators. The raw materials used are expensive and often dangerous. Similar chemical plants, when carelessly run, have been extremely hazardous; explosions, burns, and poison gas inhalation are all possible.

In 1972 the Works endured a bitter strike, during which management personnel ran the largest plant for four months. Management and workers disagree about the blame for deteriorating labor-management relations, but all agree there is "a wall between management and workers" now. A new Works Manager was appointed in early 1973 and he rotated many senior managers into new jobs. Included in this rotation were the superintendents of all three Production plants and the superintendent of the Maintenance Department.

The Production Department is charged with operating the plants and with "getting out the pounds." Their success in this task is vital to the corporation as a whole, for the largest plant is responsible for 50 percent of corporate profits in some years. Corporate Headquarters watches the Production Department carefully, and constantly seeks more output in times of booming markets.

Production operators work 12-hour shifts in a complex schedule that rotates responsibilities for manning the plant at night and on holidays and weekends. Much of their work involves monitoring production processes, "watching" rather than "doing." Their jobs are often boring, though boredom is punctuated by periods of panic when something goes wrong. Production operators are expected to do routine maintenance on their equipment and to trouble-shoot problems before calling in Maintenance mechanics.

Production workers are typically younger, less skilled, more militant union members, and paid less than Maintenance workers. Many Production operators believe that Maintenance mechanics have a soft job. They think delays in attention to their technical problems result from Maintenance laziness or incompetence, and that equipment breakdowns are often the result of poor work by mechanics. Production operators think Maintenance should be paid at the same scale and work the same hours as Production, and they envy mechanic opportunities to travel over the site and do interesting jobs.

The Maintenance Department is responsible for keeping plant equipment in good repair, so its use will not endanger workers or output. Since the technology is complex and the process is dangerous, mechanics play an important role. Indeed, the Maintenance Department is the largest at the Works.

Mechanics ordinarily work 8-hour shifts, operating as individuals or in small teams all over the site. They seldom remain in one spot for long, and the job involves varied and complex "doing" activities which are often more interesting than Production jobs. Maintenance workers are for the most part older, more experienced, more skilled, and better paid than Production operators. Many Production operators aspire to jobs as mechanics and transfer into that department when possible.

Maintenance workers have little patience with Production operators. They believe that equipment breakdowns could be avoided if Production workers would do minimal routine maintenance or avoid deliberately mistreating the equipment. They resent Production pressures to do nonessential repair tasks ahead of schedule. They regard many of the Production workers as irresponsible "young bucks," who do not have enough sense to treat their equipment right.

Maintenance and Production workers come together in a variety of circumstances. There are day-to-day contacts as mechanics make routine repairs in Production facilities. These contacts produce friction over who is to blame for breakdowns, why repairs have been delayed, who is to clean up after they are finished, and so on. Operators and mechanics also meet in scheduled shutdowns for major repairs and overhauls. These shutdowns are carefully planned in advance, and elaborate standard operating procedures apply to them. Equipment under repair, for example, is "tagged" with written explanations of its status so it cannot be misused, and mechanics use their personal locks to immobilize critical elements, like valves, whose untimely use could create danger. Production and Maintenance workers also come together in emergency situations, where unforeseen problems require immediate action.

Squabbling between Production operators and Maintenance mechanics has not produced major escalations of conflict. But management of both departments was uncomfortably aware that the combination of continued bickering, complex technology, and dangerous raw materials could produce serious problems. Several minor accidents could already be traced to tensions between the two departments.

The Riverview Chemical Works situation can be analyzed in terms of the questions listed at the end of Chapter 2. These questions direct attention to (1) elements of the interface, and (2) dynamics of representative interaction and interface development.

Elements of the Maintenance-Production Interface

The primary *parties* in this case are the Maintenance and Production Departments, each of which has interests and internal characteristics that affect their interface. Maintenance managers are concerned with keeping the installation running at low costs, since their performance is evaluated by cost criteria. Mechanics want to preserve their higher wages, better hours, and general status. Maintenance operates in small teams that deal with varied jobs, and its members are loosely knit together by a shared sense of craftsmanship. Maintenance mechanics look down on Production operators as young, inexperienced, and sometimes willfully incompetent.

Production managers are concerned with "getting out the pounds." Production operators resent the pay and working-hour advantages of Maintenance, and they want the union to equalize wage rates. Production work requires operators to remain in the same area in boring and lonely tasks. Relations between Production management and workers have been strained, in part because Production workers have little on-the-job autonomy. Production operators often blame equipment problems on poor maintenance and attribute delays in repair work to the mechanics' laziness or incompetence.

Department *representatives* include practically all operators and mechanics at different times. Both departments are represented by managers at formal interface meetings. The senior manager of Maintenance once managed a Production Department, so he is sympathetic to Production problems. His personal style is low-key and cooperative; he listens more than he talks, and he is not very assertive. The senior manager of Production is committed to participative management in his department, and he pursues his objectives with great energy. Both managers are relatively new to their roles, and both are interested in constructive change within and between their departments.

Maintenance and Production are closely interdependent, and their *interface* involves high stakes for both. Efficient, safe production requires joint work by the two departments, though the personnel involved in a given joint task may not come together again soon. Production operators remain in one place but mechanics move all over the Works, so ongoing task relations are infrequent. Boundaries defined by task requirements are seldom reinforced by physical, social, or control boundaries. Proximity shifts as mechanics come and go; social bonds are difficult to develop in fleeting contacts; control over behavior is formally and informally lodged in departments and not in the interface. The boundary around day-to-day interface contacts between Production and Maintenance is neither well defined nor stably composed.

That boundary is also very open to disruptive inputs or outputs. Operators are called away or distracted by other work;

mechanics are summoned to deal with high priority repairs elsewhere. Important information or resources may fail to reach the right place at the right time.

Interaction between operators and mechanics is partially organized by formal rules and procedures, such as sitewide safety regulations ("Always wear helmets and safety shoes") and procedures for handling equipment under repair ("tagging" repairs, locking critical valves). But shared norms and agreements for new situations are difficult to develop when contacts are fleeting. There are frequent arguments about unregulated matters, such as who should clean up what and who is to blame for continuing breakdowns.

This analysis suggests that the Production-Maintenance interface for day-to-day interactions tends toward loose organization and weak definition. The interface is not clearly defined; its external boundaries are open to disruptive inputs or outputs; few shared mechanisms for regulating internal interface activity exist. There are two exceptions to this underorganization: planned shutdowns and emergencies. Shutdowns for major maintenance are carefully planned and controlled: Production and Maintenance personnel work together on well-defined joint tasks, within an interface that is much more tightly organized than day-to-day encounters. In emergencies, the interface becomes more tightly organized by informal agreement: operators and mechanics implicitly join together for the duration of the crisis. Without the formal planning of the planned shutdown or the informal stimulus of emergency, however, the department interface tends to be underorganized and so permits either too much or too little conflict.

Several aspects of the *organizational context* affect events at the Production-Maintenance interface. The organizational reward system emphasizes partially conflicting performance criteria for the two departments: Costs are emphasized for Maintenance, and "pounds" are important to Production. When conflicts involve lower-level employees, such as mechanics and operators, the nearest common superior may be five levels away in the organizational hierarchy. Management has also been obsessed with labor-management relations, focusing more attention on negotiations with the union than on department interfaces.

On the other hand, the organization as a whole takes indicators of productivity and safety very seriously, and evidence of poor performance or dangerous behavior generates immediate attention from upper ranks of the hierarchy. Even minor accidents prompt discussion at the highest levels of plant management, and productivity below expectations can touch off elaborate investigations.

Several less direct contextual influences also affect the interface. Some department representatives identify with the larger organization, and so work for productive department relations. Managers in particular become committed to corporate goals; operators and mechanics have less to gain from corporate success, since upward mobility into management ranks is very unlikely. But just the fact of upper-level concern about the interface is enough to moderate potential problems, as representatives worry about the threat of attention from upper levels.

Dynamics at the Maintenance-Production Interface

Problems at the interface between Production and Maintenance take the form of bickering and withdrawal rather than escalation or suppression. The issues are task-related: Representatives argue about who is responsible for breakdowns, who should clean up the mess, and when repairs should be finished. The outcomes can benefit one department at the expense of the other, but the costs and gains involved are small.

These squabbles at the interface have potential for escalation. The parties distort communications to favor themselves and to denigrate the other party. Operators blame breakdowns on poor previous work by mechanics, and mechanics blame problems on lack of routine maintenance by operators. Problematic events confirm each department's negative stereotypes of the other. Mechanics explain operator "negligence" in terms of their youth and incompetence; operators explain mechanic "laziness" in connection with their excessive privileges. Distorted communications and negative stereotypes combine to fuel continued bickering. The seeds for escalation of conflict are present, but the squabbles have not escalated into outright fighting. Why have the problems remained minor?

Two factors inhibit escalation of conflict between Production and Maintenance. At this point Riverview Chemical Works is dominated by its concern about "the wall between management and workers"—a conflict that cuts across the departments. Workers from both departments are allied for the conflict with managers; neither workers nor managers want to risk their solidarity by investing in interdepartmental strife. Conflict between the two departments is also inhibited by shared organizational goals (e.g., low costs, high productivity), and by recognition that their joint performance is carefully monitored by upper management. Excessive conflict would hamper the attainment of organizational goals and draw unwelcome attention from bosses.

But even the low level of interface conflict concerned management. The performance of the Works was not high by company standards, and squabbling at the Production-Maintenance interface contributed to reduced output. And the potential costs of continued conflict were exceptionally high. Mistakes in maintenance and operation of such a complex and dangerous installation could cost millions of dollars and many lives.

MANAGING CONFLICT AT THE RIVERVIEW CHEMICAL WORKS

How may the above analysis be used to manage the relations between the Production and Maintenance Departments more productively? We turn now to subsequent events at the Riverview Chemical Works.

The new Manager of Riverview Chemical Works was charged with "turning the plant around" in terms of labor-management relations and production performance. Labor-management relations were extremely poor after the 1972 strike. Plant performance, in terms of productivity, costs, and safety, was among the poorest in the Corporation. The new

Works Manager focused his attention initially on the problem of relations between management and the union. Problems between Production and Maintenance were seen as relatively minor at the outset.

Attention to labor-management relations eventually paid off in reduced conflict. To the frustration of management, however, conflict at department interfaces—notably that between Production and Maintenance—grew more obvious and difficult to control as labor-management relations improved.

The Works Manager recruited external consultants to help diagnose and improve employee relations. The head of the Maintenance Department invited those consultants to work with his department, focusing on its internal operation.

Work with the Maintenance Department revealed substantial internal tensions at the middle management level. Several middle managers were frustrated and angry with upper management, though their feelings were largely unexpressed. Team-building activities within the Department encouraged discussion of internal problems, improved relations among Department managers, and spread recognition of how easily Department members could fall into destructive conflict.

Enthusiastic about their improved teamwork, Maintenance managers suggested meetings with Production managers to work on interface problems. The Production managers were sceptical, but willing to cooperate provided they could first diagnose and improve their internal relations. So team-building activities were also held for the Production Department.

Ultimately Production and Maintenance managers spent several days together with external consultants, discussing problems in joint work and developing a shared diagnosis of their interface. They agreed on steps to improve coordination of joint work. Since many problems at the interface involved lower level managers and hourly workers, they also agreed to hold similar meetings at lower levels to diagnose problems and develop solutions. These meetings were carried out with aid from internal consultants, who were respected by managers and workers alike. These meetings promoted better understanding and recognition of each other's problems by both operators and mechanics.

Although the interface meetings improved relations between operators and mechanics in the short term, continued pressure from Corporate Headquarters for increased production at reduced cost generated further antagonism between Production and Maintenance personnel. Eventually tensions between the Departments prompted a substantial reorganization of the Works.

Under the leadership of the Assistant Works Manager, newly promoted from the largest Production plant, the Works was reorganized into a "team management" structure that deployed most Maintenance personnel within Production plants, where they would share responsibility with Production for operating and maintaining the installations. With the aid of the internal consultants, the Assistant Works Manager evolved the new design in consultation with virtually all those affected. Although the reorganization took more than a year to conceive and implement, the process permitted influence by all parties concerned and produced little overt resistance to change.

The reorganization had some costs—the large and mobile force of Maintenance workers who could be moved quickly to trouble spots, for example, was a casualty of the change. But most managers agreed that those costs were outweighed by gains in cooperation and coordination. The years after the reorganization have been the best in Works history in terms of productivity, costs, safety, and employee relations—a result aided (but not solely determined) by improved relations between Production and Maintenance.

Developing the Production-Maintenance Interface

Intervention to develop the Production-Maintenance interface began with work on internal conflicts in the Maintenance Department. Maintenance managers realized that similar problems existed at the interface. A workshop designed largely as a reframing intervention—emphasizing diagnosis of departmental dynamics, education about conflict management, and increased internal communications—also affected perspectives on the interface and its problems.

The same team-building process was used to prepare the Production Department for work at the interface. In both team-building meetings the Departments examined internal conflicts that had previously been suppressed. These meetings paved the way for interface discussions by dealing with tensions that might otherwise have been ventilated on other parties.

Bringing together managers from the two Departments amounted to an intervention in itself. The meeting focused resources on newly recognized interface problems, and defined a clear boundary around important representatives of both Departments and the external consultants. The external and internal consultants helped manage discussions in interface meetings, and meeting outcomes included agreement about common tasks and goals, shared understandings of past controversies, joint action plans for future problems, and the beginnings of informal norms for managing future conflicts. The emergence of the internal consultants as credible resources, particularly at the lower levels, provided a new resource for managing interdepartmental conflict. These meetings reduced the bickering and increased understanding at the Production-Maintenance interface. The meetings helped create a better-defined, more inclusive, and more tightly organized interface.

Works Reorganization for Team Management

Pressures from the larger context created more problems at the Production-Maintenance interface, and eventually management undertook more extensive redefinition and reorganization of the Works. The move to "team management" eliminated Maintenance as a party and relocated the task interface much lower in the organization. Redistributing the personnel of Maintenance across the different plants established task interdependence between mechanics and operators working together over longer periods within a single department. The change reinforced task interdependencies with geographic proximity; social bonds could be built over continuing interaction; authoritative control over both sides further defined the interface, for common superiors in the new organization were much closer hierarchically to operators and mechanics. The new arrangement also encouraged tighter organization of interfaces: Constant interaction encouraged informal norms, and closer supervision made formal rules and procedures enforcement more feasible.

The organizational restructuring had costs. No longer were large groups of Maintenance workers easily available to handle crises, and the specialization possible in the old arrangement was more difficult in the new. But the new structure permitted closer control and tighter organization of important interdependence between maintenance and production work.

Figure 4.2 illustrates these changes at the Riverview Chemical Works. The interface at the outset was loosely organized (indicated by dotted oval line) and representatives bickered or withdrew from each other. Interventions that defined and tightened interface organization (dashed boundary) produced more problem-solving activity. The organizational restructuring for "team management" incorporated both parties into a single department, so that Production and Maintenance issues were solved within a single department.

MANAGING CONFLICT AT DEPARTMENT INTERFACES

What can be done about escalating, destructive conflict between departments? What options are available to remedy extremes of passive collusion and cooperation? This section proposes general approaches to managing conflict problems between departments.

Reducing Departmental Conflict

Conflict-reducing actions may focus on the immediate interaction among departmental representatives, or on longer-term forces and constraints that encourage escalation.

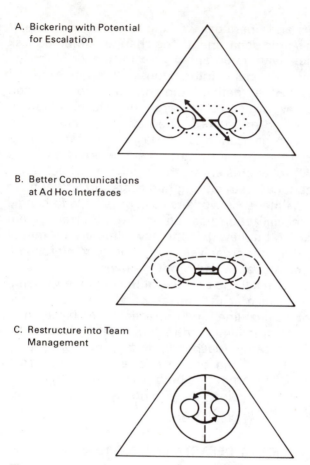

A. Bickering with Potential
   for Escalation

B. Better Communications
   at Ad Hoc Interfaces

C. Restructure into Team
   Management

Fig. 4.2. *Production and maintenance at Riverview Chemical Works.*

Changing representatives' interaction: three strategies.   Three of the four classes of intervention discussed in Chapter 3 may be used to influence immediate patterns of interaction among representatives. Representatives' perspectives may be reframed by introducing new information or interpretations; resources available at the interface may be reallocated to alleviate underlying scarcities; representative behaviors may be altered to reshape issues and tactics that promote excessive conflict. The right intervention or combination of interventions will interrupt self-reinforcing patterns of representative perception, communication, and behavior that maintain or escalate destructive conflict.

Strategy 1. *Alter representatives' perceptions.* Educative or persuasive interventions can provide alternative interpretations or new information to representatives. New information, for example, can debunk representatives' stereotypes of their own department's task competence or the other department's incompetence. Representatives who recognize their own contributions to interface problems are better prepared to recognize commonalities with their opponents, instead of continually focusing on differences. Representatives can also be educated about larger forces that encourage conflict and self-reinforcing conflict dynamics, and so become better able to control their own contributions to unintended escalations. Actions that help department representatives understand and reinterpret the conflict can also enable them to reduce it.

Strategy 2. *Alter representatives' communications.* Improving the quantity of communications can increase the flow of relevant information from both sides, so that decisions are based on more than unrealistic stereotypes. Communication quality can be improved by training representatives to send clear signals and to listen effectively. For example, requiring representatives to demonstrate that they understand another's proposal before they can make a counterproposal can reduce the tendency for salvos and countersalvos that miss each other's point. Interventions can also focus on the communications process itself, educating representatives about their mutual distortions of information (e.g., Blake, Shepard, and Mouton, 1964).

Strategy 3. *Alter representatives' immediate behaviors.* Patterns of representatives' behavior can interlock in cycles of conflict escalation. Representatives can escape deadlocked positions by breaking down large and unresolvable issues into smaller and less inflammatory subissues, or by seeking alternatives to entrenched positions that will benefit both departments or enable each to save face. Representatives can also learn de-escalation tactics: Announcements of tension-reducing intentions can be clear; risk of exploitive responses by other representatives can be reduced; low-risk initiatives for starting de-escalation can be identified; representatives can be selected or trained for skills in handling volatile situations. Without careful limitation of the stakes and risks in conflict reduction, well-intentioned initiatives may boomerang into worse conflict if the other party is distrusting or tempted to exploit the opportunity.

Excessive conflict in representative interaction may call for altering representatives' perceptions, the communications between them, or their immediate behaviors. Successful interventions interrupt ongoing chains of mutually reinforcing perceptions, communications, and actions—unsuccessful attempts can fail to alter the pattern, or even make it worse. Representative interactions shape immediate outcomes, but those interactions occur within the constraints provided by their interface, which is itself influenced over time by those outcomes.

Changing interface development: three strategies. Three intervention strategies from Chapter 3 can alter the interplay of parties, context, and interface to reduce conflict. Perspectives within those elements can be reframed; resources can be shifted, expanded, or contracted; underlying structural and cultural forces can be realigned. Such changes alter the mix of constraints and pressures provided by interface definition and organization.

Strategy 4. *Alter the interface.* Changing the way the interface is defined or organized is an obvious route to reducing interdepartmental conflict. Interventions can emphasize the importance of superordinate goals, for example, and so define more clearly the departmental task interdependence that created the interface in the first place. More resources invested at the interface can reduce conflict-promoting scarcities or expand resources for managing tensions. Interface boundaries can be redefined to include department representatives or third parties who will moderate escalation. Interventions can tighten interface organization to control the conflict: External boundaries can be closed to disruptive inputs and outputs; formal rules and procedures for deciding controversial questions can be promulgated; norms and values that limit escalation can be negotiated across departments. Tighter organization, clearer superordinate goals, expanded interface resources, and changed composition can all contribute to controlling interdepartmental conflict.

Strategy 5. *Alter one or both departments.* Reframed departmental perceptions or changed internal characteristics can also reduce interdepartmental conflict. Department interests can be reoriented by revealing unrecognized interests in cooperation or by altering perceived incentives for conflict. Department mobilization for conflict can be altered by opening department boundaries to new information, rotating personnel through different departments, reducing internal conformity and obedience to militant department leaders, or debunking unrealistic stereotypes that promote escalation. Interventions that change one department can reduce conflict even when other departments do not change immediately, but changes in one party seldom persist if corresponding changes in the other are not eventually forthcoming

Strategy 6. *Alter the organizational context.* Forces from the external context can also be realigned to reduce interdepartmental conflict. Attention from higher up in the organizational hierarchy on interface conflict can resolve immediate disputes by intervention from superiors, and long-term hierarchical attention can retard escalation in the future. Reward systems by which organizations recognize department contributions can be revised to create incentives for less conflict or disincentives for escalation. Organizational restructuring can relocate critical department interfaces or eliminate problematic interdependence, and so render conflicts moot. The organizational context defines the task interdependencies that compel department contact and conflict, so revision of organizational arrangements can drastically revise the existence or the character of department interfaces.

Better defined and more tightly organized interfaces, less mobilized and antagonistic parties, and organizational contexts structured to control escalation can interact to reduce conflict

TABLE 4.1

Reducing conflict at department interfaces

Changing representatives' interaction

1. *Alter perceptions*	Debunk representatives' stereotypes of own department's virtue and other's incompetence or malevolence
	Reconceive situation to emphasize similarities and impersonal forces contributing to conflict
	Recognize interlocking dynamics and own contributions to escalation
2. *Alter communications*	Increase the quantity of relevant information exchanged by representatives
	Improve the quality of information flow
	• representatives send clearer signals about intentions
	• representatives listen more carefully to others
	Communicate about communications problems
3. *Alter behavior*	Unfreeze deadlocked positions
	• break up enlarged issues and solve easiest subissues first
	• propose mutually beneficial face-saving alternatives
	Adopt de-escalating tactics
	• plan de-escalation strategy
	• clear messages about tension-reducing intentions
	• counters against exploitation by other representatives
	• identify low-risk initiatives
	Train/recruit representatives for de-escalation skills

Changing interface development

4. *Alter the interface*	Define interface superordinate goals that require departmental cooperation
	Expand resources to reduce conflict-inducing scarcities or provide for conflict management
	Define interface boundaries to include moderate representatives or third parties interested in conflict reduction

TABLE 4.1   (continued)
Reducing conflict at department interfaces

	Tighten interface organization to control unintended escalations • close boundaries to disruptive inputs and outputs • promulgate rules and procedures for handling controversy • negotiate norms and values shared across representatives
5. *Alter one or both departments*	Reframe department interests to recognize unseen common interests or reduce importance of conflicting interests Reduce departmental mobilization for conflict • open department boundaries to new information • rotate personnel across departments • reduce internal conformity and militant leadership • debunk unrealistic stereotypes within departments
6. *Alter organizational context*	Focus attention from hierarchical superiors on conflict to solve specific issues and prevent future escalations Change organizational reward systems to provide disincentives for excessive conflict between departments Redesign organization structure to reduce interdependence or compel cooperation between departments

among representatives. The elements are interdependent, and changes in one over time produce complementary changes in others or pressures to return to the initial state. Table 4.1 summarizes interventions for reducing conflict at department interfaces. The list of possible interventions is not exhaustive, but it does provide a variety of options for managers faced with excessive conflict between departments.

Promoting Departmental Conflict

Interventions can promote productive conflict in place of either withdrawal from interaction or suppression of differences between departments. As in conflict reduction, conflict promotion activities can alter the dynamics of representatives' interaction, or reshape the development of the interface.

Changing representatives' interaction: three strategies.   Interventions that redirect behavior, reframe perspectives, or reallocate resources can promote productive conflict as well as reduce destructive escalations. The targets of such interventions are self-reinforcing cycles of representatives' perceptions, communications among representatives, and their immediate behaviors that produce withdrawal from important interdependencies or suppression of critical differences.

Strategy 1. *Alter representatives' perceptions.* New information or novel interpretations can promote more constructive engagement. When differences are suppressed, for example, actions that clarify unrecognized differences or contradict assumed similarities between departments can spark constructive debate. Representatives can examine systemic forces and their own contributions to unrealistic peace. Suppression may be countered in part by understanding its operation and its impact on the interdependent operation of departments.

When too little conflict is a consequence of withdrawal, representatives' perceptions explain and justify departmental avoidance. The realism of stereotypes that suggest that interaction will lead to disaster can be examined. Systemic forces underlying avoidance and representatives' contributions can be analyzed. The more representatives perceive themselves as active participants and contributors to withdrawal or suppression, the more they can alter those patterns.

Strategy 2. *Alter representatives' communications.* Changing the quantity and quality of information exchanged between representatives can also promote more constructive debate. When conflict is suppressed, much noncontroversial information may be shared between department representatives, but information that might produce disagreement is systematically suppressed and distorted. Representatives can be trained or encouraged to reduce their censorship of controversial communications, so that information is presented more often and more clearly. Or representatives may be encouraged to pursue information, by actively investigating areas of potential disagreement. Explicit discussions of communication processes and the dynamics of information suppression may also promote constructive debate.

When representatives withdraw from differences, the quantity and quality of information may be restricted by their avoidance. Interventions can expand the absolute amount of communication, or encourage representatives to confront avoided issues and to listen for unrecognized differences. Discussions of withdrawal dynamics and their impact on vital information exchange can also promote productive engagement.

Strategy 3. *Alter immediate representative behavior.* Constructive conflict can be promoted by interventions that reshape the issues in question or the actions of representatives at the interface. When the problem is conflict suppression, for instance, issues can be consolidated and enlarged, and unrecognized trade-offs can be articulated to demonstrate the need for debate. Representatives' tactics for counteracting suppression include planning to raise controversial issues, commitments to departmental objectives, tactics for countering harmonizing efforts, bargaining or problem-solving tactics appropriate to the issues, or recruitment and training of representatives with skills for constructive conflict.

When the problem is conflict avoidance, on the other hand, selecting a few issues can focus discussion, and emphasizing previously unseen gains of engagement can keep representatives involved. Tactics for reducing withdrawal include formulating objectives and plans for engagement, plans for countering representatives' withdrawal, bargaining or problem-solving tactics appropriate to the issues, and activities to enhance relevant skills of representatives.

Changed interaction patterns among representatives spring from alterations in mutually supporting perceptions, communications, and actions. Interventions that influence one aspect of interaction may require supportive changes in other aspects. But altered perceptions, improved communications, or new behaviors among representatives can all serve as catalysts for rapid shifts in conflict outcomes. Increased constructive conflict will persist when supported by several aspects of representatives' interaction and by complementary interface developments.

Changing interface development: three strategies   Reshaping department interfaces to promote productive conflict may involve reframing perspectives, reallocating resources, or realigning underlying forces. The focus for such intervention may be the interface itself, one or both departments, or the organizational context within which they are embedded.

Strategy 4. *Alter the interface.* Interventions can redefine or reorganize the interface and so alter its impact on representatives' interaction. Conflict suppression is most often associated with clearly defined and tightly organized interfaces, when departmental and contextual pressures for conflict cannot compete with interface pressures for peace and harmony. Interventions that clarify the different goals of different departments can surface suppressed conflict. Reallocating resources to emphasize scarcities can compel increased competition at the interface, or focus more time and energy on recognizing and managing differences. Interface boundaries can be redefined to exclude passive representatives or to include representatives interested in productive conflict. Interface constraints on representatives' behavior can be loosened: Boundaries can be opened to stimulating inputs and outputs; rules and procedures that prevent debate can be relaxed; informal norms and values that impose excessive politeness on representatives can be renegotiated. Clear definition and tight organization that constrain interface debate and support suppression can be altered to promote productive conflict.

Withdrawal from conflict, in contrast to suppressed conflict, is common at vaguely defined and loosely organized interfaces, when representatives can avoid departmental and contextual pressures for conflict. Interventions can promote better interface definition by emphasizing the interdependence of departments and the costs of avoidance. Contracting resources available at the interface can emphasize scarcities that make withdrawal costly, and resources can be expanded to manage differences and keep representatives in interaction. Interface boundaries can be redefined to include representatives and third parties who actively explore differences. Interface organization can be tightened for better control: Boundaries can be closed to irrelevant invasions and dissipation of personnel and resources; rules and procedures to control withdrawal can be promulgated; informal norms and values that encourage open debate can be negotiated. Interventions that clearly define the interface and tighten its organization can inhibit withdrawal or denial of critical differences.

Strategy 5. *Alter one or both departments.* Department perspectives can be reframed to reduce overly positive stereotypes, to clarify unrecognized conflicts of interests, or to reduce perceived interests in suppression or withdrawal. Departments can be reorganized internally for interface conflict: Departmental boundaries can be defined more clearly; internal department organization can be altered to provide less support to conflict suppression or withdrawal. Underorganized departments, for example, can be mobilized for more engagement by aroused leadership, increased internal structure, and enhanced informal cohesion. Overorganized departments can open their boundaries and loosen their internal organization to permit more attention to external interdependencies.

Strategy 6. *Alter the organizational context.* The constellation of external forces operating on the interface and the parties can also be reshaped to promote more constructive debate. In problems of suppression of conflict, the larger organization may not recognize potential conflicts. Interventions that focus attention from organizational superiors on suppressed conflict can encourage more open debate, and hierarchical pressure for more discussion of controversial issues can be productive over time. Organizational reward systems can provide incentives for productive conflict, and disincentives for suppression. Organizations can redesign their structures to combine departments (and so legitimate suppression), or to emphasize departmental differences (and so press for more conflict).

When too little conflict is a result of withdrawal, attention from organizational superiors can encourage more focused engagements. Organizational reward systems can provide incentives for engagement and disincentives for avoidance. Organizational structures can be designed to reduce the interdependence of some departments (and legitimize their withdrawal) or to increase their interdependence (and so promote engagement).

The behavioral symptoms of withdrawal and suppression at department interfaces are rather similar—too little productive conflict among representatives. But suppression occurs in the context of overorganized interfaces, and withdrawal occurs at underorganized interfaces, so their intervention implications are quite different. Table 4.2 summarizes interventions for promoting productive conflict at department interfaces. Conflict promoting interventions, like those for conflict reduction, affect ongoing events and processes that interlock in cycles. They are consequently likely both to alter other aspects of those cycles, or to be altered themselves over time.

TABLE 4.2
Promoting conflict at department interfaces

	PROBLEMS OF SUPPRESSION	PROBLEMS OF WITHDRAWAL
Changing representatives' interaction		
1. *Alter perceptions*	Clarify unseen differences or unrealistic similarities	Examine assumptions about costs of interaction
	Examine systemic forces for suppression	Examine systemic forces for withdrawal
	Examine representative contributions to suppression	Examine representative contributions to withdrawal

TABLE 4.2 (continued)
Promoting conflict at department interfaces

	PROBLEMS OF SUPPRESSION	PROBLEMS OF WITHDRAWAL
2. *Alter communications*	Expand exchanges of controversial information Improve quality of exchange: • send uncensored messages Discuss suppression dynamics	Increase amount of absolute communication Improve quality of exchange: • speak to avoided issues Discuss withdrawal dynamics
3. *Alter behavior*	Define positions: • enlarge fragmented issues • articulate suppressed trade-offs Surfacing tactics: • plan to raise issues • commit to objectives • suppression counters • bargaining/problem-solving tactics Train/recruit skilled representatives	Define positions: • focus on few relevant issues • emphasize unrecognized gains of engagement Engagement tactics: • plan to engage other • commit to interaction • avoidance counters • bargaining/problem-solving tactics Train/recruit skilled representatives
Changing interface development		
4. *Alter the interface*	Clarify goal diversity between departments Constrict resources for scarcity; expand for managing Define boundaries to include conflict raisers	Emphasize department interdependence Constrict resources for withdrawal; expand for managing Define boundaries to include conflict engagers

TABLE 4.2 (continued)
Promoting conflict at department interfaces

	PROBLEMS OF SUPPRESSION	PROBLEMS OF WITHDRAWAL
	Loosen organization: • open boundaries for stimulation • relax rules and procedures restricting debate • relax norms and values compelling politeness	Tighten organization: • close boundaries to husband resources • enforce rules and procedures restricting withdrawal • negotiate norms and values compelling engagement
5. *Alter one or both departments*	Clarify divergent interests; de-emphasize similarity Mobilize for more conflict: • arouse leadership • create internal structure • build internal cohesion	Clarify importance of interaction; de-emphasize threat of contact Mobilize for more engagement: • strengthen leadership • loosen internal constraints • reduce isolationism
6. *Alter organizational context*	Focus hierarchical attention on suppression Alter organizational reward system to reward productive conflict, punish suppression Restructure organization to integrate or clarify differences of departments	Focus hierarchical attention on withdrawal Alter organizational reward system to reward productive conflict, punish withdrawal Restructure organization to separate or emphasize interdependence of departments

SUMMARY

This chapter first defines simple department interfaces, emphasizing task interdependence among relatively equal departments insulated from the larger society by a common organizational context. Analysis of department interfaces involves examining their elements—interface definition and organization, departmental interests and mobilization, representatives' roles and personal characteristics, and organizational superiors, reward systems, and design—and the dynamics of interaction among those elements at two levels—the interaction of department representatives, and the development of department interfaces.

To illustrate this analysis, I describe the relations between Maintenance and Production at the Riverview Chemical Works. The Departments and their representatives, the larger organizational context (the corporation), the definition and organization of the Production-Maintenance interface, and the dynamics of representative interaction and interface development all helped shape events at the Works. The next section follows the efforts to manage departmental conflict at the Works over several years, and analyzes these efforts as interventions to build a more effective department interface and later to restructure the organizational context for better management of departmental differences.

The last section discusses conflict management at department interfaces in more general terms, briefly suggesting strategies and tactics for either reducing or promoting conflict. There is not enough room here to discuss this catalogue of interventions in detail; however, some interventions will be considered more specifically in succeeding chapters.

Department interfaces are in many ways the simplest interfaces. Their differences and their interdependencies center on organizational tasks, so the reasons for conflict and the importance of conflict management between them are easily recognized. Simple department interfaces are not plagued by power differences, nor by invasion from the larger context, and they benefit from the attention and guidance of superiors who are concerned with their joint performance and who are respected by representatives of both departments.

Two characteristics distinguish department interfaces from other forms of simple interfaces, which I discuss in subsequent chapters. First, although all interfaces bring together interdependent parties, the interdependence of departments is defined by, and centrally concerned with, organizational tasks. Consequently, successful conflict management intervention can often focus in large measure on "getting the job done." Second, the organizational context exerts an important and even-handed effect on both parties. Both departments share some commitment to the goals of the organization, and that commitment tends to moderate problems at the interface. So conflict between departments is typically less extreme than at many other interfaces.

Level Interfaces

5

Level interfaces bring together parties from different levels of the organizational hierarchy. This chapter describes characteristics of level interfaces that distinguish them from other interfaces, and examines interlevel conflict using the frameworks of Chapters 2 and 3. Here I focus on the special problems of managing conflict between unequally powerful parties.

The first section considers conflict at level interfaces in general terms. The second section illustrates interlevel conflict between workers and managers in a transit authority, and applies the framework of Chapter 2 to analyze these relations. The third section describes interventions to improve worker-management relations at the transit authority, and considers the impact of the interventions on representatives' interaction and the development of the interface. The following section examines interventions for managing unequal conflict in more general terms. The summary reemphasizes the problems unique to level interfaces.

ANALYZING LEVEL INTERFACES

Level interfaces bring together parties that differ in formal organizational power. Virtually all complex organizations and societies grant some parties more formal authority and access to organizational resources than others. Doctors have more formal power in hospitals than orderlies; managers in manufacturing firms wield more formal authority than workers. Organizational hierarchies in general define unequal distributions of formal power.

What is power? Generations of scholars have debated the implications of different definitions (e.g., Lukes, 1974; Clegg, 1979). For the purposes of this book, *power refers to the ability of one party to get another to behave in ways incompatible with the latter's immediate interests.* The exercise of power can produce either positive or negative consequences. Sometimes the use of power mobilizes energy, commitment, and effective action by leaders and their followers. On other occasions power use results in coercion, obstruction, apathy, and resistance (McClelland, 1975; Kanter, 1979). Upper parties can mobilize lower parties to pursue a vision contrary to their own immediate interests: Gandhi inspired thousands to risk their lives in the Indian Independence Movement for national and spiritual goals. Or upper parties may coerce lower parties into sullen and apathetic obedience. "Slaves," writes McClelland, "are the most inefficient form of labor ever devised by man." (McClelland, 1975:263)

Does the allocation of formal power by organizational hierarchies define *real* power in organizations? Do organization charts and formal reporting relations determine *actual* as well as *theoretical* power? Formal position has an impact on power distribution on organizations: Chief executives can exert more influence on middle managers than vice versa. But the formal distribution of power does *not* account for all organizational power differences: Secretaries with little formal authority often control activities of executives. Understanding conflict at level interfaces requires attention to both informal and formal aspects of power.

Formal definitions of power differences are comparatively easy to see. Organizational ranks are endowed with explicit authority and responsibilities, granted control over critical resources, or cleared to handle sensitive information. But *informal* factors also influence the relative power of the parties. Parties may unofficially control important information, special expertise, critical "connections," or unique competencies needed by the organization, and so wield power despite low positions in the formal hierarchy (Mechanic, 1962). Formal definitions of upper and lower parties may only partially reflect the realities of informal influence. Branch organizations sometimes dictate terms to corporate headquarters; workers sometimes force management to accept their demands. Control over the outcomes of conflict at level interfaces is *not* always obvious from formal definitions of upper and lower parties.

   Simple level interfaces are defined by (1) task interdependencies and (2) unequal formal power between upper and lower parties that (3) may be influenced by contextual forces even though they (4) share a common organizational context. Level interfaces, like department interfaces, bring together parties that must interact because of *organizationally defined interdependencies.* Workers and managers must interact if organizational activities are to be coordinated; corporate headquarters and branch organizations must interact if corporate resources are to be effectively utilized. But level interfaces also bring together *formally unequal parties to whom the distribution of power is a central concern.* Workers and managers are often greatly concerned about controlling each other; branches and headquarters worry about mutual influence. Level interfaces *share a common organizational context* that defines their differences in formal power. Workers and managers work in the same plant, and headquarters and branches belong to the same corporation. But their unequal rank within the formal hierarchy increases the likelihood of *influence by forces in the larger context.* Workers often turn to international unions for support against management; branches sometimes seek support from local communities in controversies with headquarters.

Elements of Level Interfaces

What are the bases for level interfaces in organizations? What underlying forces define upper and lower parties? One explanation for hierarchical differences emphasizes *coordination* of complex organizational activities. In this view, rational use of resources requires different levels of authority and responsibility. Organization design is a matter of analyzing coordination requirements and rationally designing appropriate hierarchies and levels (e.g., Miller and Rice, 1967; Galbraith, 1977). Another explanation for power differences focuses on the continuing *contest* for political control. From this perspective, the design of organizational hierarchies reflects struggles for dominance among contending coalitions (March, 1962; Braverman, 1974; Hecksher, 1980).

Both perspectives are useful in analyzing level interfaces. Analysis of organizational departments, for example, suggests that their power grows as they become recognized for solving critical organizational problems. Power in this view is based on (1) ability to resolve important uncertainties, (2) lack of substitute sources for that ability, and (3) centrality in the organization (Hickson et al., 1971). When business organizations face uncertain markets, effective marketing departments become more powerful. Note that organizational power in this theory depends on both task relevance (e.g., ability to resolve uncertainty) and political positioning (e.g., centrality, essentiality). Individual influence may also rest on both task and political factors. Kanter (1979) argues that individual power in organizations is derived from job characteristics and political alliances. When job definitions permit individuals the discretion to solve problems of high relevance to the organization and then be recognized for it, they become more powerful in a productive sense. Positive power also depends, in her analysis, on the availability of good political connections with sponsors higher in the hierarchy, with hierarchical peers, and with subordinates. Both political and task considerations affect the power of parties at level interfaces.

Upper and lower parties. The interests and characteristics of *parties* to level interfaces are defined by both task requirements and power inequalities. The focus here is on the impact of power inequalities, since task requirements were discussed in Chapter 4. Formal power distribution defines upper and lower parties; the terms "upper" and "lower" will be used even when the actual power distribution is not clear.

Upper parties tend to identify with the organization that grants them power, and to pursue its interests as their own (Collins, 1975; Smith, 1974). Managers often adopt organizational goals as their own, and devote an enormous amount of time and energy to organizational problems. Upper parties are usually responsible for managing the organization that grants them authority, so they are experienced and skillful in mobilizing for conflict at level interfaces. With fewer people at the top, upper parties are coherent and cohesive. Power apparently encourages pride, assertiveness, initiative, and strategic thinking (Collins, 1975; Nord, 1976). Upper parties often develop characteristic attitudes to lower parties over whom they exercise power: They remain psychologically distant; they attribute subordinate competence to their own supervision; they tend to denigrate lower parties, and they are likely to exercise rather than restrain their power (Kipnis, 1972; Rosenhan, 1973).

Lower parties, in contrast, are often alienated from organizational objectives and primarily concerned with protecting themselves from organizational demands (Collins, 1975; Nord, 1976). Workers, for example, are more likely than managers to perceive conflict between their interests and those of the organization. Since their tasks typically require fewer organizing and managing skills, lower parties may be less prepared to mobilize themselves for conflict. Within organizations, lower parties are often larger than upper parties, and so more difficult to organize. The experience of having little power shapes their perspectives and personal characteristics: caution, apathy, emotionality, passivity, and short time orientations are all responses to the experience of powerlessness (Collins, 1975; Nord, 1976). Lower parties may also magnify the skills and strengths of upper parties beyond reality (Zimbardo et al., 1973).

The effects of power differences on parties may be illustrated by two experimental simulations that produced strikingly different effects. Zimbardo and his colleagues (1973) created a realistic prison in which "guards" and "prisoners" (both groups composed of college students) were to spend two weeks. The prisoners staged an early and ineffectual rebellion, but the guards soon expanded their formal power superiority to an overwhelming degree of dominance. Within a week they were like brutal, capricious, and sadistic tyrants, requiring prisoners to comply with their slightest whim. The prisoners, in contrast, became so passive, apathetic, and withdrawn that the experimenters terminated the experiment before it was half over. Since guards and prisoners had been assigned at random from the same population of college students, the experimenters concluded that extreme situational power differences can rapidly produce drastic characteristics in upper and lower parties, *even when they begin with no discernible differences.*

In another simulation, this time of a society, participants were separated into upper, middle, and lower classes with appropriately different access to food, shelter, money, transportation, and the like (Brown, 1978). But the upper party was unable to prevent the lower party's mobilization and resistance, and conflict rapidly escalated into outright warfare. The actual power of upper and lower parties became more equal over time, in contrast to the prison simulation, and party characteristics never diverged to the extent visible in the prison simulation. Major differences among the parties are less likely if power differences are not extreme.

Upper and lower representatives.   The roles and personal characteristics of upper and lower representatives may also vary dramatically. The upper party frequently assumes lower party compliance. Guards expect to be obeyed by prisoners; managers expect compliance from workers. Lower party representatives often have organizational roles (e.g., worker, subordinate) that contradict their party role (e.g., union steward, staff association representative). The simulation prisoners were never able to create a representative role acceptable to both parties; representatives appointed by lower parties in the society simulation were recognized only grudgingly by the upper party.

The skills and personal characteristics of representatives from upper and lower parties also affect conflict at level interfaces. Upper and lower parties are often so different that their representatives are ill-equipped to understand one another.

Mulder (1976) points out that placing a worker on a board of directors can confirm the directors' stereotype of worker incompetence; a worker's effective leadership over other workers does not necessarily prepare the worker to operate effectively in board discussions of financial and policy matters. The experience of different power positions may also produce personal characteristics that contribute to problems at the interface. Proud, assertive, upper representatives with high initiative who disdain lower parties may work poorly with cautious, apathetic, or emotional lower representatives who see upper parties as basically malevolent.

Level interface definition and organization.   Level interfaces are defined by both organizational tasks and the distribution of formal organizational power. The extent to which the interface controls representative behavior is important in the *definition* of its boundaries. Appropriately defined boundaries allow both interface and party influence over representatives. Strongly defined interfaces may compel representatives to betray their parties, such as the willingness of some prisoners in the prison simulation to "rat" on their fellows. Weakly defined interfaces permit representative defection or noncompliance. Representatives in the society simulation, for example, cheerfully reneged on solemn promises made at the interface at the whim of their parties.

Boundary definition can be strengthened by other criteria. The guards control over the prisoners, for example, was reinforced by their constant proximity and the prisoners' identification with their subordinate status—formal interface definitions converged with geographical and social definitions. On the other hand, interface definition may be undermined by divergent criteria. Upper and lower classes in the society simulation had little direct contact, strong intraclass social bonds but little interclass acceptance, and opposed objectives. Small wonder the upper and lower representatives barely acknowledged their interdependence at the interface.

Level interfaces can be composed in symmetrical or asymmetrical terms, and can include few or many representatives. The guards controlled the composition of interfaces with the prisoners, and carefully retained numerical and physical superiority at meetings when prisoners might have gained influence by weight of numbers. A variety of interface compositions were tried in the "minisociety," ranging from bringing all the parties together (which produced a near riot) to meetings of single representatives (which produced deception and denials of commitments).

Level interfaces can vary widely in degree of *organization*. Overorganized interfaces have closed external boundaries and tightly regulated internal activities that suppress overt conflict. The prison simulation, for example, became relatively closed to the external world: Occasional "visitors" were permitted, but only with careful monitoring and control. Activity at the guard-prisoner interface was tightly, albeit asymmetrically, regulated. Prisoners had to comply not only with formal prison rules but also with the informal whims of the guards. Constraints on guards were comparatively loose, although those who were "nice" to prisoners were ridiculed by the other guards. The interface organization suppressed conflict and created tight regulation of prisoner behavior.

Underorganized level interfaces, in contrast, exert little boundary control over inputs and outputs and little internal regulation of representatives. In the society simulation, for example, negotiations between upper and lower representatives were constantly disrupted by other party members, and "leaks" of confidential discussions produced mistrust and escalation. Sometimes underorganization permits explosions of intense conflict. In other situations, the lack of shared regulatory mechanisms results in lower party apathy, upper party abdication, and mutual withdrawal from controversy. The lower party in the society simulation considered "going to the beach" for the duration of the simulation; the upper party actually abandoned the site to go out to dinner at a crucial point. Escalated power struggles or apathy and abdication are both possible at underorganized level interfaces.

Appropriate organization requires external boundaries that control relevant inputs and outputs, and internal regulations that limit conflict without suppressing important differences.

Moderate control over boundary permeability permits relevant and stimulating inputs from the parties and the larger context, and allows outputs of important information and personnel. Shared formal and informal organizing mechanisms legitimate interlevel differences and provide channels for airing and resolving them. It is *legitimation* of power differences that is crucial, and neither the prison nor minisociety simulations developed jointly accepted interfaces at which power differences were accepted and managed constructively.

Level interface context.   Upper and lower parties are embedded in the same organizational context, though their attitudes to that context may vary. Hierarchical superiors may not have credibility with both parties: Inviting top management to resolve conflicts between workers and managers may seem to workers like inviting the fox to guard the chickens. It is possible to create organizational structures, such as grievance procedures and appeal systems, that span power differences (e.g., Scott, 1965). But such structures must be protected from subversion by upper parties and suspicion of favoritism by lower parties. It is the larger organization that creates level differences and interdependencies in the first place, and so alternative organization structures may reduce the potential for interface tensions. Decentralizing decision making from corporate headquarters to divisions, for example, may reduce the level of conflict and confusion at their interface.

Forces from the context beyond the organization may quickly become important at level interfaces, even though the definition of those interfaces and parties is initially internal to the organization. Lower parties often appeal to external resources to offset the formal power advantage of upper parties. Prisoners in the simulated prison sought help from lawyers, chaplains, and parents, while guards and wardens closely controlled and minimized visiting rights. As power becomes more equal or as conflict escalates, upper parties also may seek external support: Managers seek regulation by state and federal governments when conflict with workers gets out of hand.

Dynamics at Level Interfaces

Two dynamics are important at level interfaces: (1) Immediate behaviors of representatives can interlock to produce too much or too little conflict, and (2) the interplay of interface, parties, and context can create too much or too little constraint on representatives' behavior.

Upper and lower representatives' interaction.   Representatives' actions can produce stable patterns of constructive interlevel bargaining and problem-solving. But power differences can also provoke explosive struggles over power, upper party abdication and lower party apathy, or extremes of upper party dominance and lower party submission.

Power struggles link upper and lower parties in cycles of perception, communication, and action with potentials for explosive conflict. The issues in such struggles are frequently linked to power distribution, at least in symbolic terms. Upper party proposals that minisociety lower parties work for extra food and privileges were rejected primarily because the latter refused to accept implicit legitimation of their lower status. Party perceptions are skewed by their hierarchical position: Lower parties fear upper parties as wholly malevolent and overpowering, and upper parties often stereotype lower parties as weak and subhuman. Both parties bring to authority relations strong feelings derived from their experiences as parents and children (Bion, 1959). Communications between unequal parties are *particularly* vulnerable to distortion and restriction. The lower party's fear reduces its communication to upper parties, particularly of information that might provoke retaliation; the upper party's ignorance of lower party concerns blinds them to areas of controversy. When lower parties voice long-suppressed antagonisms, upper parties are often surprised into responding with injured innocence or outrage. Lower parties able to protect themselves are more likely to confront upper parties; violence is more often initiated by strong social protest groups than by weak ones (Gamson, 1975). Initial conflicts between upper and lower classes in the society simulation were verbal and mild; disputes became more polarized, emotion-laden, intense, and physical over time. As power struggles progress, parties focus on obstructive uses of power, frustrating other parties rather than pursuing their own goals (Kanter, 1979).

Too little conflict is associated with dominance and submission or with apathy and abdication. In both patterns potential issues between the parties may never become articulated. Submissive lower parties dare not challenge upper parties, and dominant upper parties are blind to their issues. Apathetic lower parties do not care enough to raise issues, and abdicating upper parties avoid potential trouble.

Both patterns can be self-reinforcing. The dynamics of *dominance and submission* often produce escalating oppression. Mulder (1976) has found experimentally that upper and lower party attitudes complement each other: As inequalities increase, upper representatives become *more* interested in dominance and lower representatives become *less* resistant to oppression. This pattern can produce a spiral of increasing inequality and oppression, as ever more dominant upper parties lord it over ever more submissive lower parties. Thus, violence is most often initiated by upper parties when social protest groups are weak (Gamson, 1975). Oppressive cycles may be enjoyed by upper parties, but they produce sullen and listless lower parties whose behavior must be closely supervised.

Abdication and apathy, on the other hand, involve reduced communications, perceptions that the other party can be neither influenced nor educated, and general withdrawal from joint activity. Upper classes in the society simulation eventually abandoned the society, abdicating their elite roles to "fiddle while Rome burns." The lower classes considered "going to the beach to play" for the duration of the simulation. Withdrawal reduces interdependent activity. No society or organization can long survive if interdependent levels cease to interact.

Obviously such runaway destructive dynamics are not inevitable, or few organizations would survive. Limited conflicts at level interfaces are more common. Upper and lower representatives can recognize conflicts of interest, and bargain and compromise to resolve those differences. When power differences are accepted as legitimate, and issues are not defined as threats to that legitimate distribution, representatives may bargain on task issues without undercutting their position within an accepted hierarchy. Bargaining processes to manage interlevel conflict produce *negotiated leadership,* in which lower parties agree to limited subordination and upper parties accept limited domination.

An alternative dynamic involves problem-solving at level interfaces, in which lower representatives surrender immediate conflicting interests for larger or longer-term common interests with upper parties. Power distributions are usually less threatened by problem-solving over common interests, but acceptance of power differences as legitimate remains fundamental. Problem-solving dynamics at level interfaces give rise to *facilitative leadership,* in which the joint resources of upper and lower parties produce outcomes valuable to both (e.g., Berlew, 1980).

Dynamics of interface development.   Patterns of representative interaction influence and are influenced by interface organization. That organization is also affected by party characteristics and by influence from the larger context. Figure 5.1 summarizes the patterns of interface development associated with different patterns of representative interaction.

Too much conflict at level interfaces (A) is associated with highly mobilized parties (solid boundaries) that perceive their interests as conflicting; underorganized interfaces (dotted boundary) that provide little control over boundary permeability or representative interaction (divergent arrows); and party links to external allies who support their struggle (arrows from outside agencies). The actual power differences between the parties (represented by vertical distance) is often relatively small (or the struggle would be short-lived). Conflict between upper and lower parties in the society simulation followed this pattern, and it may also be observed in extreme labor-management struggles or die-hard resistance to unfriendly corporate takeovers.

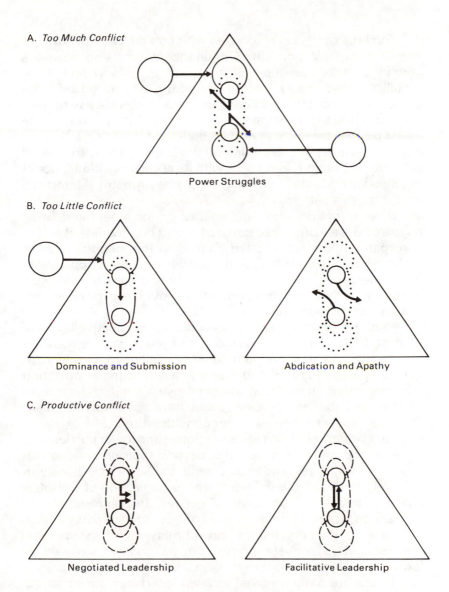

Fig. 5.1. *Conflict at level interfaces.*

Too little conflict is associated with two different patterns of interface organization (B). Dominance/submission relations involve a mobilized upper party (solid boundary) and a demobilized lower party (dotted boundary), separated by large power differences (vertical distance) at an interface asymmetrically organized to constrain lower parties tightly but regulate upper parties loosely (half dotted, half-solid boundary). Links to outside agencies are controlled by the upper party (arrow from outside). The prison simulation, with its escalating dominance of prisoners by guards at an increasingly asymmetrical interface, illustrates this pattern.

Patterns of abdication and apathy, on the other hand, bring together loosely organized parties (dotted boundaries) at an underorganized interface (dotted boundary) that permits them to withdraw from controversy and interdependence. If upper party had gone out to dinner and lower party had gone to the beach simultaneously, the society simulation would have run down for lack of commitment from both parties.

Interface developments can encourage productive levels of conflict (C). In negotiated and facilitative leadership, representative bargaining and problem-solving involve moderately organized parties (dashed boundaries) that recognize conflicting and common interests at moderately organized interfaces (dashed boundaries). External parties are not involved unless they are relevant to issues under consideration.

Level interfaces bring together upper and lower parties who differ in important characteristics beyond their unequal formal power. Power issues tend to be central, explicitly or implicitly, in their relations, and the definition and organization of the interface reflects the relative power of parties. The representatives' interaction may produce explosive changes toward power struggles or expanding dominance and submission, for communication restrictions between parties can be greatly increased by lower party fear and upper party blindness. External third parties and forces are often involved at level interfaces, for organizational contexts are frequently unable to contain interlevel tensions.

A LEVEL INTERFACE AT THE COLLEGE CITY TRANSIT AUTHORITY

Relations between management and workers at the College City Transit Authority illustrate some problems of conflict at level interfaces.

The College City Transit Authority is a semipublic agency charged with providing coordinated transport services to a six-township area. The area includes a city of about 100,000 people as well as smaller towns and a large university. The Authority operates a trunk line bus service and a passenger-responsive service of smaller vehicles. The services are supported by levies from the townships and grants from state and federal governments as well as rider fares.

The Executive Director of the Authority reports to a Board appointed by local government officials. This Board is responsible to voters, who approve operating levies, and to the "riding public." During the early seventies the Authority expanded dramatically after funds became available to launch an innovative passenger-responsive service. In 6 years the work force employed by the organization grew from 30 to 250—more than an 8-fold increase.

Before the expansion the Authority's work force was largely male and lower middle class. Many workers were black. New hires were drawn from a different population—ex-students at the local university. They were predominantly white and highly educated; many were politically "progressive" and some were explicitly committed to radical social change; a substantial fraction were militantly feminist women. The workers had been represented for years by the local unit of an international union of public employees. The Authority's workers represented a tiny segment of the local's membership, and so got little attention.

In 1975 a group of new workers organized a competing organization, largely to extract concessions from the international union. To their surprise, they won a representation election. The independent Transit Workers Union was born, with a slate of officers almost exclusively from new hires. These officers had considerable education, political sophistication, energy for innovation—and no experience in collective bargaining. They were committed to innovative work organization and governance, though a sizeable minority of the rank and file preferred economic gains. The older members of the work force were willing to tolerate the strange ideas and behavior of the new union leaders if they got better wage agreements.

The Executive Director of the Authority was nationally known for innovation in transportation, and he was hired to manage the new passenger-responsive service. He was a mercurial figure, with small patience for individuals who misunderstood or challenged him.

Many managers came up through the ranks, beginning as drivers. The Director of Operations was an ex-driver who had served on the union bargaining team. The Personnel Manager had also represented the union in the past. The third member of the management bargaining team was a lawyer, who represented the municipal government in negotiations with various unions. Together the management bargaining team boasted years of collective bargaining experience, many on behalf of the international union. The management team understood clearly the processes of collective bargaining. They were also impatient with delays, for negotiations were an added burden to their already crowded work schedules.

Shortly after the creation of the new union, its bargaining team began negotiations with management representatives. The union team proposed a variety of innovations for managing the Authority. Management rejected most of them as frivolous or as gross infringements of management prerogatives. The initial positions of management, on the other hand, assumed that negotiations start low and compromise upward; some of their initial offers were less than the present contract. The union regarded these offers as farcical and "a slap in the face." Each challenged the other's good faith.

As negotiations continued, tensions intensified. The union committee wanted wide-ranging discussions of issues, and accused management of hiding behind a "united front." The management committee expected the union to take clear positions and to bargain with a single voice, and accused the union of "not doing their homework." Representatives of both parties lost their tempers and personally attacked each other. The union sought to influence the public with abusive stories in local newspapers, and went behind the Director's back to the Board. Management sent letters to the union rank and file suggesting that the union team was not representing them effectively.

The deadline for a strike approached with few issues resolved. Ultimately verbal agreement on a contract was reached a few minutes before the strike deadline, in a tumultuous meeting with scores of strike-ready workers hanging in the windows. But subsequent disagreements about the verbal agreement resulted in serious problems in formalizing it. The final written contract required fourteen months of further acrimonious debate. The resulting relations between union and management were strained—the Executive Director and the union president were notorious for public shouting matches, and both sides expected a long and bitter strike at the 1977 negotiations.

Events at the College City Transit Authority may be examined in terms of interface elements and dynamics.

Elements of the Worker-Management Interface

The two primary *parties* to this interface are management and union officers. Management has interests in running the organization, in preserving their prerogatives, and in avoiding problems that hamper performance. The Executive Director is a central figure: His combative style generates tensions within management that may be displaced to the union, and it also evokes confrontations with union leaders. Many managers are old union members, but they support free enterprise as an economic system. Management attitudes to the union have been shaped by the 1975 negotiations: They see union activists as so personally abusive and ideologically radical that there is little hope of cooperation with them.

Union officers are interested in more resources for their members and in redistributing power and decision making in the work place. The leadership group is cohesive and homogeneous, but the rank and file is diverse and not entirely supportive of their leadership. The union leaders are avowed socialists, ideologically well to the left of management. The 1975 negotiations confirmed union suspicions of management; many feel that they should have struck in 1975, and that a firmer stance is necessary now.

The two parties are *represented* in contract negotiations by their bargaining committees. Management's representatives are all veterans of many negotiations, and two are long-term employees who have been union officials. They have more experience but less formal education than most of the union committee. The Executive Director supervises them closely, and agreements must be approved by him and by the Board.

The union representatives have less experience in collective bargaining. Several are personally charismatic, articulate, and fiery. They are eager to demonstrate their effectiveness to the rank and file. Role pressures on both parties encourage militant representation, and personal characteristics of some representatives—particularly from the union—encourage explosions.

The level *interface* at College City Transit Authority is defined by formal power and task interdependence. Buses do not roll unless managers and dispatchers can coordinate the activities of drivers and mechanics. Interface boundaries are partially defined by law: Collective bargaining legislation sets many parameters for negotiations. But the geographical proximity of negotiations, interdependent organizational tasks, and control boundaries set by law have not created a strongly defined level interface. On the contrary, strong social bonds and mobilization for a power struggle have reinforced party boundaries at the expense of the interface, and representatives' behavior is much more influenced by party membership than by the bargaining interface. Interface composition also contributes to conflict escalation, for some of the union's most articulate and combative members belong to its bargaining committee.

The boundaries of the interface are comparatively open. The Executive Director looks over the shoulder of the management committee and the rank and file participate actively in union meetings. Activity within the interface is only loosely regulated. General procedures for bargaining are defined by law and administrative procedures, but formal rules and roles specific to this interface have not been developed. Few informal control mechanisms have evolved to regulate interface activity. The parties began with very different theories and expectations; management came prepared for bargaining and the union came to problem-solve and brainstorm. Their interaction has produced more antagonism than shared agreements. Conflict has eroded even general norms of politeness against shouting matches and personal abuse. The union-management interface is quite underorganized.

The *organizational context* of the Transit Authority does not greatly moderate union-management conflict, for the union understandably regards upper levels of the hierarchy (e.g., the Director) as allies of the management committee. Present organizational structures and reward systems emphasize level differences, even though union members were promoted to management during the expansion.

But third parties exist in the *larger context* with interests in reduced conflict: State and federal governments, for example, may be expected to intervene in serious escalations. Management is concerned about the Board, the municipal government, the voters, and the riding public. Union officers fear that the rank and file may recall the old international union if they fail to deliver better wages. Both parties have attempted to influence each other's constituencies: The union addressed the Board and the voters in the media, and management approached the rank and file in letters. Contextual forces—allies and third parties—are of considerable concern to both sides.

Worker-Management Dynamics

The *interaction among representatives* escalated over time. Representatives' disagreements were increasingly conceived as "big" issues: The union perceived management to insist on continued "capitalist" control; management perceived the union as "radical crazies" and "socialists" committed to complete takeover of the workplace. Settlement of any single issue became contingent on settlement of all of them—representatives did not "sign off" specific issues as they were discussed but instead kept all open to the last minute. The resulting confusion and misunderstanding prolonged negotiations until long after "agreement" had been reached.

Behavior at the bargaining table contributed to the power struggle. Representatives were wary of each other at the outset. The union had little bargaining experience, and management was not familiar with the new union. Initial presentations were not reassuring. Union representatives felt management was unreasonably stingy, and reacted angrily. Management representatives thought the union demanded unreasonable changes, and dismissed them with contempt. Early disagreements contributed to mutual misunderstandings, less recognition of each other's legitimate interests, angry personal attacks, and efforts to subvert each other's constituencies. These results combined to produce increasingly intense conflict and increasingly overt obstruction of each other's activities.

The interplay of parties, context, and interface promoted *looser interface organization.* Initial party differences predisposed representatives to be suspicious. Task and legal requirements defined some interface boundaries, but little shared commitment to common goals or norms constrained representatives. Early conflicts reinforced initial suspicions, and both sides sought support from external allies and so contributed to more tension. The combination of mobilized parties, loose interface organization, and polarized context encouraged rapid escalation of the power struggle.

But the conflict stopped short of a strike in 1975. Two factors contributed to this limit. Both parties were cautious about their relative strengths: Management was not sure the Board would support a hard line, and union officers were not sure the rank and file would follow them out on noneconomic issues. External forces also pressed against a strike: Managers worried about antagonizing the riding public, and union officers feared international union competition for rank and file loyalties. Agreement at the last minute was reached, but continuing bargaining problems led both sides to predict a strike in 1977.

MANAGING CONFLICT AT THE COLLEGE CITY TRANSIT AUTHORITY

One consequence of the 1975 negotiations was a "Quality of Work Committee," composed of union and management representatives. Many issues of workplace governance raised by the union were rejected as inappropriate for collective bargaining by management. The union proposed a joint committee to work on such issues outside the collective bargaining framework, and management conceded that provision in the 1975 contract to gain agreement on the larger package.

Federal interest in such cooperative committees in the public sector made funds available to support the Committee's development. Consultants from the nearby university were retained for training, consultation, and evaluation of the Committee's operations. The Committee first met shortly after the formal end of negotiations (but long before a mutually acceptable written contract was ready). Members of the union executive and the management bargaining teams were included, though an effort was made not to duplicate the collective bargaining interface. Initial meetings gave ample evidence of residual distrust and antagonism between the parties.

The consultants worked for the next two years with the Committee. The Committee defined goals, created procedures for managing tasks, diagnosed the state of the organization, and managed conflicts among its members. After several workshops and much conflict during regular meetings, the Committee gradually evolved a climate of trust and cooperation among its members that astonished the rest of the Authority. Union and management representatives abided by rules of confidentiality within the Committee. Eventually management representatives volunteered information about clashes of views among senior managers, and union representatives shared internal union problems at Committee meetings. Relations among union and management representatives in the Committee produced several cooperative projects. The Committee reviewed bus routes, initiated changes in pay distribution, assisted the Safety Committee, and began long-term projects to improve job design, organizational communications, and problem-solving in several departments. Within a year the Committee was widely known as an example of cooperative union-management relations in spite of continuing warfare in the rest of the organization.

Shortly before the 1977 negotiations, discussion in a Committee meeting revealed that both parties expected negotiations to culminate in a deadlock and a long strike. Given the temper of the two sides, a strike seemed likely regardless of substantive issues. The Committee decided to try to prevent a deadlock based on antagonism and past history rather than substantive disagreement.

The Committee and their consultants proposed a workshop for the bargaining committees. The workshop would be run by an external consultant unknown to either party (but recommended by the Committee's consultants), whose fee would be shared by union and management. The consultant would interview both bargaining committees, and propose a workshop which would be implemented only if both parties agreed to participate. The objective was to prevent escalation during negotiations based on misunderstanding instead of substantive differences.

The prenegotiations workshop took place the week before negotiations began. Short lectures on the dynamics of col-

lective bargaining were offered as background. Supervised by the external consultant, union and management teams shared perceptions of each other and of "dirty tricks" each had played in the previous negotiations. Each party excelled at listing the other's dirty tricks, but each also grudgingly recognized items on the other's list. Eventually representatives negotiated several ground rules to govern upcoming negotiations: (1) a procedure for relieving union negotiators from late shift work (a sore point left over from the last negotiations), (2) agreement to advise each other before communicating with each other's constituencies (commonly listed as a "dirty trick" in the past), and (3) agreement to meet regularly during negotiations with Quality of Work Committee consultants to examine the negotiation process. Both parties anticipated difficult negotiations, but both were pleased with the workshop. As a management representative put it, "This has cleared the air of a lot of left-over stuff from last year."

The representatives brought radically different initial positions to the negotiations. But these differences did not evoke the antagonistic misunderstandings and personal attack common in previous negotiations. New members of the union bargaining committee later accused old hands of trying to scare them with inflated horror stories of management's past behavior. The management team described union representatives as "statesmanlike." Representatives of both parties agreed that the negotiations were a vast improvement. They devised several innovations in procedure, including splitting into subgroups to explore complex issues and meeting with the consultants to discuss the process of negotiations as agreed in the workshop.

In spite of the improved climate of negotiations, agreement was not reached on all the issues before the contract deadline passed. After extended negotiations, the union finally struck. The strike decision was not taken in anger or as a result of personal conflict between representatives. But both parties questioned the other's strength in a showdown:

Management was not convinced the union could actually take the rank and file out, and the union thought management might collapse in the face of an actual work stoppage. The state labor relations agency intervened almost immediately, and their fact finder proposed a settlement that was accepted (though both parties felt it favored the union) after nine days of strike.

The resumption of normal operations was peaceful. Managers described their relations with the union as "surprisingly good"; relations after a strike in 1977 were greatly improved over relations without a strike in 1975. Management did not like the wage provisions of the new contract, but they blamed that package on the third party. Management and union described each other in terms of "reluctant respect," and expressed optimism about their future relations.

These events can be analyzed as interventions at two level interfaces between management and union at the Transit Authority.

The Quality of Work Committee Interface

The Quality of Work Committee was created by the 1975 negotiations, with management and union as primary parties. The overall interests of the two parties had not changed, but the Quality of Work Committee focused on common interests in improved safety, better role definitions, and other areas not appropriate for adversarial resolution. Most representatives who met in the Committee were not on bargaining committees, and their roles were defined from the beginning as cooperative rather than combative.

Interface boundaries were defined initially by the need for a cooperative forum and concern with the breakdown of relations between the parties. Training and extensive process consultation from the university consultants helped define a Committee that could influence members from both parties. In time, initial agreement about task and control boundaries were supplemented by social bonds among Committee members that separated them from the union-management power struggle in the rest of the Authority. Strict confidentiality for information shared in meetings and elaborate procedures for choosing and initiating new members provided boundary controls that limited disruptive inputs and outputs. Formal rules and procedures to control internal conflict were enforced with aid from the consultants. Shared understanding of Committee goals and values and the evolution of trust among members helped to informally constrain internal conflict.

The university consultants played important roles in managing ongoing communications and in helping formulate plans for changing the larger organization. That consultation was supported by external agencies, such as the federal government, interested in cooperative strategies for managing labor-management relations. So the Committee benefited from larger social forces that compelled attention to conflict and cooperation in public sector labor relations.

Patterns of behavior within the Committee differed greatly from interaction elsewhere in the organization. Differences between Committee managers and union representatives increased flows of accurate information, for representatives learned to explore rather than attack differences. Committee members had realistic perceptions of each of their parties, and could discuss at length forces influencing each side. Committee members had learned and were able to use problem-solving tactics in place of the threats and coercion more common elsewhere in the Authority.

Events at the interface produced a very visible enclave of labor-management cooperation in the midst of an organizational battlefield. Committee members wanted to reproduce the climate of the Committee in the larger organization, but that change required influencing events at the bargaining table as well as in the organization as a whole.

Negotiations as a Level Interface

The bargaining committee interface was not initially affected by events within the Quality of Work Committee, though members of the different committees were in contact with each other. But as the 1977 negotiations drew near, several factors affected the bargaining interface. The union reconstituted its bargaining committee, replacing half its members with new and relatively unalienated representatives. The Quality of Work Committee offered an alternative model that particularly impressed new union representatives. And the Committee also launched its effort to reduce negotiations conflict.

The negotiations interface was badly underorganized by the end of the 1975 negotiations. Conflict among the parties left little but the minimum legal structure to define the interface, and the parties recognized few shared tasks or social bonds. The 1975 negotiations produced few formal or informal mechanisms for regulating interaction among representatives. The Quality of Work Committee proposed the prenegotiations workshop as an attempt to build more interface organization. Initial interviews were designed to set constructive representative expectations as well as solicit information, and the consultant pressed representatives to set reasonable goals for the event. Workshop activities were designed to strengthen the interface boundary and to tighten interface organization. The Executive Director and other union members were excluded from the workshop to minimize external disruptions. The consultants closely supervised initial interactions to prevent escalation, but encouraged dealing with more difficult issues as the workshop progressed. By the end of the workshop representatives were creating formal procedures and informal norms to control future negotiations.

Ultimately the negotiations interface was affected by both the Quality of Work Committee and the prenegotiations workshop. But ambiguity about power differences remained. The strike tested both the resolve and the resources of both parties—and clearly established their ability to hurt each other. Since little animosity had developed in negotiations, the parties could recognize their mutual dependence and accept face-saving alternatives proposed by the state fact finder with little debate.

Changing perceptions and internal characteristics of the parties (in part touched off by the success of the Quality of Work Committee), changes in the interface organization promoted by

A. Power Struggle between
Union and Management
Bargaining Committees

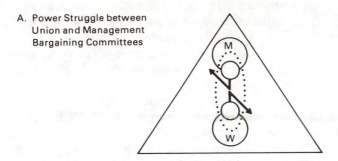

B. Problem-Solving among
Workers and Managers on
Quality of Work Committee

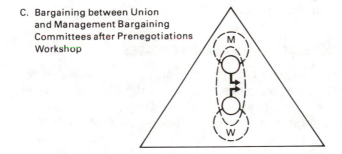

C. Bargaining between Union
and Management Bargaining
Committees after Prenegotiations
Workshop

Fig. 5.2. *Workers and management at College City Transit Authority.*

Quality of Work Committee and consultant interventions, and pressures from contextual forces such as the Committee, the consultants, and the state mediator, combined to reduce conflict at the bargaining table. Conflict remained, as evidenced by the strike. But that strike was a test of relative strengths that is inevitable and legitimate in collective bargaining. The rapid return of workers and managers to an improved relationship suggests the strike was perceived as appropriate, in contrast to previous more antagonistic interactions.

Figure 5.2 summarizes the changing interfaces at the College City Transit Authority. After the 1975 negotiations (A), highly mobilized (solid lines) workers and management bargained within an underorganized bargaining interface (dotted line), and representatives' interactions created an escalating power struggle (divergent arrows). At the end of the 1977 strike, two interfaces had emerged (B and C). The Quality of Work Committee (B) brought together representatives of less mobilized parties (dashed lines) in a moderately bounded and organized interface (dashed lines) characterized by problem-solving patterns of interaction (arrows). The bargaining interface (C) also linked somewhat mobilized parties (dashed lines) in a moderately bounded and organized interface (dashed lines) characterized by bargaining dynamics (arrows).

MANAGING CONFLICT AT LEVEL INTERFACES

Conflict at level interfaces can generate particularly serious problems; unequal power obscures tensions which can become extreme. In this section I deal first with ways of reducing conflict that has escalated into a destructive power struggle, and then turn to ways of promoting productive conflict to counteract upper party dominance or abdication and lower party withdrawal or submission.

Reducing Interlevel Conflict

When there is too much conflict at a level interface, it is because power has become a central issue without permitting the upper party to dominate debate. On the other hand, when there is relative parity in a power struggle between parties, neither party gains a decisive advantage, and both may ultimately become exhausted.

Changing representatives' interaction: three strategies. Interventions that redirect behavior, reframe perspectives, and reallocate resources can all interrupt power struggles at level interfaces. To do so, intervenors can alter the polarized perceptions, restricted communications, and coercive tactics of the representatives.

Strategy 1. *Alter representatives' perceptions.* Upper and lower representatives develop distorted pictures of the situation and each other that justify their continuing and escalating interlevel conflict. Emotional stereotypes of each other may be altered to undercut the rationale for intense conflict. Upper representatives may recognize the legitimacy of lower party aspirations and concerns; lower representatives may accept upper parties as ignorant rather than consciously malevolent. Interventions may educate representatives about their own contributions to the dynamics of power struggles, enabling them to avoid unintended escalation. Reframing perceptions can clarify legitimate differences, so representatives recognize what actions and demands will be seen as abuses of power or prerogative. New information reduced the stereotypes of ideological inflexibility held by both sides of the Transit Authority.

Strategy 2. *Alter representatives' communications.* Power struggles cause drastic restrictions on the flow of trustworthy information between upper and lower parties. Intervention can encourage the upper party to actively search for information about the lower party's concerns, or carefully attend to veiled lower party communications. Lower parties can be encouraged to present their concerns more clearly, before explosions of frustration threaten upper parties. Both parties can discuss ways in which their communication is restricted, and either can invent mechanisms to improve information flow.

Strategy 3. *Alter representatives' actions.* Power struggles give rise to polarized issues and entrenched commitment to alternatives that affect the distribution of power among the parties, and to spirals of increasingly coercive tactics by representatives. Interventions can distinguish power implications from other issues, so they can be managed separately. Alternative solutions can be introduced to break deadlocks. These alternatives must preserve power parity among representatives, but also offer mutually beneficial or mutually face-saving resolutions. Intervenors can also change the tactics of one or both representatives to moderate power struggles. Representatives can shift to behaviors that emphasize clear and credible messages about intentions, procedures for safeguarding both parties against abuses, explicit recognition of legitimate differences, counters for power grabs that unbalance negotiations, and low-risk initiatives that build trust. Representatives on both sides can be trained or recruited for skills in interrupting destructive power struggles.

Changed perceptions, communications, and behavior can interrupt the dynamics of power struggles. But representatives' behavior occurs within the constraints of the interface. Changes in their immediate behavior may be cancelled by interface forces and events. The improvement in relations among bargaining committee representatives, after the College City Transit Authority prenegotiations workshop, would not have persisted if the formal and informal character of the interface had not also changed.

Changing interface development: three strategies. Interventions to reframe perspectives, reallocate resources, or realign underlying structures can change the interplay of parties, context, and interface. These interventions shape events in the long run.

Strategy 4. *Alter level interfaces.* Power struggles occur at interfaces that are relatively weakly defined or loosely organized. When no accepted forum for discussion exists, creating new interfaces can reduce excessive interlevel conflict. Many organizations, like the Transit Authority, have created joint labor-management committees for problem solving (Walton and Schlesinger, 1978). Interface boundaries can be reinforced: Successful labor-management committees combine new social bonds, increased geographical proximity, and shared task goals to reinforce interface boundaries defined by collective bargaining mandates. Boundaries can be redefined to include new representatives, such as the consultants at the Transit Authority, or to balance upper and lower representation when asymmetries contribute to power struggles.

Interventions can close external boundaries and tighten internal regulation to constrain conflict. Cooperative labor-management committees, for example, require careful boundary management. Inputs that threaten representatives or undercut parity can set off new escalations, and trust can be badly sabotaged by "leaks" of confidential information (Kochan and Dyer, 1976). Tightening shared internal controls can increase lower party security and reduce ambiguity faced by upper parties. Formal rules and procedures provide standards for both: Grievance procedures and appeal systems can be designed that are fair to both sides (Scott, 1965; Gillers, 1980a). Informal mechanisms, such as norms that equalize the status of representatives, or informal friendships and trust among representatives, can also reduce tensions. Interface climates can encourage mutual trust and understanding among representatives, and informal acceptance of party differences is often central to moderating power struggles.

Strategy 5. *Alter upper or lower parties.* Intervention can be designed to reshape a party's perceptions of its interests at the interface. Lower parties may discover an interest in upper party survival: Unions sometimes accept wage cuts if they believe the company is really bankrupt. Upper parties can find reason to listen to lower parties: Worker participation sometimes increases productivity dramatically (e.g., Coch and French, 1948). Intervenors can reduce tension by recruiting less militant leaders or by attending to differences within parties that are obscured by the power struggle. Diversity within the transit workers rank and file moderated the union leaders' ideological enthusiasm for challenging management, particularly when shouting matches at the bargaining table became less common. Party stereotypes that create pressure on representatives can also be debunked: Credible information can contradict stereotypes of lower parties as radical and irresponsible, or stereotypes of upper parties as malevolent and power hungry. Discussions of perceptions in the Transit Authority prenegotiations workshop, for example, debunked provocative stereotypes on both sides. More generally, recognition of legitimate aspirations and differences on both sides can forestall power struggles based on reading each other out of the human race.

Strategy 6. *Alter the surrounding context.* Interventions can affect either the organizational context of power struggles, or the larger context affected by continuing interlevel conflict. Hierarchical superiors are not often seen as neutral third parties to level interfaces, at least by lower parties. But organizational structures, such as well-designed grievance systems or appeals procedures (Scott, 1965), can limit abuses of power. Many organizations promote the legitimacy of their hierarchies of power by creating avenues for lower representatives to move upward, thus absorbing protest and gaining skilled membership at the same time (e.g., Hecksher, 1980; Edwards, 1979). More fundamental restructuring of the organizational context may significantly redistribute power: Workers can acquire control of organizations or form cooperatives, and so gain formal power over their managers (e.g., Zwerdling, 1980).

Power struggles promote involvement with forces in the larger societal context. Lower parties often recruit allies to balance the formal power of upper parties. Union locals establish alliances with internationals; minority parties form coalitions; small businesses form trade associations. Third parties can moderate power struggles by enforcing rules, arbitrating or mediating conflicts, or facilitating communications (e.g., Laue and Cormick, 1978). Less directly, recognition of forces and events in the larger context can produce new perspectives on power struggles. A long history of struggle between management and workers in the steel industry may be replaced by cooperative ventures, in response to international competition that threatens the existence of jobs and companies.

Conflict reduction interventions include strategies to interrupt escalating cycles of representative perception, communication, and action, or to alter the interplay of upper and lower parties, their interface, and the larger context. Table 5.1 summarizes interventions for reducing power struggles. These interventions may be used singly or in combination. Over time, successful interventions will affect and be affected by dynamics not part of the original focus of attention.

TABLE 5.1
Reducing conflict at level interfaces

Changing representatives' interaction

1. *Alter perceptions*	Debunk representatives' stereotypes: • alter views of upper parties as malevolent, omniscient • alter views of lower parties as illegitimate, radical Educate representatives about: • dynamics of power struggles • their contributions to escalation Clarify perceptions of legitimate differences among parties
2. *Alter communications*	Encourage upper parties to hear lower party concerns Encourage lower parties to present concerns clearly prior to explosions that threaten upper party Discuss restrictions in communications and invent solutions
3. *Alter actions*	Separate power distribution issues from others and manage them separately Search for alternatives that do not threaten balance of power while providing mutual benefit or saving face Train or recruit representatives to defuse power struggles: • clear and credible messages about intentions • explicit legitimation of differences in power • tactics for countering power grabs • safeguards against abuses of power • low-risk initiatives to demonstrate good faith

TABLE 5.1   (continued)
Reducing conflict at level interfaces

Changing interface development

4. *Alter level interface*

Redefine the interface more clearly:
  - create new interface to include warring representatives
  - reinforce existing boundaries with others
  - compose interface to balance party representations
  - include peacemakers

Tighten interface organization:
  - close boundaries to inputs and outputs that undermine parity
  - create formal procedures that forestall abuses and legitimize the allocation of resources
  - encourage informal links and legitimation of differences among parties

5. *Alter one or both parties*

Alter party perceptions of their interests:
  - clarify lower party interests in upper party survival
  - clarify upper party stakes in lower party

Control party mobilizations to prevent sudden polarization into defensive united fronts

Debunk unrealistic party stereotypes:
  - alter lower party perceptions of upper party as malevolent, power-hungry
  - alter upper party perceptions of lower party as radical, irresponsible

6. *Alter context*

Change the organizational context:
  - control actions by superiors that escalate conflict
  - design formal procedures that protect both parties from abuses
  - create avenues of upward mobility for lower parties
  - redistribute formal and actual power to reduce abuses and expand organizational stakes for parties

TABLE 5.1 (continued)
Reducing conflict at level interfaces

Manage links to the larger context:
- recruit external allies
- limit escalatory recruitment of external allies
- use third parties to balance power, enforce rules, facilitate communications, or mediate specific issues
- recognize and plan for larger societal developments that alter power balances at the interface

---

Promoting Interlevel Conflict

Too little conflict at level interfaces may be associated with dominance and submission or with abdication and apathy. The former dynamics produce increasing power differences; the latter encourage decreased contact.

Changing representatives' interaction: three strategies. Productive conflict between representatives can be encouraged by interventions that affect cycles of their perception, communication, or action. But problems of dominance and submission and problems of apathy and abdication call for quite different interventions.

Strategy 1. *Alter representatives' perceptions.* New information or interpretation of events can alter excessive dominance and submission. Emotion-laden stereotypes can be reframed: Upper parties can reorient their perceptions of lower parties as less than human; lower parties can reexamine their beliefs in upper party irresistibility. Intervention can educate representatives about their own contributions to dominance and submission dynamics, so they are more able to control them. More generally, intervention that clarifies the legitimate rights and duties of both parties can set the stage for limiting the spirals of power abuse and passive acceptance.

Abdication and apathy can also be changed by new representative perceptions. Upper views of lower parties as dangerous or irrelevant and lower stereotypes of upper parties as uninterested can be revised by new information. Representatives can be educated about their contributions to abdication dynamics. Recognizing their responsibilities for continuing engagement can reduce the temptation to avoid controversy in the future.

Strategy 2. *Alter representatives' communications.* Productive conflict can also be encouraged by changes in the quantity and quality of communication between representatives. Extreme dominance produces one-way flows of information, in which upper representatives give many orders but get little valid information in return. Upper representatives who encourage controversial messages from below and resist the temptation to punish bearers of bad news are more likely to hear about problems and controversies in the future. Third parties can be either conduits for controversial information or safeguards for lower parties: Beckhard (1967) has designed a "confrontation meeting" that communicates large amounts of information up the hierarchy in a short period. Analysis of interlevel communication restrictions can aid both sides to counteract unintended lapses of communication.

Abdication reduces the flow of information from both sides, and so requires intervention that encourages both parties to raise and discuss controversial issues. Expanding interaction can identify issues that need attention, and focusing on potential controversies can reveal unrecognized interdependencies. When representatives analyze withdrawals from communication, it improves understanding and generates ideas to promote future engagement.

Strategy 3. *Alter representatives' actions.* At interfaces characterized by dominance and submission, lower perspectives on issues and alternatives may remain unarticulated and unrecognized. By raising the awareness of lower party issues and alternatives to upper party proposals, intervenors can catalyze more constructive engagement at the interface. Issues whose resolution will affect the distribution of power can be separated from other issues; resolutions that increase power imbalances between upper and lower parties, for example, should be avoided when dominance promotes too little conflict. Representatives can utilize tactics to reduce spirals of dominance and submission: Upper representatives can make explicit commitments to rules that reduce power imbalances; lower representatives can use power-building tactics, such as mobilizing strong party support; representatives can explicitly recognize legitimate rights and duties at the interface; tactics for recognizing and countering dominance-inducing initiatives can be devised.

Cycles of abdication result in failure to discuss controversial issues and to identify alternatives to withdrawal. Intervenors can clarify different perspectives on the issues, or separate out and deal with power implications of issues that encourage avoidance. "Participative" managers sometimes bend over backward to avoid dominance, for example, and so confuse their subordinates into paralysis. Clarifying expectations with respect to specific issues can reduce withdrawal problems. Tactics for interrupting cycles of abdication can also be invented: Upper representatives can experiment with more active leadership styles; lower representatives can press for clearer expectations; both sides can explicitly confront lapses into withdrawal; clearly articulated responsibilities can reduce the temptation to avoid problems.

The dynamics of dominance and abdication are maintained by interlocking patterns of representatives' perceptions, communications, and behavior. Interventions that interrupt these cycles change, and are changed by, other aspects of representative interaction—when the latter are affected by the development of the level interface.

Changing interface development: three strategies.   The interplay among parties, context, and the interface itself shape the definition and organization of that interface over the long term. Dominance and submission are associated with asymmetrical interfaces; abdication and apathy are linked to underorganized interfaces.

Strategy 4. *Alter the interface.* Dominance occurs within interfaces that are strongly defined for lower parties but weakly defined for upper parties. Intervenors can establish interface definitions for upper parties by demonstrating upper dependence on lower parties, or they can weaken interface definitions for lower parties by emphasizing the limitations of upper control. Interface composition can be varied to reduce dominance problems: Assertive lower representatives, upper representatives who listen, and third parties who balance relations can be included; representatives who contribute to dominance and submission patterns can be excluded.

Problems of abdication and apathy can benefit from interventions that define interfaces and representatives' responsibilities clearly, and so hamper withdrawal from controversial issues. Creating an explicit forum for dealing with issues can reduce avoidance: The passive resistance of the foremen to a management-sponsored shift toward a more participative management style in one plant gave way to productive discussion only after the plant manager actively encouraged the foremen to raise their objections in regular meetings. Interfaces can also be composed for more engagement: Assertive representatives and third parties who will raise issues can be included, and representatives who avoid conflict can be excluded.

Interfaces can be reorganized by altering boundary permeabilities and internal regulations. Dominance and submission are associated with asymmetrical interface organization—open boundaries and loose regulation for upper parties, and closed boundaries and tight controls for lower parties. Interventions can rebalance asymmetrical organization. In a communications group created to share information across levels, Alderfer (1977a) found boundary management to be critical: Powerful organizational groups (e.g., managers, union representatives) often sought to penetrate the group, with disruptive results if they succeeded. Asymmetric internal controls can be rebalanced for productive conflict: Formal procedures that constrain both parties equally can be promulgated, and informal norms can reward initiatives from lower parties and punish bullying by upper parties. The communications group developed an elaborate set of formal and informal mechanisms that regulated all members similarly, and so balanced potentially asymmetric interface organization.

Problems of abdication often occur at underorganized interfaces, and so need interventions that close boundaries to irrelevant inputs and to critical losses of information and personnel. Closing the boundary around the plant manager-foreman discussions of participative management reduced external disruptions and encouraged the parties to deal with differences. Underorganized interfaces can also benefit from tightened formal and informal internal regulation. Formal procedures for managing interface meetings (e.g., Robert's Rules of Order) and key roles (e.g., conveners, chairpersons) can focus discussion on controversial issues and reduce avoidance of controversy. Informal norms that support disagreement and debate can be encouraged, particularly as experience demonstrates that neither party will abuse its strength or that the engagement has constructive outcomes.

Strategy 5. *Alter upper and lower parties.* Interventions that increase submissive lower party recognition of their divergent interests, or that promote internal cohesion, leadership, and mobilization, can produce lower party challenges to dominant upper parties. Perceptions of upper parties as overwhelmingly strong and malevolent can be debunked. Organizing Indian farmers for collective action produced initiatives that influenced other villages and government bureaucrats (Tandon and Brown, 1981), and training high school students in negotiation skills produced more effective debate with school administrators (Chesler and Lohman, 1971). Altering lower party characteristics that support continued passivity can encourage productive conflict.

Interventions for upper parties vary with different problems. Dominant parties can profit from education about long-term consequences of oppression and about their interests in more constructive conflict. Upper party mobilization can be reduced, and their perceptions of lower parties as subhuman can be changed. Interventions in the prison simulation, for example, might have emphasized long-term interdependence between guards and prisoners, or reduce the guards' fear of a revolt, or emphasized prisoners as fellow human beings.

At interfaces characterized by abdication and apathy, on the other hand, upper parties and lower parties alike withdraw. Interventions can clarify upper and lower party interests in leadership and decision making, and internal leadership and cohesion can be mobilized in both. In abdication at level interfaces, the parties can be mobilized to engage each other rather than be allowed to retreat from their differences.

Strategy 6. *Alter the organizational or larger context.* Appeal to the larger organizational hierarchy is not very useful in reducing dominance and oppression, because superiors usually have limited information and little interest in undermining their own authority. However, superiors who are committed to reducing excessive dominance may have a big impact: Top administrators of youth detention facilities in California instituted a new grievance system that rebalanced the distribution of power between prisoners and staff, even though the staff argued that "everything that is being done is for the (prisoner's) benefit" (Gillers, 1980a:30). Changes in organizational reward systems or alterations in organizational structure can redistribute formal power and so reduce interface dominance. Corporate decentralization, for example, often delegates important responsibilities and improves the balance of power at branch-headquarters interfaces.

Abdication sometimes creates performance problems that draw attention from hierarchical superiors. Managers who exercise too little power over their workers are often more visible to upper levels than managers who exercise too much, given the nature of organizational information flow. Organizational procedures and reward systems can be designed to encourage interlevel engagement. Participative gain-sharing plans, for example, encourage constructive conflict among workers and managers for enhanced productivity, and gains are then distributed to both parties (Lawler, 1980). Changes in organizational structure can redraw party definitions and formal power distributions for more productive conflict. A state department reorganization in 1965, for example, collapsed six hierarchical levels and improved both upward communication and program autonomy significantly (Warwick, 1975).

Third parties from the larger context can be drawn into problems at level interfaces. Extremes of dominance and submission attract attention from external agencies, even when lower parties are too submissive to seek external aid. Political parties, academic researchers, investigative journalists, union organizers, community activists, and government ombudsmen sometimes offer their resources to oppressed parties. Or lower parties may alert outside agencies by "blowing the whistle" on organizational abuses of power. Escalating dominance and submission, once visible to agencies in the larger context, are likely to draw external intervention.

Abdication evokes less external intervention, because it creates internal inefficiencies that are less visible to the larger context. Both parties move away from the problem rather than call attention to it. Management lapses at the Three Mile Island nuclear reactor, for example, would not have become externally visible if their potential consequences had not been so shattering.

The larger context of social, economic, and political forces and trends is often difficult to influence. Some parties have sufficient leverage to alter those patterns: Multinational corporations have reportedly threatened to abandon plants in developing countries if their governments would not suppress union organizing. But many parties have little direct influence on the larger context, and so must cope through awareness of larger forces and their implications: Militance in Third World labor movements has implications for employer dominance in Third World plants, and energy shortages have implications for abdications that waste energy. Changes in the distribution of social power can be foreseen and used for productive conflict at level interfaces; failing to take larger social changes into account may set the stage for explosive conflict problems.

Interrupting the dynamics of interface development can involve redefining or reorganizing the interface directly, altering the interests and mobilization of one or both parties, or shifting the contextual forces on parties and interface. Successful interventions produce better defined and organized interfaces to control power struggles or abdication, or less asymmetrical interfaces to moderate dominance and submission.

Table 5.2 summarizes interventions for promoting productive conflict at level interfaces. These interventions may be used alone or in combination, and their impacts affect different aspects of the interface over time.

TABLE 5.2

Promoting conflict at level interfaces

	DOMINANCE/ SUBMISSION	ABDICATION/ APATHY
Changing representatives' interaction		
1. *Alter perceptions*	Debunk stereotypes: • view of uppers as irresistible • view of lowers as subhuman Educate about oppression dynamics: • potential explosions • own contributions Recognize legitimate rights and duties of both	Debunk stereotypes: • view of uppers as uninterested • view of lowers as dangerous, irrelevant Educate about abdication dynamics: • avoidance patterns • own contributions Recognize responsibilities of both
2. *Alter communications*	Alter one-way flow: • safeguard lower communicators • encourage upper search Communicate about restriction of communications	Increase interaction: • promote discussions of controversial issues • pursue ambiguities Discuss atrophy of communications

TABLE 5.2 (continued)
Promoting conflict at level interfaces

	DOMINANCE/ SUBMISSION	ABDICATION/ APATHY
3. *Alter actions*	Separate and manage dominance issues first Articulate lower alternatives Power-balancing tactics: • upper self-limitation initiatives • lower power-building initiatives • explicit legitimation of rights and duties • tactics for countering dominance/submission Train/recruit representatives able to listen (upper) and speak up (lower)	Separate and manage abdication issues first Articulate unseen alternatives Engagement tactics: • low-risk engagement initiatives • explicit discussion of responsibilities • tactics for countering withdrawal Train/recruit representatives able to recognize and assert issues

Changing interface development

4. *Alter level interface*	Redefine interface to balance parties: • clarify shared objectives, costs of dominance • add boundaries to restrain upper/subtract to allow lower discretion • include resources to balance relations: assertive lowers, listening uppers, third parties	Redefine interface to control withdrawal: • clarify shared objectives, costs of withdrawal • add boundaries to reinforce existing interaction • include active participants, exclude conflict avoiders, include third parties who promote engagement

TABLE 5.2   (continued)
Promoting conflict at level interfaces

	DOMINANCE/ SUBMISSION	ABDICATION/ APATHY
	Balanced interface organization: • close upper boundaries to arbitrary influence • open lower boundaries to challenge • promulgate formal procedures that apply equally to upper and lower representatives • promote norms and values to reward lower initiatives and punish upper bullying	Tighten interface organization: • close boundaries to distracting invasions and to loss of critical resources and personnel • establish procedures and roles for focusing discussions • promote informal norms and values that reward initiatives from both representatives
5. *Alter one or both parties*	Reframe perceived interests: • raise lower party awareness of different interests • clarify upper stakes in lower mobilization Balance mobilization: • mobilize lowers to pursue their interests • demobilize uppers to prevent further escalation	Reframe perceived interests: • clarify lower interests in engagement • clarify upper stakes in engagement Mobilize for engagement: • mobilize lowers to pursue interests in engagement • mobilize uppers to pursue interests in engagement

TABLE 5.2   (continued)
Promoting conflict at level interfaces

	DOMINANCE/ SUBMISSION	ABDICATION/ APATHY
	Debunk party stereotypes: • views of subhuman lowers • views of malev- olent, irresis- tible uppers	Debunk party stereotypes: • views of dan- gerous, irrele- vant lowers • views of unin- terested uppers
6. *Alter context*	Rebalance organiza- tional context for dominance: • superior com- mitment to more equal re- lations • procedures that limit power dif- ferences (e.g., grievances) • organizational redistributions of power (e.g., decentralizations) Involve external forces: • inform inter- ested third par- ties about abuses (e.g., whistle-blowing) • redirect external forces to pro- mote power balance • utilize external developments to promote power balance	Focus organizational context on abdica- tion problems: • superior com- mitments to more en- gagement • procedures that limit withdrawal (e.g., participa- tive gain-sharing plans) • organization re- structures that collapse levels (e.g., flatter designs) Involve external forces: • inform third par- ties of costs of avoidance • redirect external forces to pro- mote en- gagement • recognize and utilize external developments to promote engagement

SUMMARY

Level interfaces bring together parties that differ in their formal organizational power, although their actual inequalities are modified by their informal power. Power differences are central at level interfaces. These power differences spring from both job activities and political alliances, and they can produce positive or negative uses of power at the interface.

Conflict management at level interfaces may be required to deal with too much conflict, which is associated with power struggles, or too little conflict, which is associated with oppression or abdication. Intervenors can reduce destructive conflict or promote productive conflict by interrupting the interaction among representatives, or by altering the interplay of interface, parties, and contexts. Over time, these interventions interact and influence each other as well.

Several aspects of conflict management at level interfaces deserve final emphasis. First, managing power is critical to changing problematic conflict at level interfaces. The effect of interventions on the distribution of power is closely linked to their effect on the conflict. Even "statesmanlike" negotiations could not prevent a strike at the College City Transit Authority, given the parties' need to test each other's strength. Second, the unequal position of the parties in the organizational hierarchy affects organizational credibility as a third party, and so enhances the importance of external third parties. Events at the Authority were greatly influenced by external third parties, ranging from consultants to state and federal governments. Third, interventions that establish or preserve parity among upper and lower parties are often critical to reducing conflict in power struggles, or to promoting conflict in dominance/submission relations. Without the security of parity, upward spirals of warfare or downward spirals of oppression are difficult to interrupt. The strike at the Authority reinforced the parity between management and union. Finally, level interfaces seem particularly vulnerable to rapid and explosive instability. Extreme restrictions on communications between upper and lower parties allow covert antagonism and mobilization to proceed to extremes before they suddenly become visible. Strong feelings and harsh words were common between workers and managers at the College City Transit Authority. Managing conflict at level interfaces may require great skill in communications and in coping with the emotionally volatile relations associated with power and authority.

Culture Interfaces

6

Organizations are embedded in larger contexts, and differences created by the world outside can affect events within the organization. Individuals and groups with different cultural backgrounds must often work closely together in organizations, and their cultural differences may result in misunderstandings, personal prejudice, institutional discrimination, or cultural isolation. This chapter focuses on cross-cultural relations within organizations, and on interventions to manage organizational problems of culturally-based conflict.

The chapter is organized by the frameworks of Chapters 2 and 3. The first section deals with problems of conflict at culture interfaces in general. These problems are illustrated in the tensions between majority and minority groups in the South Side Hospital Laboratory. The third section examines conflict management activities at the South Side Hospital, and more general discussion of interventions to manage conflict at culture interfaces is offered in the fourth section. A final section summarizes the chapter and highlights the unique characteristics of culture interfaces.

ANALYZING CULTURE INTERFACES

Just what is "culture"? The term has been defined in many ways, but here it refers to the web of beliefs, norms, and values that allow members of a common culture to assign meaning to their own and other's behavior (Geertz, 1973). Shared culture sets common expectations about the symbolic implications of actions, so individuals can interpret each other's behavior and judge it as appropriate or inappropriate to the situation. Applying the cultural expectations of one culture to interpret behavior grounded in another may lead to ludicrous misunderstandings. American Peace Corps volunteers in Ethiopia, for example, sometimes misinterpreted the common sight of men holding hands in the street, even though they had been told that Ethiopian and American norms differ in the expression of affection between men.

Cultural differences are established early. We grow up in a cultural context and are taught from early childhood a set of beliefs, norms, and values which enable us to understand and interact appropriately with the people around us. The language we speak, the myths we learn, the rituals we participate in, the values we aspire to, all provide symbolic frameworks by which we assess the meaning of our own and others' acts. Cultural assumptions acquired in early childhood often have deeply rooted connotations of good and bad: "It is *wrong* to cheat," or "It is *good* to be punctual." Subsequent contacts with cultures that attach different values or connotations to those activities ("Cheating is clever if you don't get caught" or "Punctuality is measured in hours not minutes") may result in highly charged misunderstandings (see Hall, 1959).

Individuals who live in culturally homogeneous settings, where most people share common assumptions, often believe those assumptions are shared by "everyone" (or "all right-thinking people"). Contacts with different cultures may produce shock. Peace Corps volunteers faced with Ethiopian handholding customs became more aware of how tightly U.S. norms restrict the expression of affection among males, and of how deeply rooted and emotionally charged such unrecognized cultural assumptions may be.

The roots of cultural differences are outside organizations, but organizations may have to deal with conflicts imported from the larger society. A culture interface may arise from contact between two relatively independent cultures. The rise of transnational corporations and increasing global interdependence, for example, often bring individuals from very different cultures (e.g., American, Japanese, Saudi Arabian) into close contact within organizations. Cultural differences may also be based on assumptions within a culture about appropriate roles (e.g., men and women, young and old), and changes in those assumptions may produce tension at interfaces. Culture interfaces also develop between subcultures (e.g., blacks, Jews, Appalachians, WASPs in U.S. society) or between minority and majority subcultures (e.g., blacks and whites in the U.S.).

Conflict at culture interfaces can produce complex problems. Different cultural assumptions may result in misunderstandings and communication problems that in the extreme can produce "culture shock." Individuals in culture shock are unable to understand the cultural context that surrounds them, and they may become depressed or unable to act as a result (Lundstedt, 1963). Cultural differences may be associated with prejudice and personal bigotry, or with institutional discrimination. The former involves overt and covert antagonisms associated with cultural differences on the part of individuals (Allport, 1954). Institutional discrimination incorporates bias into organizational and institutional arrangements, so discriminatory results are achieved without the necessity for personal bias by individual representatives. Thus, the web of educational, occupational, residential, and political discrimination against black people in the U.S. creates a sort of push-buttom racism that may be operated by individuals who are themselves not personally prejudiced (Knowles and Prewitt, 1969; Chesler, 1976). More generally, too much conflict at culture interfaces produces *cultural polarization,* accompanied by personal bias, distorted communications, and fighting between representatives. Too little conflict is associated with either *cultural homogenization,* in which cultural differences are ignored and suppressed so that potentially valuable perspectives remain unexplored, or *cultural isolation,* in which representatives withdraw from interaction at the expense of their organizationally defined interdependence. Productive conflict between cultural representatives can produce *multicultural problem-solving,* in which explorations of cultural differences contribute to mutually beneficial outcomes, or *multicultural bargaining,* in which negotiations over cultural differences produce mutually acceptable compromises in spite of conflicting interests among the parties.

Simple culture interfaces are defined by the combination of (1) organizational task interdependence and (2) cultural differences imported from the larger context between (3) relatively equal parties who (4) share a common organizational context. The representatives of different cultures interact *for reasons of organizationally defined interdependence.* American, Saudi Arabian, and Japanese managers must work together effectively if a transnational corporation operating in all three countries is to perform well; men and women doctors must be able to operate together effectively if patients are to survive their ministrations. But culture interfaces are also in part defined by *cultural differences imported from the larger context.* Organizations are not responsible for cultural differences between the United States, Japan, and Saudi Arabia, nor have they created current changes in American perceptions of appropriate roles for men and women. But organizations become microcosms of the larger society at internal culture interfaces. Cultural differences do not necessarily imply power differences, and simple culture interfaces *bring together relatively equal parties.* In reality some of the most difficult to manage interfaces combine culture and power differences; minority-majority interfaces, such as black-white contacts in the U.S., often present complex combinations of culture and power differences (see Chapter 8). Finally, the definition also assumes that the parties *share a common organizational context.* The representatives of different nationalities, subcultures, or cultural roles have common organizational goals and expectations.

Elements of Culture Interfaces

Cultures emerge from efforts to solve the problems of living in society, and cultural features may be based in factors like climatic conditions (e.g., the Eskimos), availability of food (e.g., the South

Sea Islands), terrain (e.g., Bedouin nomads), and availability of land (e.g., frontier Americans). The social experiences of Eskimos, South Sea Islanders, Bedouins, and frontier Americans are sufficiently different to make misunderstandings among them quite likely, if they come in contact. Histories of contact also shape cultural relations. Relations between blacks and whites in U.S. organizations have roots 300 years deep; relations between men and women are based on millennia of contact. Culture interfaces in organizations are shaped by the history of the larger society as well as by past events in the organization (Alderfer, 1977b).

Cultural parties.   Cultural characteristics and assumptions are derived from social experiences. Men and women, for example, begin learning early what characteristics and attitudes are culturally appropriate to their genders. U.S. gender stereotypes call on women to be personal, emotional and intuitive, oriented to relationships, supportive, and vulnerable; men, in contrast, are expected to be impersonal, analytic and intellectual, task-oriented, competitive, and strong (Kanter, 1975). Early training in such characteristics is brought to culture interfaces in organizations.

Early training of the parties is often reinforced by unrealistic expectations from the other parties. Kanter (1975) has described stereotypic roles assigned to women in male-dominated organizations that reinforce dominant cultural expectations. Women may be fitted into several stereotypes: "mother" (who brings cookies and takes care of her "boys"), "pet" (who is cute and not a competitor), "sex object" (whose desirability also breeds resentment), and "iron maiden" (who is tough and dangerous). Such stereotypes reinforce cultural characteristics, and sufficient reinforcement may sometimes induce parties to accept dominant stereotypes as valid. The Clarks's (1958) famous study of Southern black children who chose white over black dolls illustrates black acceptance of negative white stereotypes.

Parties to culture interfaces in organizations may be difficult to identify, for organizations may have little reason to locate cultural representatives in physical or task proximity—unlike members of departments or levels. The existence of a culture interface must often be inferred from the relevance of cultural differences to conflict problems, or from societal histories of tension outside the organization. Since cultural parties in organizations are often dispersed, they may remain unmobilized or even unknown to each other unless conflict escalates to extremes. The interests of cultural parties may be diffused and unclear, unless cultural issues inside and outside the organization press parties to define their concerns. Challenges to white male dominance of U.S. organizations in the larger society have mobilized blacks and women as parties to pursue their interests in some organizations. Similarly, transnational corporations are becoming increasingly aware of cultural parties and problems at culture interfaces (e.g., Heenan and Perlmutter, 1979).

Cultural representatives.   Almost any member of a cultural party may become a representative, since potential cross-cultural contacts and conflicts are dispersed through the organization along with cultural differences. This dispersion has two important implications. First, roles of culture representatives are seldom well-defined, since cultural parties are not sufficiently organized to recognize the need for representative roles until after serious problems have erupted. Second, in the absence of party organization and recognized representatives, active roles at culture interfaces are often taken by self-identified representatives with extreme positions on cultural differences. Racially militant whites and blacks, ethnocentric Americans, Japanese, or Arabs, male and female chauvinists are likely to challenge each other at nascent culture interfaces. Such challenges clearly identify culture interface problems, but they seldom create a good climate for calmly exploring important differences.

Personal characteristics of cultural representatives may be important to their ability to work at culture interfaces. Some personality traits, for example, are associated with prejudice against outgroups: authoritarianism, dogmatism, intolerance of ambiguity, low cognitive complexity, and low self-esteem (Ashmore and DelBoca, 1976). Representatives with such characteristics may have problems understanding and working with representatives of other cultures. On the other hand, experience in living and working in other cultures may help individuals understand their own cultural backgrounds and to tolerate representatives of different cultures.

Culture interface definition and organization. Since cultural differences are defined by external forces, culture interfaces are seldom formally defined by organizations—unless serious problems draw organizational attention. People tend to interact *within* their cultures rather than across them (Amir, 1976), so culture interfaces do not develop socially defined boundaries unless cross-cultural interaction begins for other reasons. Culture interfaces in most organizations are weakly defined as a multitude of interpersonal contacts, unless problems encourage explicit efforts to mobilize parties and define their interface more clearly.

The composition of culture interfaces may include various mixes of representatives. Interface compositions skewed in favor of one party may lock minority representatives into stereotyped roles by virtue of numbers alone. Kanter (1976) has pointed out that lone women or lone blacks are inevitably highly visible representatives whose behavior is interpreted by majority representatives in cultural rather than personal terms. As long as the composition of the organization as a whole is skewed and minorities are dispersed within it, culture interfaces are likely to reinforce the tendency to stereotype minorities.

Overorganized culture interfaces have closed external boundaries and tight internal regulation of representatives' behavior. Closed external boundaries inhibit inputs from or outputs to parties: Overorganized interfaces may bring together managers of different nationalities but suppress discussion of relevant cultural differences, and so sacrifice important information for the sake of surface homogeneity. Formal rules and procedures may be invoked ("You're out of order—let's keep on the task at hand") to constrain exploration of culturally based misunderstandings. Informal expectations may also limit interaction: Kanter's (1975) roles for women ("mother," "sex object," "pet," and "iron maiden") may be paired with complements ("son," "lover," "master," and "victim") that constrain the contributions possible from both. Overorganized interfaces enforce a kind of cultural homogenization that suppresses important and relevant differences in perspective and resources. Interface organization that systematically favors one party may create the push-button racism or sexism of institutional discrimination, by which even unprejudiced majority representatives may benefit from and reinforce unfair advantages.

Underorganized interfaces, in contrast, have open external boundaries and loose internal regulation. Open boundaries permit disruptive invasions or loss of critical resources, and external events may catalyze explosions of too much conflict at underorganized culture interfaces. The widely heralded generation gap, for example, was a loosely organized culture interface between young and old in the sixties in many organizations. Tensions in the larger society produced the Kent State riots and killings, and that event set off widespread escalations of conflict between students and faculties in high schools all over the country. Few formal or informal mechanisms for controlling conflict over cultural issues existed within the high schools, so conflict in many cases moved very rapidly to extremes. On the other hand, underorganized interfaces may permit mutual withdrawal from differences and cultural isolation. Efforts to integrate the trust department of a large bank, for example, foundered on the inability of either party to confront cultural differences. Several "highly qualified" black managers joined the department, but no mechanisms for discussing racial differences or their implications existed, and whites and blacks tended to withdraw from each other. Ultimately the isolated blacks despaired of working effectively in the department, and left.

Culture interface context.   The context of the culture interface includes the organization in which parties and interface are embedded, interested external parties, and the larger context of social, economic, and political forces. Organizations vary considerably in their awareness of and sensitivity to problems at culture interfaces: Some U.S. organizations invest substantial resources in managing personal and institutional discrimination by race and gender; others are oblivious to those issues. Some multinational corporations actively encourage multicultural perspectives in their staffs; others do not recognize the importance of cross-cultural understanding (Heenan and Perlmutter, 1979). Organizational contexts are important in their effect on events at culture interfaces. Minority participants in culture interfaces emphasize the importance of top management commitment to ending discrimination (e.g., Jones, 1973). Organizational policies and structures related to cultural differences shape the development of parties and interfaces. Multinational corporate policies that limit top management positions to parent country nationals, for example, almost insure that the corporation will remain relatively unaware of other perspectives.

Social forces and trends in U.S. and world society in recent years have raised the stakes at various cultural interfaces. Minority groups have mobilized within U.S. society; increasing world interdependence has made cross-cultural problems more visible. These trends have sometimes produced third parties with interests in managing cultural conflict. The Equal Employment Opportunity Commission, for example, regulates institutional discrimination at work, and a variety of agencies are concerned with cross-cultural conflicts within multinational corporations. Culture interfaces are influenced by contextual forces ranging from organizational pressures to interested third parties to social trends.

Dynamics at Culture Interfaces

Two levels of dynamics occur at culture interfaces. Immediate interaction among representatives produces too much, too little, or appropriate and productive conflict at interfaces. Longer-term interplays among conflict outcomes, party interests and characteristics, interface definition and organization, and contextual forces alter the interfaces within which representatives act.

Dynamics of culture representatives' interaction.   Interaction between representatives of different cultures may set off escalating cycles of misunderstanding and action that culminate in intense conflict and *cultural polarization.* Initial perceptions on both sides may pivot on past histories of conflict or on negative perceptions of cultural differences. Tensions between minority students and the administration at San Francisco State College (Chalmers, 1974) in the late sixties involved administration views of students as radical and irresponsible, and student perceptions of the administration as deceitful and racist. Communications between cultural representatives may be restricted by a combination of culturally based misunderstanding and conflict-based distortion. Conservative San Francisco State trustees and radical black students and faculty used rhetorics that were mutually inflammatory, regardless of the content of their proposals. Representatives may formulate big issues, commit to inflexible positions, and adopt tactics of increasing coerciveness. Conflict escalated at San Francisco State from negotiations to name-calling to strikes and closures to violent confrontations between students and police. Events that appear trivial from one perspective seem cataclysmic from another: Delays in opening the San Francisco State black studies program resulted in student strikes, faculty firings, police occupations, and violent clashes. The parties can entrench themselves in positions that are extremely difficult to give up: San Francisco State students and faculty struck for over four months, and antagonisms remained long after classes reopened.

At other culture interfaces, interaction among representatives can suppress cultural differences for a *cultural homogenization* that ignores culture differences relevant to the parties and their interdependence. Representatives do not perceive, or do not admit to perceiving, significant differences between the parties; communications about differences are suppressed or limited to noncontroversial discussions; representatives' actions are carefully controlled to prevent cross-cultural challenge or exploration. Treating the new black female resident in one hospital as "just one of the gang" of white male doctors, for example, suppresses her unique perspectives on patients (many of them black and/or female) and on medical practice, from which all might learn. Cultural homogenization is often based on good intentions, but the results are often problematic. Black females are seldom very comfortable as "honorary white males," and the fiction cannot easily be maintained by either side. So cultural homogenization requires maintaining a fiction that simultaneously deprives both sides of resources that are potentially relevant.

A third conflict problem at culture interfaces occurs when representatives withdraw from differences, thereby reducing interaction and encouraging *cultural isolation* of the parties. Representatives perceive cultural differences as threatening or offensive; they reduce communication and selectively accept data to fit their perceptions; they seek safe distances from the threat and so reduce interaction. An extreme form of such isolation is "culture shock" in which a representative despairs of communicating and retreats into depression (Lundstedt, 1963). Protecting new black managers in a bank's trust department from racist white customers, for example, isolated them from the department's most important business. Failure to examine cultural differences relevant to business activity isolated them further: Much trust department business was done in recreational clubs, to which the blacks did not or could not belong. Well-intended avoidance of cultural differences sabotaged the effort to integrate the department by so isolating the new managers that they eventually left.

Productive conflict at culture interfaces involves perceiving and explicitly recognizing cultural differences, encouraging communication about those differences when relevant, and encouraging representatives to resolve differences without escalation, suppression, or avoidance of conflict. When the mix of party interests is perceived to balance in favor of common interests, representatives may engage in *multicultural problem-solving* which includes relatively open communications, positive mutual perceptions, and tactics that generate alternatives beneficial to both cultures. For example, Alderfer et al. (1980) describe problem-solving in a multicultural consulting team that used its own race and gender differences to aid diagnosis of cultural problems in a larger organization. When the balance of interests of cultural parties at an interface are perceived as more in conflict, representatives may engage in *multicultural bargaining* that combines guarded communications, perceptions focused on differences and relative strengths, and tactics designed to manipulate goals and commitments for acceptable compromises without losing sight of underlying common interests of both parties. Conflict between blacks and whites at the University of Michigan in 1970, for example, culminated in negotiated settlements after black students and faculty established their capacity to disrupt university functioning, and so brought white administrators to the bargaining table (Chalmers, 1974).

Dynamics of culture interface development. Representatives' interactions influence and are influenced by culture interface organization and definition, which emerges in turn from the interplay of interface, parties, and contextual forces.

Figure 6.1 portrays patterns of interface development associated with different dynamics of representative interaction. Too much conflict at culture interfaces produces cultural polarization (A). Highly mobilized cultural parties (solid boundaries) square off within a poorly defined and underorganized interface (dotted boundary) and recruit allies from the larger context (arrows from outside) to support escalating conflict (divergent arrows). The escalation of conflict at San Francisco State College between white trustees and black student leaders is an example of cultural polarization that followed this path. Ultimately students, faculty, and outside groups mobilized to fight administrators, trustees, and state government at an interface that provided little regulation of the naked force employed by representatives. Initial differences between parties were drastically expanded, and all paid a high price in the ensuing organizational shutdowns.

Too little conflict may take either of two forms (B). Cultural homogeneity brings together relatively unmobilized cultural parties (dotted boundaries) in an overorganized interface (solid boundary) that suppresses exploration of cultural differences (short arrows). In such situations apparent "integration" may reflect enforced homogeneity and institutional discrimination in which structural forces reproduce dominance of one cultural party by another. Making the black female doctor "one of the

A. *Too Much Conflict*

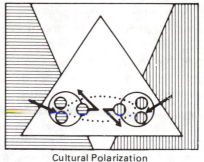

Cultural Polarization

B. *Too Little Conflict*

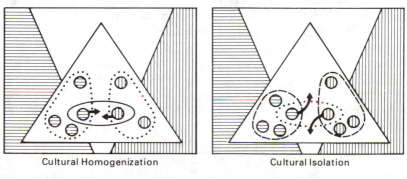

Cultural Homogenization Cultural Isolation

C. *Productive Conflict*

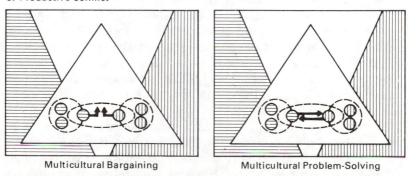

Multicultural Bargaining Multicultural Problem-Solving

Fig. 6.1. *Conflict at culture interfaces.*

gang" prevents discussion of differences that may be quite relevant to both parties. Cultural isolation, in contrast, brings together parties that may be moderately organized (dashed boundaries) at an underorganized interface (dotted boundary) that
permits withdrawal from important cultural differences and reduced interaction across cultures (wandering arrows). The result
undercuts the organizational interdependence of the parties. Although the bank discussed earlier was committed to integrating
its trust department, failure to actively confront cultural differences between white and black managers resulted in isolation of
the latter and their eventual departure.

In productive conflict patterns (C) both multicultural bargaining and multicultural problem-solving bring together moderately
organized parties able to take in new information but also able to
recognize and act on behalf of their own interests (dashed boundaries). These parties interact within a clearly defined and
moderately organized interface (dashed boundary) that limits
debate without suppressing differences or permitting avoidance.
Problem-solving interactions (long arrows) involve open exchanges of information, trust and friendliness, and exploration of
options that generate mutually beneficial outcomes and understandings. The consulting team mentioned earlier was able to
develop increased understanding of its own and others' cultural
differences and problems through examining its members' relations. Bargaining interactions (compromising arrows), in contrast, involve guarded exchanges of information, suspicion and
perception of differences, and manipulation, coercion, and defensive tactics for creating compromise on options where perceived interests conflict. Eventual negotiations between University of Michigan administrators and black students and faculty
achieved compromises that partially met the needs of both parties without producing the extended organizational disruptions
seen at San Francisco State.

The dynamics of culture interfaces have several unique attributes. First, since culture interfaces are rooted in the external
context, they are particularly sensitive to external events and to
linkages with external forces. Second, cultural assumptions are
often inarticulate but associated with strong feelings, so

seemingly trivial events may have important symbolic content to one party and evoke strong reactions that astonish the other party. Third, since cultural differences are often not central to organizational divisions, cultural parties may be organizationally dispersed, relatively unmobilized, and represented by extremists. These factors contribute to low organizational awareness about culture interfaces, punctuated with sudden eruptions linked to external events.

A CULTURE INTERFACE AT THE SOUTH SIDE HOSPITAL

Relations between the minority and majority staff members in the Laboratory of the South Side Hospital are an example of problems at a culture interface.

> *South Side Hospital is a medical facility of National Health Care, a health maintenance organization that offers prepaid medical care to individuals and organizations in several states. As the costs of medical care have increased across the country, National Health Care has grown rapidly, since it offers reasonably priced services in comparison to many other medical systems. The South Side Hospital is relatively new, and was opened to handle the expanded clientele in a large Midwestern city.*

> *There is a high proportion of black residents on the South Side. The central city population is nearly half black, though the surrounding metropolitan area is almost entirely white. In the last fifty years most of the people financially able to do so have moved out of the central city, leaving behind poor blacks and poor whites. The city has a long history of racial tension, and severe riots occurred in its black ghettoes during the late sixties. Many Hospital clients are members of minority groups.*

> *The Hospital opened with a small and temporary Laboratory facility, established to handle routine work. Six technicians were employed under the temporary supervision of Ms. Grey, an experienced black laboratory technician. Most of the other technicians were also black and held high school de-*

grees. Since none of the technicians had advanced training, more complex tests were handled by another facility.

National Health Care decided in 1973 to expand the services available at the South Side Hospital Lab. A young white laboratory technologist, named Ms. Williams, was hired to manage the Laboratory. She was told that she could hire new or train old personnel, and redesign and systematize Lab procedures. But she was to improve and expand Laboratory services as rapidly as possible.

Ms. Williams decided to expand Laboratory services by quickly hiring new personnel who could soon qualify as laboratory technologists. Certification as a technologist requires a college degree, though the degree need not be in a medical field. Hospital policy did not require technologists (rather than technicians) to staff the Laboratory, but Ms. Williams believed that hiring more highly trained personnel was critical to improving Lab services. Most of the New Hires held college degrees, but some of these degrees (e.g., a B.A. in English) were of arguable relevance to Laboratory work. All the New Hires with college degrees were white.

By 1976 the Laboratory had expanded to a staff of fifteen, which was split into two antagonistic groups. One group, led by the original supervisor, Ms. Grey, included the original staff and other minorities (six blacks, a Polynesian, and a first-generation Jewish immigrant). All the members of the "Old Guard" were technicians, with less professional training than technologists. The other group was led by Ms. Williams, and included the five newly hired white technologists. The Old Guard believed that the New Hires owe their positions to racial prejudice rather than superior qualifications.

In 1976 the Laboratory jobs were reclassified for consistency with other National Health Care facilities. This reclassification was intended to bring the South Side job classifications up to the levels at other facilities, but the actual impact was to grant more pay and responsibilities to New Hires. The Old Guard's job titles and definitions remained unchanged, and several of them—including Ms. Grey—were "redlined" to receive no pay raises. The Old Guard believed that the reclassification results were motivated by racial bias on the part of Ms. Williams. Now new people with less experience got more pay for doing the same work as the Old Guard.

Old Guard members began to demonstrate their antagonism with slowdowns and minor insubordination. Ms. Williams retaliated with disciplinary actions, and those actions were interpreted as further harassment by the Old Guard. Ms. Williams formally disciplined Ms. Grey for eating lunch in the Laboratory. While formal rules did prohibit eating in the Laboratory, the Old Guard argued that everyone else broke the rule with impunity—so the disciplinary action was intended as harassment. Ms. Williams also transferred Ms. Goldstein, a close colleague of Ms. Grey, against her will. Both Ms. Grey and Ms. Goldstein filed formal grievances about these actions. After token efforts to use internal grievance procedures, both women filed suit with external agencies charging Ms. Williams with racial and religious discrimination. They asked for relief from her harassment.

National Health Care had encountered problems of minority relations in the past. Several years prior, National Health Care had agreed with the Equal Employment Opportunity Commission, after another discrimination suit, to arrange systematic performance reviews and to promote minority personnel to higher organizational positions. The new suit posed a serious problem for National management, for they had not yet complied with the previous agreement. They feared that new suits would create serious problems with EEOC and/or the public image of the organization. They decided to settle the two suits out of court, "giving in" (in the eyes of Ms. Williams) to the Old Guard.

Ms. Williams believed that she had been abandoned by upper management. Her immediate superior, Ms. Thomas, had chosen to stay away from the Laboratory so she could remain unbiased in the eyes of the union and the EEOC. Ms. Williams saw no option but to go ahead with her original plan to upgrade Laboratory performance and capabilities.

*The Old Guard was jubilant at the settlements. They inter-
preted them as confirmation of their assessment of Ms.
Williams. In their view the best solution to continuing problems in the Lab was for management to fire Ms. Williams.
The union steward, who had been on the original Laboratory
staff, agreed and so recommended to management. The Old
Guard enthusiastically planned new suits, and carefully doc-
umented Laboratory events in preparation for that
eventuality.*

*Meanwhile, Laboratory performance declined seriously.
Tests were misperformed, samples were lost, and the medical staff increasingly protested low-quality work, even
though the New Hires were working themselves into a lather
to compensate for Old Guard alienation.*

Events in the South Side Hospital Laboratory can be examined in terms of interface elements and dynamics.

Elements of the Old Guard-New Hire Interface

The *parties* of the Old Guard and the New Hires came from
different cultural contexts and historical experiences. The Old
Guard was composed of minority group members, who shared
the common experience of discrimination from the dominant
culture. They were also less educated in a society that places a
high value on education. In the immediate situation, Old Guard
members shared occupational interests in challenging the promotions of the New Hires; more generally, they shared interests
in challenging institutional discrimination against minorities—
an interest reinforced by the societywide awakening of minority
and particularly black consciousness over the previous decade.
Experience in the larger society reinforced their experience in
National Health Care to feed their suspicions of the white
majority.

The New Hires, in contrast, were young, attractive members
of a dominant culture, well-socialized into the concern with performance and advanced training characteristic of medical systems. Most of them exhibited little overt prejudice against

minorities, and they were insulted to be accused of racism when they were most consciously concerned with improving performance. The New Hires did not recognize that they might be beneficiaries of institutional discrimination.

The leaders and primary *representatives* of the two parties embodied their differences. Ms. Grey was the informal as well as the formal leader of the Laboratory prior to 1976. A woman of considerable interpersonal power, she was willing to directly challenge the authority and competence of the New Hires, and to fight for her own and the Old Guard's rights. Ms. Williams was younger and more highly trained than Ms. Grey, but less able to generate informal support from her subordinates. She was willing to press for improved Laboratory performance. Whether she was actually racially biased remained unclear, though she was at best naive about the racial implications of some of her decisions.

The *culture interface* between Old Guard and New Hires was nominally defined by task interdependence, shared physical space, and common authority within the Laboratory. But the conflict undermined Old Guard commitment to Laboratory tasks and annihilated the legitimacy of Ms. Williams's authority. Social bonds defining the interface were swamped by the tensions between the parties; party boundaries, in contrast, were strongly defined by shared social bonds.

The interface was also underorganized, and increasingly so as the conflict continued. Its external boundary was open to invasion by allies and third parties: Upper management, the medical staff, the union, and external agencies all sought to influence events in the Laboratory, and events in the Lab were virtually advertised to interested external parties. There were few mechanisms for regulating interaction between the parties. Formal procedures and rules provided little constraint on behavior, though a grievance procedure had been created for union matters, and National Health Care had recently appointed a regional EEOC officer to manage equal opportunity issues. But neither of these mechanisms effectively regulated conflict between the Old Guard and the New Hires. Nor were informal mechanisms for managing conflict available. The parties shared few norms or understandings that could control conflict, and their initial engagement undercut rather than facilitated the development of common beliefs or expectations.

The *context* contributed to the problem. The organization admitted to past institutional discrimination, and more recently had failed to implement measures to counter that discrimination. The Old Guard was influenced by the growing sophistication about discrimination in the city's black population, and they took advantage of outside institutions created to counter institutional discrimination, such as the EEOC and the state Civil Rights Commission. This strategy played to management weakness, for another lost suit or even an investigation could have compromised the organization with federal and state regulators and with its large minority client population. Other third parties also influenced events at the Laboratory: The union watched with interest and offered support to the Old Guard, and the medical staff increasingly complained about reduced Laboratory performance.

Old Guard-New Hire Dynamics

Ms. Williams and Ms. Grey found themselves locked into *escalating sequences of perceptions, communications, and actions.* From Ms. Williams's viewpoint, the dominant issue was the improvement of Laboratory performance. From Ms. Grey's perspective, prejudice was central, and the new hiring decisions reeked of racial bias. When the issues are so conceptualized, it is not surprising that conflict results. As conflict continued, events were easily interpreted as personal attacks: Insubordination by the Old Guard was a personal challenge to Ms. Williams; "redlining" Ms. Grey's salary was an explicit punishment to her; and so on.

The conflict was self-reinforcing. Communications between the two parties decreased drastically; Ms. Grey and Ms. Williams were barely on speaking terms. Each new event was interpreted to fit mutual negative stereotypes; the New Hires' behavior was attributed to prejudice, and the Old Guards' actions were explained as irresponsible vindictiveness. The representatives engaged in escalating coercion: Ms. Williams was insubordinate; Ms. Grey invoked disciplinary procedures; Ms. Williams appealed to external agencies; and so on. Each new action by one representative confirmed the other's perceptions of the first's intransigence, and so justified counterinitiatives, which contributed in their turn to further misunderstanding and polarization.

The escalation of the representatives' conflict was enhanced by an interplay of parties, interface, and context that *loosened remaining interface organization.* Party characteristics at the outset made conflict probable. Minority personnel who have been running a facility cannot be expected to look with favor on the promotion over their heads of young and inexperienced personnel from the dominant majority, even given strong rationales for hiring outsiders. The New Hires were not prepared to respond in a meaningful way to Old Guard challenges. The Old Guard was initially mobilized for managing Laboratory tasks, and they were able to carry that mobilization over informally for challenging the relatively unmobilized and unaware New Hires.

The transition to Ms. Williams's leadership made no provision for creating an interface between the two cultures, in part because their existence may not have been obvious to her. Old Guard and New Hires shared physical space in the Laboratory, but little effort was made to develop shared goals or values that would hold them together. Formal rules for organizational conflicts at culture interfaces had not been developed, and the interaction between Old Guard and New Hires produced few shared norms and values by which they could regulate disputes. On the contrary, the more the two parties interacted, the more they undermined general expectations that might have regulated their contact. The organizational context provided no credible moderator of their conflict. The organization admitted past institutional discrimination, but had done little to remedy it; the labor-management grievance system was not appropriate for cultural issues, in part because almost all the people involved belonged to the union. Ultimately the involvement of external agencies, in the form of EEOC suits and threats to the larger organization, catalyzed efforts to reduce the conflict and tighten culture interface organization within the Laboratory.

CONFLICT MANAGEMENT AT THE SOUTH SIDE HOSPITAL

Interventions to manage the conflict were tried with various degrees of success at the South Side Hospital.

By the fall of 1977, the South Side Hospital Laboratory was a mess. The Old Guard and the New Hires barely spoke to one another. The performance of the Laboratory as a medical service had declined badly. Management was all but paralyzed—upper management was concerned about threatening attention from the EEOC, and Ms. Williams had no credibility with either the Old Guard or the union. The Old Guard was planning new suits with external agencies, and cheerfully neglecting all but minimal performance requirements.

Upper management saw few attractive alternatives. Transferring or firing Ms. Williams, as demanded by the Old Guard and the union, seemed neither fair to her nor a viable response to an organizational problem. But the situation could not be permitted to continue. In desperation, management asked a team of organization development consultants, then working with top management, to intervene in the Laboratory.

Two consultants—a white male and a white female—interviewed Ms. Williams, her supervisor, personnel managers, and union representatives about the situation. Ms. Williams felt abandoned by upper management and unable to influence the situation—she was willing to accept help from any source. Personnel and union representatives were skeptical—they doubted that much could be done, but they were willing to have the consultants try.

The consultants proposed three meetings to clarify concerns and "clear the air" on both sides, and to develop shared solutions to Laboratory problems. The initial meeting would focus on the present state of the Laboratory as seen by New Hires and Old Guard. A second meeting would focus on desired states of relations. A third meeting would develop strategies for reaching shared goals. Although there were sharp exchanges between group representatives in the first two meetings, the discussions went much as planned. At the third meeting, however, an initial argument between representatives over a recent incident inspired the union representative—supposedly attending as a silent observer—to an impassioned speech. She argued that the meetings were making things worse, that the union should take jurisdiction over the problem since all Laboratory employees were union members, and that nothing would change as long as management "remained prejudiced against certain parties." The New Hires responded indignantly that the union was itself biased, that it certainly did not represent them, and that they would not continue as long as the union representative remained in the meeting. Then they left.

Aghast at this explosion, the consultants decided not to bring the parties together again immediately. They began interviewing representatives of the two groups to explore underlying causes and possible resolutions to the conflict. But they soon discovered that they had little credibility with the Old Guard, who were not prepared to trust white consultants perceived to be allies of management.

The consultants asked a third consultant—a black male—to work directly with the Old Guard. He was able to develop good rapport with the Old Guard, but he found it increasingly difficult to work with the other two consultants. The consulting team itself fell prey to internal conflict. When the consultants presented their analyses of interview data, they were attacked by both the New Hires and the Old Guard, who could agree that the consultants had not been helpful, if nothing else.

While the external consultants were struggling with the Laboratory, upper management had galvanized the Personnel Department into implementing the agreement reached with the EEOC several years before. Management did not want to be equally vulnerable to future suits. The Personnel Department had started training managers for the regular performance appraisals called for by the EEOC agreement.

Ms. Williams's immediate supervisor, Ms. Thomas, had remained almost completely aloof from the problems in the Laboratory. In response to pressure from upper manage-

ment and requests from the external consultants, Ms. Thomas began to attend meetings of the Laboratory staff to discuss the development of the new appraisal system. She agreed to develop standards and procedures for appraising the performance of Laboratory employees, provided they would participate in that process so the resulting system would be relevant to them and their jobs.

Over the next several months, Ms. Thomas spent considerable time in the Laboratory. She discussed job definitions and performance criteria with the Old Guard and New Hires, and she and they together developed standards for assessing employees' contributions. She agreed to participate in appraising employee performance with Ms. Williams, and to join her to discuss appraisals with each employee. Overt conflict between the Old Guard and the New Hires was reduced during this period, and Laboratory performance improved. The threat of new suits to be filed with external agencies did not materialize.

These events can be considered as two related sets of activities focused on Laboratory problems: (1) interventions by the external consultants, and (2) interventions by various levels of management.

Consultant Interventions

The consultants came to the Laboratory from elsewhere in the National Health Care organization, at least ostensibly without bias in favor of either party. But—they were asked to intervene by management; they initially talked to individuals who might be expected to favor the New Hires; they were both white; the female consultant intentionally developed a supportive relationship with Ms. Williams early in the consultation. It is not surprising that the Old Guard doubted their neutrality.

The consultants initially worked with both parties together, scheduling meetings to jointly diagnose problems and formulate shared goals. They called meetings to share information and to develop joint solutions, on the assumption that they could organize the interface for constructive dialogue. Hindsight suggests that they tightened interface organization enough to promote constructive interaction in the first two meetings, but the interface boundary was sufficiently open and interface organization sufficiently loose to permit the union representative to catalyze runaway escalation in the third meeting. The resulting conflict gave the consultants pause about bringing the parties together again.

They turned instead to working with the parties separately, through individual and group interviews—only to discover their lack of credibility with the Old Guard. The Old Guard identified the senior white male consultant with top management—"cold, distant, not very interested in us"—and the white female consultant with Ms. Williams—"young, sexy, biased." The new black male consultant quickly developed rapport with the Old Guard and almost as quickly lost rapport with the other consultants. Ultimately the consultant team became a microcosm of the Hospital, with each consultant identified with a different party. The resulting tensions within the consulting team itself disrupted their ability to work together. Contact between consultants and Laboratory resulted in consultant cultural polarization rather than Laboratory multicultural bargaining or problem-solving—a fate not uncommon for multicultural third parties struggling to manage issues of symbolic importance to them as well as to their clients.

Management Interventions

Hospital management played an important role in both creating and solving Laboratory problems. Had management seriously undertaken measures to counter institutional racism after its initial agreement with EEOC, for example, promotions from the ranks of the Old Guard would have been encouraged and the controversial recruitment of the "qualified" white New Hires might never have occurred.

Management's decision to settle the Old Guard suits out of court contributed to increased conflict, in the short term, for it was construed as censure of Ms. Williams and admission of the

Old Guard charges. But the suits also awakened management to the potential importance of the issues. The organization as a whole could not afford wide publicity about institutional racism, particularly publicity backed up by unfavorable EEOC decisions.

The consultants' efforts to intervene in the Laboratory brought little joy to either Laboratory or consultants. But their efforts may have had important symbolic implications: Their entry symbolized management concern, in the form of resources previously employed by top management of the corporation. Although Old Guard and New Hires both eventually rejected the consultants, neither was blind to the implied attention of upper management.

The creation of a performance appraisal system and commitment to promoting minorities were explicit organizationwide responses to the EEOC agreement. Implicitly, these changes also responded to important symbolic issues in the dispute between Old Guard and New Hires. Public commitment to those goals could be construed as a management acknowledgement of past sins, a promise to avoid their repetition, and recognition of the importance of culture interfaces in the organization.

Finally, the intervention of Ms. Thomas in the Laboratory could be seen by both parties as responding to their interests. Ms. Williams could interpret her presence as long-missing management support, and the Old Guard could see her presence as protection from the prejudice of Ms. Williams. Ms. Thomas brought the parties together for a task of immediate personal relevance to both—the creation of a system to fairly evaluate their contributions to Laboratory work. This task encouraged interdependent work by both parties, since they shared a common investment in accurate description and fair assessment of their work. The combination of shared formal rules and procedures for appraisal and the inclusion of Ms. Thomas as a (relatively) neutral participant in the appraisal process offered tighter and more legitimate regulation of the appraisal interface at which the Old Guard had to engage Ms. Williams.

Events in the Laboratory can be conceived as a shift from conflict suppression to conflict escalation at a culture interface—from cultural homogeneity to cultural polarization as portrayed in Figure 6.2. Cultural homogenization at the expense of impor-

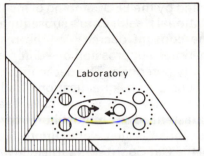

A. Too Little Conflict: Homogenization
   and Institutional Discrimination

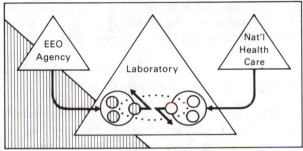

B. Too Much Conflict: Cultural Polarization
   and Open Warfare between
   Old Guard and New Hires

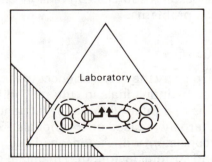

C. Productive Conflict: Multicultural
   Bargaining over Performance Standards
   and Appraisal Procedures

Fig. 6.2. *Culture interface at South Side Hospital Laboratory.*

tant differences is illustrated by the EEOC finding of institutional discrimination, and by National Health Care's subsequent failure to fulfill their half of the consent decree (A). The result was inattention to—and sometimes suppression of—differences between minority and majority personnel. The decision to upgrade the Laboratory by hiring people with "qualifications" rather than train already employed minority staff would have been challenged at interfaces characterized by multicultural bargaining and problem-solving. But those issues were suppressed in the South Side Hospital until the Old Guard was sufficiently enraged and mobilized to undertake external suits that threatened devastating publicity (B). The ensuing consultant interventions did not produce problem-solving, for distrust and antagonism by then ran very deep. But management interventions did create a climate for multicultural bargaining, in which the parties recognized sufficient common interests to compromise and continue working together (C).

MANAGING CONFLICT AT CULTURE INTERFACES

Too much or too little conflict call for interventions to change culture interfaces. Too much conflict requires intervention to reduce cultural polarization and fighting; too little conflict calls for promoting confrontations that reduce cultural isolation or homogenization. These interventions may redirect behavior, reframe perceptions, reallocate resources, or realign structural forces to manage conflict problems.

Reducing Intercultural Conflict

Much attention has been paid by the social sciences in the United States to the parts played by individuals in cultural conflict and polarization. Explanations and interventions for influencing racism, for example, have largely focused on individuals. This emphasis on individuals is consistent with American ideology, but it also ignores systemic and societal factors that maintain cultural conflicts, and so focuses attention where it is least likely to change patterns of racism or cultural dominance (Chesler, 1976).

Real changes require understanding and intervention in both the dynamics of representatives' interaction and the patterns of interface development.

Changing representatives' interaction: three strategies. Immediate interactions among cultural representatives involved in too much conflict typically involve emotionally loaded misunderstandings, strongly charged negative stereotypes, and overtly discriminatory actions. Interrupting cycles of cultural polarization requires interventions that alter perceptions, improve communications, or change the actions of representatives.

Strategy 1. *Alter representatives' perceptions.* Perceptions can be changed with new information and interpretations of the situation. Negative stereotypes of the other party are sometimes based on sheer lack of information: Some male biases about women colleagues, for example, can be altered by more opportunity for work-related contact (Kanter, 1975). Other cultural stereotypes are related to personal characteristics: Weissbach (1976) found experiences that increased individual self-acceptance or insight, confronted individual values inconsistent with prejudice, or increased individual cognitive complexity, all reduced racial prejudice. Educating individuals about the dynamics of cultural polarization can help them recognize culture-based misunderstandings and moderate the escalation of cultural conflict. For example, representatives who understand the phases of culture shock—initial euphoria at being in a new culture, subsequent crises of misunderstanding and frustration, depression and withdrawal, and eventual recovery and better understanding—can guard against expressions of frustration that escalate misunderstanding and conflict.

Strategy 2. *Improve cross-cultural communications.* Misunderstandings and distortions based on cultural differences can be reduced by more information exchange. Expanded communications do not automatically improve relations; some forms of interaction can confirm or reinforce past problems. Amir's (1969) review of studies of contact across ethnic differences suggested that cross-cultural contact promotes better relations when, among other factors, representatives have equal status, communications are intimate rather than casual, and interaction outcomes are rewarding rather than tension-laden, unpleasant, or status-reducing for either representative. Interventions can also expand the representatives' capacity to communicate about the communication process and its blocks. The factor underlying a confusing but escalating argument between American and Indian colleagues, for example, turned out on examination to be American negative interpretation of an Indian head movement intended to be affirmative.

Strategy 3. *Alter representatives' actions.* Cross-cultural tensions can sometimes be reduced by redefining cultural issues, proposing new alternatives, or altering representatives' tactics. Issues at cultural interfaces often carry powerful symbolic overtones for one or both parties—a kind of emotional booby trap that may blow up in the representatives' faces. Choosing to upgrade South Side Hospital Laboratory performance by recruiting "qualified" personnel had considerable symbolic importance to U.S. blacks, for "qualifications"—here as elsewhere—often appears to be a code word for "white" rather than a measure of performance. Interventions that separate out culturally loaded issues can prevent unintended escalations of conflict. Defining needed skills and recruiting staff to fill those needs could have reduced Old Guard suspicions that prejudice against minorities controlled promotion. Posing new alternatives that allow the parties to shift from entrenched positions without losing face can permit de-escalations. The alternative of a new appraisal system, jointly designed and monitored by a more senior manager, permitted Old Guard and New Hires to work together. Representatives can be recruited or trained for tactical skills in limiting conflict or interrupting escalation. Credible messages about depolarizing intentions can be sent: Ms. Thomas's request that both parties participate in designing the new appraisal system is an example. Cultural differences can be explicitly accepted: New Hire recognition of Old Guard sensitivities about discrimination, for example, might have reduced escalation in the Laboratory. Tactics for identifying and resolving misunderstandings might have developed "early warning" agreements by which problems could be identified and discussed before they became polarized. Tactics for interrupting escalation dynamics between cultures can be created, such as low-risk initiatives to defuse culturally important symbolic issues.

Interventions that interrupt self-fulfilling dynamics of cultural polarization may focus on perceptions, communications, and actions singly or in combination. But in the long run different aspects interact with each other, and with the interface settings in which they occur.

Changing interface development: three strategies. Cultural polarization is most obvious at underorganized interfaces, with poorly defined external boundaries and loosely regulated internal interaction. Interventions to reduce cultural conflict can focus on the interface itself, on culturally defined parties, or on contextual forces that impact both.

Strategy 4. *Change culture interfaces.* Interface boundaries and compositions can be redefined to reduce tensions. Since organizations are often oblivious to cultural differences until major problems arise, many culture interfaces in organizations remain unrecognized by organizational criteria. Recognizing culture interfaces can be an initial step to better understanding and conflict reduction, as in the creation of an EEO office in National Health Care. Bringing polarized parties together at a new interface often requires clear and compelling superordinate goals. The creation of new performance standards for both parties offered such a shared goal in the South Side Hospital Laboratory. Interface boundaries can also be redrawn to include new resources. The Old Guard would not have participated in developing new performance standards to be administered solely by the New Hires, so the inclusion of Ms. Thomas as a monitor was very important. Since initial cultural party dispersion makes it easy for extremist representatives to emerge, redrawing interface boundaries to exclude some representatives or include moderates can also be central to conflict reduction.

Tightening interface organization may involve closing interface boundaries or tightening control over representatives' interactions. The open boundaries of culturally polarized interfaces permit inputs and outputs that disrupt negotiations and escalate conflicts. Klein, Thomas, and Bellis (1971), for example, brought together Black Panthers and white police representatives to improve mutual understanding at a time of high tension in their city. But events in the city so worried police officers that they insisted on wearing their guns to meetings, and the third parties finally terminated the meetings to avoid making things worse. Third party failure to control the input of union representatives at meetings between Old Guard and New Hires similarly increased conflict. Sometimes boundaries have been closed around cross-cultural negotiations by physical distance: Workshops that have been located in other countries to permit undisturbed negotiation among Irish Catholics and Protestants and among Ethiopians, Somalis, and Kenyans (Doob and Foltz, 1973; Doob, 1970). Interface organization can also be tightened by establishing formal and informal internal regulatory mechanisms. Aronson and his colleagues (1978) devised a "jigsaw" teaching technology that emphasized interdependence in multicultural teams of elementary students for academic performance, and so enhanced the performance of minorities (majorities continued as before) and the attitudes of both groups toward each other. Levi and Benjamin (1977) developed problem analysis procedures that firmly controlled interaction between Arabs and Israelis at controversial points, but also provided flexibility for developing creative alternatives to deadlocked positions. As polarization is reduced, shared interface norms that regulate escalation (e.g., "Don't react until you understand") may emerge, and parties can learn to avoid issues that are particularly culturally sensitive.

Strategy 5. *Change one or both cultural parties.* Interventions can alter party interests, perceptions, or organization. Cultural polarization emphasizes differences in party interests, and interventions can clarify common interests or reduce interest differences among parties. Common interests in the definition of Laboratory performance standards, for example, encouraged cooperation between Old Guard and New Hires. Stereotypes of other parties sometimes have roots in group pressures for conformity rather than in personality dynamics of individuals, and interventions that alter group dynamics can reduce the impacts of group stereotypes (Allport, 1954). The need for tight cohesion in the Old Guard to defend itself from New Hire exploitation may have been reduced by the support of external agencies, and so set the stage for improved relations within the Laboratory. Parties can also create representative role definitions and pressures that encourage moderate representative behavior. Representatives who do not need to speak for their entire cultural heritage, for example, are less prone to extreme positions or stereotyped action, and role definitions that do not isolate individuals as single tokens at an interface can also reduce tension between representatives (Kanter, 1976).

Strategy 6. *Alter the context.* Forces from the organizational context and the impact of societal forces can also be altered by interventions. Recognition of culture interfaces and cross-cultural issues by the organizational hierarchy can reduce conflict, particularly when authoritative encouragement of improved relations is backed up by clear rewards and punishments (Amir, 1969; Jones, 1973). Admonitions to officers of a Southern police force who made racial slurs on other officers had little impact, but the slurs stopped overnight when the superintendent announced he would personally sit on a committee to review such cases. Formal structures and policies of the larger organization can be altered to respond to cultural differences. Racial integration in U.S. Army units near the end of World War II had a dramatic effect on the perceptions of blacks and whites (Stouffer et al., 1949). More recently, the promulgation of organizationwide affirmative-action policies has sometimes had an important effect on culture interfaces in organizations. Creating organizational departments to deal with cross-cultural issues in and outside organizations can reduce tensions and promote quicker recognition of new issues. The decision to appoint an EEO officer in National Health Care may help prevent unrecognized escalations and cultural polarizations in the future.

The larger context outside the organization is particularly relevant to cultural parties and culture interfaces because of the external roots of cultural differences. Cultural parties understandably look outside the organization for allies—to race- and gender-based support organizations, or to representatives of national cultures. National Health Care's concern with the cultural polarization in the Laboratory was partly due to the organization's large minority client population. Cultural conflicts in the larger society may also create third parties concerned with conflict management. The Equal Employment Opportunity and Civil Rights Commissions are third parties formed in response to social conflicts, but are highly relevant to organizational interfaces. Third parties may have difficulty understanding the complexities of cultural relations, or in establishing credibility across cultural differences, unless they can successfully manage those differences within themselves—the third party may have to become an effective culture interface to intervene effectively (Alderfer et al., 1980). Large-scale trends in larger context cross-cultural relations are often beyond direct influence of all but the largest intervenors, but those forces may foreshadow the cultural conflicts of tomorrow. Organizations burned by past inattention to black-white or male-female relations can insure against future heat by a wary eye on future trends: National, religious, and North-South (world regions) differences seem likely bets as future culture interfaces of note.

Table 6.1 summarizes interventions for reducing conflict at culture interfaces, either by interrupting cycles of representa-

TABLE 6.1
Reducing conflict at culture interfaces

Changing representatives' interaction

1. *Alter perceptions*

Debunk representatives' stereotypes:
- views of others as immoral or crazy
- enhanced self-acceptance, insight, cognitive complexity, or value consistency to reduce prejudice

Educate representatives about:
- dynamics of tokenism and the distortions involved in cross-cultural perception
- phases of culture shock
- own contributions to cultural polarization

TABLE 6.1 (continued)
Reducing conflict at culture interfaces

2. *Alter com-munications*	Increase contact among representatives with: • equal status • intimate rather than casual communication • rewarding rather than unpleasant or tension-laden outcomes Expand representatives' capacity to communicate about cross-cultural communication processes and blocks
3. *Alter actions*	Separate symbolic issues that are "emotional booby traps" for one or both cultures and manage separately Pose alternatives to deadlocked positions that permit cultural "face-saving" or mutual benefit Recruit or train representatives with depolarizing skills: • credible messages about depolarizing intentions • explicit recognition of sensitive cultural differences • tactics for identifying and handling misunderstandings • tactics for managing unintended escalations

Changing interface development

4. *Alter the interface*	Define the culture interface more clearly: • clarify superordinate goals important to both cultures • define interface boundaries recognized by organization • include resources that promote spanning cultural gaps • exclude extremists unwilling to depolarize relations Tighten interface organization to control interaction: • close boundaries to inputs and outputs that reinforce cultural antagonisms

TABLE 6.1   (continued)
Reducing conflict at culture interfaces

	• use physical separation to limit external invasions • create formal procedures that limit conflict and emphasize interdependence • encourage norms that discourage hasty assumptions about differences, particularly moral ones
5. *Alter one or both parties*	Clarify party interests in common and de-emphasize conflicts of interest Reduce group-based pressures for conformity and antagonistic stereotyping of outgroups Encourage party demobilization through reduced leadership militance, increased examination of internal differences Create representative roles that encourage moderation and multiple representatives
6. *Alter context*	
• Organization	Encourage recognition of cultural issues and support for reduced polarization by hierarchical superiors Organizational rewards and punishments to reduce polarization Redesign organizational structures and policies to encourage depolarization: • integrate segregated divisions • promulgate and implement affirmative action policies • create organizational units to deal with cross-cultural issues in and outside organization
• Larger context	Invite external allies to encourage depolarization Involve external third parties to mediate or manage conflict: • parties with external power base • parties composed as an effective culture interface in themselves Monitor emerging cultural differences to anticipate significant culture interfaces of the future

tives' interaction or by intervening to define and tighten the organization of the interface within which interaction occurs. These interventions can be employed singly or in combination. Over time, however, change activities will evoke complementary changes at both levels of analysis, or be overwhelmed by countervailing forces.

Promoting Intercultural Conflict

Too little conflict at culture interfaces may involve either suppressing relevant cultural differences in cycles of cultural homogenization, or withdrawing from cultural interdependence in cycles of cultural isolation. Interventions to promote more productive debate can focus on either (1) interrupting the dynamics of representative interaction, or (2) altering the interplay of parties, context, and interface.

Changing representatives' interaction: three strategies. Cultural homogeneity and cultural isolation both emerge from self-reinforcing cycles of representatives' perceptions, communications, and actions at the interface. Interventions that alter any of these aspects can promote more productive engagement.

Strategy 1. *Alter representatives' perceptions.* New information and perspectives on situations can be provided. For problems of cultural homogenization, intervention can debunk perceptions that minimize differences between the cultures. The Old Guard at the South Side Hospital Laboratory, for example, were made aware of significant differences between themselves and the New Hires. Intervention can also educate representatives about the dynamics of cultural homogenization, and so help them recognize those patterns and their own contributions to them. Educational experiences have been designed, for instance, to help individuals learn about their own and others' cultural assumptions and differences (Birnbaum, 1975). Awareness of cultural differences may be all that is needed for representatives to assert their differences at the interface, just as minority awareness in the South Side Hospital paved the way for Ms. Grey to challenge Ms. Williams.

Cultural isolation, on the other hand, may require debunking stereotypes of unbridgeable differences and clarifying representatives' similarities. Educating representatives about the dynamics of isolation can enable them to control their own withdrawal. If white or black managers in the trust department mentioned earlier had foreseen the outcomes of their mutual avoidance, either could have initiated increased contact.

Strategy 2. *Improve cross-cultural communications.* Interventions can improve the quality and quantity of information exchange. In cultural homogenization, information about potentially controversial issues is censored to preserve the illusion of similarity. Expanding the amount and range of information exchanged enhances the possibility of constructive controversy, and interventions that focus on sharing information about differences can promote much debate. Third party interventions to promote discussion of the "undiscussable" in the South Side Hospital Laboratory were so successful that the resulting torrent of ideas and feelings was difficult to control. Joint analysis of factors that suppress information between culturally defined parties can reframe the representatives' perspectives and so reduce the restrictions.

In cultural isolation, communication across cultures is seriously reduced, in spite of organizationally imposed interdependence among representatives. Intervention that increases communication can interrupt the self-reinforcing pattern of withdrawal, provided the exchanges do not confirm the fears of the representatives. By discussing together the factors contributing to the decline in communication and the cultural isolation, representatives can gain new perspectives on their information exchange and promote better communications.

Strategy 3. *Alter representatives' actions.* Changes in representatives' actions can interrupt the cycle of cultural homogenization. "Emotional booby traps" inherent in culturally symbolic issues can be identified and sprung. Questioning the "qualifications" of New Hires in the South Side Hospital Laboratory, for instance, revealed that academic qualifications (e.g., a B.A. in English) were not always good preparation for Laboratory work. Tensions around the issue of "qualifications" became harder to suppress when Old Guard members found they had to train some New Hires in the very work the latter were hired to "upgrade." Raising such symbolic issues can produce more open debate at culture interfaces. Articulating alternative outcomes that are culturally relevant can also increase debate, since homogeneity limits the options perceived or considered. When the alternative of more training for Old Guard members (in order to upgrade Laboratory performance) was recognized, more debate became possible. Representatives can be trained or recruited for skill in constructively bringing to the surface cultural differences. Representatives can accomplish this by recognizing important differences between cultural parties, by expressing these differences clearly, by exercising skills for bargaining or problem-solving about their implications, and by tactics for countering any attempt to deny or suppress differences. The Old Guard and Ms. Grey identified specific issues and pursued them in the teeth of efforts by many different parties to quiet their protests—and ultimately the organization as a whole shifted to more active problem-solving and bargaining over issues of institutional and personal racial discrimination.

Interventions can also alter representatives' actions that promote cultural isolation by examining the cultural issues that contribute to the avoidance. Recognizing and dealing with the cultural issue (impact of racism) that promoted black and white withdrawal within the trust department, for example, might have permitted more mutually productive engagement. Representatives may discover alternatives that encourage their interaction without fulfilling their fears. Representatives can also be trained or recruited for skills in counteracting isolation: recognizing cultural interdependencies, expressing those interdependencies in terms understandable across cultures, skills for nonthreatening engagement, and tactics for counteracting attempts at avoidance.

Changing interface development: three strategies.   The definition and organization of culture interfaces are shaped by the outcome of the representatives' interactions, on the one hand, and the interplay of the parties, context, and the interface itself on the other. Interventions to affect that interplay may redefine or reorganize the interface, alter the parties, or refocus forces from the larger context.

Strategy 4. *Alter the interface.* Interventions can alter the definition or the organization of culture interfaces. Culturally homogeneous interfaces typically have clearly delineated boundaries that include only representatives who fit well-defined criteria. One aspect of "institutional discrimination" is the fine screen of "qualifications" imposed on those who would cross the external boundary of the interface. Relaxing the formal or informal promotion policies that limit the top management positions in transnational corporations to members of the parent country allows a wider cultural perspective in policymaking—particularly if the qualifying screen for top management does not require near-assimilation to the culture of the parent country (Heenan and Perlmutter, 1979). Redrawing boundaries of homogeneous interfaces to include more cultural diversity can produce more constructive engagement across cultural differences.

Overorganized culture interfaces may be loosened by interventions that open up impermeable boundaries or that relax restrictive rules, procedures, norms, and values. Another aspect of institutional discrimination is the proliferation of organizing mechanisms that are fair in the terms of one culture but discriminatory in the terms of another. Since culture interfaces are usually not formally defined by organizations, informal mechanisms (norms, values, and beliefs) often enforce cultural homogeneity at interfaces. Diagnostic interventions that open interface boundaries to new information or that encourage examination of informal constraints can loosen interface organization. When managers in a transnational corporation discussed data on perceived cultural diversity in the corporation, their interest in cross-cultural discussions increased, they formulated new procedures for making multicultural consensus decisions about goals, and they agreed to move toward less ethnocentric policies in the future (Heenan and Perlmutter, 1979). Opening external boundaries to new information, loosening formal rules and procedures, and negotiating more flexible norms can all contribute to reducing cultural homogeneity.

Cultural isolation, in contrast, involves interfaces that are inadequately defined and underorganized. Interventions can create new forums (or strengthen old ones) for examining cultural differences. Organizations seldom define multicultural interfaces if there are no major problems, although sometimes recognition of coming issues may evoke action. Alderfer (1977a) described the creation of a "communications" group that brought together level and culture representatives (male, female, black, white) for information-sharing about potential organizational problems. At first their task was not well defined. However, the task-defined boundaries of the group were reinforced when everyone accepted the group-developed charter and ground rules, and when social bonds developed. In addition to the level and culture representatives, an external consultant was included to promote open discussion. This set the stage for constructive debate within the interface.

Tightening the organization of a culture interface may require closing boundaries that are too open and creating formal and informal control mechanisms to constrain representatives. When disruptive inputs and outputs are controlled, representatives can concentrate on the central issues. The communications group developed elaborate ground rules for confidentiality and managing member replacements (Alderfer, 1977a). Formal and informal mechanisms for controlling interaction can be created or tightened. The communications group developed formal rules, consultant and chairperson roles, and strong informal norms and values for dealing openly with cultural differences carefully avoided elsewhere in the organization. Tighter interface organization made avoidance much more difficult within the communications group.

Strategy 5. *Alter one or both parties.* Interventions can alter party interests and organization to promote productive conflict. Culturally homogeneous parties can be encouraged to recognize differences in their interests. Clarifying cultural identities and interests, and taking a hard look at stereotypes of cross-cultural similarities, can reveal differences for interface debate (Birnbaum, 1975). Cultural parties dispersed throughout a larger organization can be mobilized to recognize and preserve their differences, and so encourage debate at critical interfaces. Many programs have prepared subordinate cultural groups (e.g., "hard-core" unemployed) for life in dominant culture organizations (e.g., Friedlander and Greenburg, 1971); fewer have taught dominant parties to work effectively with less fortunate cultures, though dominant cultures are often in better situational and personal positions to learn new skills (Triandis and Malpass, 1971). Organizing parties for more effective activity at culture interfaces may also require designing representative roles that encourage clear and vigorous representation supported by a mobilized party.

Cultural isolation and withdrawal from interface conflict can also be affected by changing the parties. Intervention can clarify party interest in continuing or increased interaction, or reduce group-based stereotypes that underpin withdrawal. Work with their parties prior to forming the organizational communications group was a condition for representatives' participation. Organizing cultural parties for increased communication may involve making them in some ways more similar to each other. Women may be more able to work in male organizations if they learn to be more assertive, intellectual, impersonal, and invulnerable to feedback; men may work more effectively with women after human relations training to develop the skills women acquire in childhood (Kanter, 1975).

Strategy 6. *Alter the context.* Interventions can reshape the pressures from organizational and social contexts. Cultural homogeneity can be reduced by explicit recognition of cultural differences by organizational superiors, or by formal organizational structures and policies that encourage cultural diversity. If transnational corporations can recognize the dangers of cultural dominance by parent countries, they can promote more multicultural awareness and exploration. Organizational policies (e.g., commitment to effective affirmative action programs) and structural arrangements (e.g., reward systems, hierarchical arrangements that offer really equal opportunities across cultural differences) can also reduce excessive homogeneity at culture interfaces (Kanter, 1976).

Forces in the larger context can also reduce cultural homogeneity. External allies or third parties concerned with intercultural relations may uncover institutional discrimination, or may support more direct confrontation of cross-cultural differences. The Old Guard at the South Side Hospital Laboratory could not have challenged the New Hires effectively without support from external regulators. Government insistence on control of transnational subsidiaries in India has driven away some corporations, but permitted productive mixes of Indian and foreign expertise in others. Homogeneity may also be undercut by trends in the larger social context; external explosions may reveal future internal problems. The riots in the sixties in black communities near the South Side Hospital might have been read as indicators of future tensions within the hospital.

Cultural isolation may also be affected by contextual factors. Pressure from organizational hierarchies to recognize and jointly explore cultural differences can encourage more interaction among representatives. The multicultural communications group described earlier began with clear support from top management. But top management commitment may be difficult to obtain in the absence of obvious problems, and withdrawal tends to submerge cultural issues as a visible problem (though performance problems based on lack of interaction may become visible as a consequence). Organizational changes in policy or structure that highlight interdependence among culturally-defined parties can also compel increased interaction and debate. Japanese companies that have built assembly plants in the United States have created special organizational forms to facilitate cross-cultural interaction among managers.

Forces in the larger context may also promote engagement between isolated cultural parties. Pressures from external cultural groups can encourage more open debate at culture interfaces. Black community group pressure on Kodak, for example, made discussion of black-white relations unavoidable inside the organization. Third party agencies in the larger context can raise questions about cultural isolation in organizations. Interventions by federal and state regulatory agencies can catalyze more interface debate. Large-scale social trends and possibilities may also intervene. If the Equal Rights Amendment is ultimately passed, organizations will have to take into account both immediate legal implications and implications of enhanced political clout for women's organizations in the longer term. Interventions that make use of long-term trends, external third parties, and allies in the larger context can all promote more constructive conflict at culture interfaces.

Table 6.2 summarizes interventions for promoting conflict at culture interfaces to deal with either cultural homogeneity or cultural isolation. Interventions at the level of interface development interact with interventions at the level of representative interaction to shape conflict at culture interfaces over time.

TABLE 6.2
Promoting conflict at culture interfaces

	CULTURAL HOMOGENEITY	CULTURAL ISOLATION
Changing representatives' interaction		
1. *Alter perceptions*	Debunk representatives' stereotypes that minimize differences	Debunk representatives' stereotypes of unbridgeable differences
	Educate representatives: • dynamics of homogenization • their contributions	Educate representatives: • dynamics of isolation • their contributions
2. *Alter communications*	Expand exchange of controversial information	Expand exchange of communications that do not confirm fears
	Encourage joint analysis of blocks to controversial communications	Encourage joint analysis of factors that reduce communication

TABLE 6.2   (continued)
Promoting conflict at culture interfaces

	CULTURAL HOMOGENEITY	CULTURAL ISOLATION
3. *Alter actions*	Identify and use emotional booby traps to energize issues	Identify and control cultural issues that encourage withdrawal
	Identify alternatives that express more diversity	Identify alternatives that permit low-threat interaction
	Recruit or train representatives to surface culture differences: • recognize culture differences • clearly express differences • bargaining/problem-solving skills • tactics for countering cultural suppression	Recruit or train representatives for cross-cultural engagement: • recognize cultural interdependencies • express interdependencies • nonthreatening engagement skills • tactics for countering cultural avoidance

Changing interface development

	CULTURAL HOMOGENEITY	CULTURAL ISOLATION
4. *Alter the interface*	Redefine interface boundary: • clarify goal diversity • expand boundary criteria • diversify composition to include challengers	Define interface more clearly: • clarify interface goals • articulate boundary criteria • include resources that encourage open debate
	Loosen interface organization: • open boundaries to both cultural parties	Tighten interface organization: • close boundaries to cultural invasion and withdrawal

TABLE 6.2   (continued)
Promoting conflict at culture interfaces

	CULTURAL HOMOGENEITY	CULTURAL ISOLATION
	• relax formal mechanisms that promote institutional discrimination • diagnose and re-negotiate informal controls that suppress differences	• create rules and procedures to encourage cultural engagement • negotiate informal norms and values to support exploration of cultural differences
5. *Alter one or both parties*	Clarify cultural interests that conflict Debunk party stereotypes of similarity across cultures Mobilize dispersed parties and leadership for challenge Create representative role definitions and support for challenging homogeneity	Clarify party interdependencies Debunk party stereotypes of unbridgeable differences Mobilize parties for better communication and understanding Create representative role definitions that emphasize continuing communication
6. *Alter the context* • Organization	Hierarchical recognition and encouragement of cultural differences Organizational redesign to reduce homogeneity: • policies that promote diversity	Hierarchical recognition and encouragement of cross-cultural interdependence Organizational redesign to reduce isolation: • policies that emphasize interdependence

TABLE 6.2   (continued)
Promoting conflict at culture interfaces

	CULTURAL HOMOGENEITY	CULTURAL ISOLATION
	• reward systems that encourage cross-cultural challenge	• reward systems that encourage interaction
	• structural resources that promote differentiation (e.g., cultural ombudsmen)	• structural resources to facilitate communication (e.g., third party mediators)
• Larger context	External allies who press for heterogeneity	External allies who press for more interaction
	Third party attention to suppression of differences	Third party attention to difference avoidance
	Utilize societal events to undercut internal suppression	Utilize societal events to undercut internal avoidance

SUMMARY

Culture interfaces are the result of forces in the external society that create different cultural identifications and assumptions among organization members. Culture interfaces bring together parties with different world views, interdependent for organizational purposes, but strongly affected by external forces beyond organizational control or even awareness.

Culture interfaces, like other interfaces, are affected by the combination of parties, interface organization, and interaction. Too much conflict at culture interfaces is associated with culture shock, personal prejudice, and cultural polarization that may produce deep antagonism and intense fighting. Too little conflict between cultures, on the other hand, is associated with enforced cultural homogeneity and institutional discrimination in some cases and cultural isolation and withdrawal in others. Both patterns deprive the parties of resources from each other. Productive conflict between culturally defined parties is associated with multicultural bargaining or problem-solving that recognizes and utilizes cultural differences without allowing too much escalation.

Interventions at culture interfaces can reduce excessive conflict, and so moderate the effects of cultural shock and polarization. Or interventions can promote productive conflict, and so undo enforced homogeneity or cultural isolation. These interventions may emphasize altering the patterns of representatives' interaction by changing their perceptions, communications, or actions. Or they may focus on reshaping interface definition and organization by altering the interplay of the parties, the context, and the interface itself. Or intervenors can combine interventions into both levels of conflict dynamics.

Several aspects of culture interfaces deserve a final emphasis. First, culture interfaces are deeply rooted in the historical experience of individuals and groups in the larger society. As a consequence, events in the larger society may dramatically affect events at culture interfaces, even in organizations with little knowledge of or direct relevance to those events. Second, cultural differences shape, in fundamental but not very obvious ways, the social identities of parties and individual representatives. As a result, issues at culture interfaces can have symbolic value well beyond their obvious importance, and representatives of one culture may be very much unprepared for the depth of feeling the issue sets off in the other representatives. Third, cultural differences are often peripheral to organizational concerns. Organizations are often insensitive to potential problems at culture interfaces until they are sufficiently serious to affect activities to which the organization is more attuned. Finally, cultural differences are often dispersed throughout the organization. This dispersion increases the likelihood of unplanned negotiations between self-appointed representatives of relatively unorganized cultural parties at informally defined culture interfaces.

Organization Interfaces

7

Until now we have been considering interfaces *within* organizations at which departments, levels, or cultures come together. In this chapter we turn to interfaces *between* organizations that are critical to the survival of the organizations involved.

Consider the challenges facing U.S. automakers in the eighties. Competing firms struggle to expand or regain market shares lost in recent years to foreign firms. Regulatory agencies threaten severe economic and political sanctions for non-compliance with federal regulations. Suppliers of critical raw materials may defy the automakers' efforts to plan ahead. Consumers may unexpectedly reject cars that were in great demand a year ago. Organizational futures hang in the balance at interfaces with forces in the outside environment.

I begin by considering organization interfaces from the perspective of the framework proposed in Chapter 2, and discuss elements and dynamics of interfaces that link organizational parties. The analysis is illustrated in the relations between the Ghetto Development Corporation and the forces in its environment. Efforts to manage conflicts between the Ghetto Development Corporation and other agencies are described and analyzed in the third section. The fourth section discusses strategies for managing conflict at organization interfaces in more general terms. The last section summarizes the chapter and highlights unique aspects of organization interfaces.

ANALYZING ORGANIZATION INTERFACES

Simple organization interfaces bring together organizations that (1) depend on each other for critical resources, (2) sometimes asymmetrically, in contexts of (3) varying organization but (4) pervasive impact. Relations between organizations are often compelled by *interdependence for critical information and resources.* General Motors and the United Auto Workers must interact for the sake of continuing labor and jobs; the oil companies that jointly built the Alaskan pipeline needed each other's resources to do the job. The organizations involved may be *equal or unequal in power* at the interface. A small plant whose entire output supplies only 5 percent of General Motors' spare parts is likely to be more dependent on GM than vice versa; or an agency providing services to the blind may be relatively dependent on federal funding sources. The larger contexts of organization interfaces are *sometimes highly organized and centralized, and sometimes chaotic.* "Mandated cooperation" may be compelled among social service agencies dependent on the same funding agency; the "free market" may allow all sorts of interaction patterns at other organization interfaces. The *larger context typically has a pervasive impact* on events at organization interfaces. Decisions in OPEC meetings have an impact on General Motors and on social service agencies, and influence their relations at more immediate organization interfaces.

Managers and academics are now paying more attention to forces outside organizational boundaries, for several reasons. First, studies of managerial practices reveal that different external conditions have been associated with quite different management behavior in effective organizations. Burns and Stalker (1961), for example, found that electronic firms in dynamic environments were more effective if they used "flexible" and "organic" management structures, while textile firms in comparatively stable environments were more effective if they utilized more bureaucratic and "mechanistic" structures. At about the same time organization theorists were heavily influenced by "open systems theory," which emphasizes transactions between organizations and their environments. Academic attention has focused on links between organizations and their environments and impacts of environment on organization structure (e.g., Emery and Trist, 1965; Lawrence and Lorsch, 1967; Thompson, 1967). Evidence has also indicated that organizational environments have themselves become increasingly complex and unstable as a consequence of social, economic, political, and technological change. Interdependent relations among organizations, and the impact of those relations on organizational functioning, have expanded (e.g., Terreberry, 1968; Schon, 1971; Pfeffer and Salancik, 1978). Finally, investigators of larger systems (e.g., communities, industries) have recently emphasized the role of interorganizational relations in decision making and resource allocation. The performance of industries (Hirsch, 1975) or the characteristics of communities (Laumann et al., 1978) are influenced by events at organization interfaces. Developments in managerial practice, organization theory, organizational environments, and larger social systems have all contributed to focusing attention on organization interfaces.

Work on organization/environment relations has generated several conceptual perspectives. Miles (1980) distinguishes between contingency perspectives and process perspectives in terms akin to the static and dynamic aspects of interface analysis. *Contingency perspectives* emphasize links between environmental conditions and organization structure and process. Effective performance, in this view, is contingent on being organized appropriately to meet external challenges. The studies contingency theory is based on compared organizations at one point in time, and found performance was linked to the "fit" between environment and internal organization (e.g., Burns and Stalker, 1961; Lawrence and Lorsch, 1967). Contingency theorists often emphasize problems of uncertainty and the importance of information processing in turbulent and unpredictable environments (e.g., Galbraith, 1977; Thompson, 1967). They often treat organizations as relatively passive recipients of environmental influence, tossed by waves of external change and complexity.

Process perspectives focus more on the dynamics of organization/environment relations, on the development of organization/environment fit over time. These studies have examined histories of organizational relations and the dynamics of influence among them. Some investigators have emphasized contests over critical resources—the control over human, material, and financial resources on which organizations depend for survival, growth, and autonomy (e.g., Pfeffer and Salancik, 1978); others have emphasized evolutionary patterns of organizational variation, selection, and retention that preserve some organizational forms and eliminate others (e.g., Aldrich, 1979). Researchers in the first, resource dependence, tradition often emphasize active manipulation of external forces by powerful organizations. Investigators in the second, evolutionary, tradition more often conceive organizations as relatively powerless victims or beneficiaries of natural selection mechanisms they cannot control.

The two perspectives are not mutually exclusive. The fit between organization and environment emerges from the dynamics of organization/environment interaction over time. Contingency perspectives are particularly relevant to understanding the elements of organization interfaces, and process perspectives are helpful in considering dynamics of representative interaction and interface development.

Elements of Organization Interfaces

The elements of organization interfaces are often larger and more complex than the elements of interfaces within organizations. The parties are organizations; representatives may often be departments; immediate contexts may be industries, communities, or interorganizational networks.

Organizations as parties. The sheer variety of organizational parties relevant to a focal organization may be breathtaking. Business firms deal with competitors, regulators, suppliers, and consumers of their products (Dill, 1958): Chrysler must worry about competitors like Ford and Toyota, federal agencies like OSHA, suppliers of raw materials like U. S. Steel, dealer networks, and finicky consumers. Social service agencies must deal with service authorizers, third party funders, client organizations, personnel associations, or competitive services.

The interests of organizational parties may be highly diverse (e.g., Laumann et al., 1978). Parties may have similar interests that encourage linkage for common goals: General Motors and Chrysler have a common interest in limiting federal safety standards that increase prices. Or parties may have complementary interests: General Motors and Exxon are in different industries but their products are complementary. Or party interests may be antagonistic: General Motors and Chrysler compete for market share, and Ralph Nader's organization challenges both on behalf of consumers. The mix of complementary, similar, and antagonistic interests perceived by organizational parties can be complex and changing over time.

Organizations vary in how they organize to deal with organization interfaces. Some organizations focus much attention on external forces and actively create environment-related strategies, structures, and processes; others do not notice external forces until they are about to be overwhelmed (Ackoff, 1974). Miles et al. (1978) suggest that organizations fall into four categories: "prospectors" emphasize innovation within broadly defined goals, and so create flexible and decentralized structures and processes; "defenders" define an environmental niche, and preserve it by specialization, centralized management, and formal hierarchy that maximizes efficiency; "analyzers" balance present strengths and innovations by using matrix structures to achieve the benefits of both product and function divisions; and "reactors" have unclear strategies, create structures and processes mismatched to strategies, or fail to respond to external changes. External challenges may find organizations strategically aware and internally mobilized, or relatively unaware and inappropriately mobilized for conflict and change at organization interfaces.

Organizational representatives.   Organizations frequently develop special subunits to cope with organization interfaces. Manufacturing firms create purchasing departments to acquire critical raw materials (Strauss, 1962); municipal governments create labor relations departments to deal with new public unions (Kochan et al., 1975). Such "boundary-spanning units" can undertake several functions: representing the organization to outsiders, scanning and monitoring external events, protecting the organization from threats, information processing and gatekeeping, exchanging inputs and outputs with other organizations, or linking and coordinating interorganizational activities (Miles, 1980). Boundary-spanning units can be permanent or temporary. An X-ray manufacturing company, for example, created a temporary boundary unit of high-status representatives to sell new equipment and train customers who might resist less educated sales staff (Callahan and Salipante, 1979).

Boundary-spanning departments are caught between two worlds. Influencing representatives of other organizations calls for skills in negotiation, political tactics, and informal influence strategies (Kotter, 1979). Superiors of boundary-spanners, who have formal authority over them, sometimes expect more compliance than the latter can concede and remain effective. Effective representatives develop considerable informal power within their organizations if important stakes are invested at their interface, and if few substitutes exist for their ability to manage tensions there (Hickson et al., 1971). Boundary-spanning units are shaped by their intermediate position, and so mirror characteristics of the organization interface.

Organization interface definition and organization. Organization interfaces can be defined by competitive interdependence that compels interaction among antagonistic organizations, or by cooperative interdependence in which both parties tend to gain from interaction, or by "mandated cooperation" in which organizations cooperate because of the requirements of a powerful third party (Laumann et al., 1978). The interests of the parties, their past histories of interaction, and the attitudes of interested third parties all contribute to defining organization interfaces. Organization interfaces can include few or many representatives. Organizations sometimes negotiate carefully defined interfaces to manage bilateral relationships: A public utility may negotiate a long-term contract for deliveries from a coal company to remove uncertainty about especially critical inputs (Galbraith, 1977). Or large groups of organizations with common interests define a common organization interface, such as trade associations or chambers of commerce. Organization interface boundaries can be defined by geographical location (e.g., local chamber of commerce), by common tasks (e.g., association of business school deans), by social identifications (e.g., NAACP), by common mandates (e.g., coordinating council of agencies serving blind people), or by combinations of these criteria.

The boundaries of organization interfaces vary considerably in permeability. Some interfaces establish and maintain close controls over materials and information. Organizations sharing technical secrets in joint ventures may develop interface boundaries that are closed to information output in sensitive areas. Other interfaces invite external inputs and outputs to interorganizational negotiations: "Sunshine laws" that compel public negotiations in the public sector, for example, permit relatively open flows of information about interface discussions.

Organization interfaces also vary in constraints on interaction among representatives. Formal interface authorities or goals can limit interaction: Funding agencies, for example, often require social agencies to cooperate when serving their clients. Formal rules and procedures to regulate interorganizational relations can be formulated and enforced: Contracts establish limits and responsibilities, and provide for penalties or dispute resolution measures in the event of noncompliance. Formal structures and authoritative mechanisms are particularly important for controlling interaction among many equally powerful organizations; trade associations or large coalitions that agree on common interests but also have interests in conflict need formal control mechanisms (Galbraith, 1977). Informal mechanisms may be sufficient to coordinate relations among a few well-established organizations: Price leadership among steel companies, for example, is a kind of coordination by informal norms that would be difficult in a less-concentrated industry. Boundary permeability and internal regulation together organize interfaces to tightly or loosely constrain the interaction of organization representatives.

Organization interface context. The immediate contexts of organization interfaces may be complex or simple, stable or changing, receptive or antagonistic (Miles, 1980). Although it is probably uncommon for organization interfaces to be enfolded in a shared context the way department interfaces are enfolded by the larger organization, organizational interaction is sometimes closely circumscribed by the immediate context. Close supervision of mandated cooperation among social service agencies by a common funding source, for example, narrowly limits their escalation, suppression, or avoidance of conflict. Or antitrust surveillance of competitors in a highly concentrated industry can stringently constrain explicit organizational cooperation.

But on the whole, relations at the interorganizational level are less tightly organized and richly connected than relations within organizations, and organizational parties are more often on their own to work out relations with each other (Trist, 1977). This situation sometimes provides opportunities for organizations to create favorable contexts for themselves. The trade association interface among large U.S. pharmaceutical corporations, for example, promoted favorable distribution channels and pricing patterns, gained legal protections for drug patents and brand names, and co-opted American Medical Association regulators. The resulting immediate context permitted high profits (Hirsch, 1975).

Forces from the larger context of social, economic, and political change can have a pervasive impact at organization interfaces. Some contextual forces and trends are beyond the influence or even the awareness of the parties. Environmental "turbulence" can affect interface events independent of organizational activities (Emery and Trist, 1965). Pharmaceutical corporations may have little awareness of Latin American wars, Third World oil coalitions, or religious revolutions. Other forces can be set in motion by organizational activities. Federal government regulation of the pharmaceutical industry expanded as the AMA declined as a regulator (Hirsch, 1975); and public reaction to media reports of corporate abuses in poor Third World countries (marketing drugs banned as unsafe in the U.S.; 6000 percent markups) may lead to further external pressures. Trends in the larger context seem to be toward increased uncertainty, increased interdependence, and increased complexity and vulnerability to disruption in a civilization based on worldwide linkages among organizations and nations (Schon, 1971; Pfeffer and Salancik, 1978; Frank, 1979). Organization interfaces can both influence and be influenced by a complex and dynamic larger context that includes events and forces throughout the world.

Organization Interface Dynamics

Research on change processes at organization interfaces is presently burgeoning and extremely complex. This section describes patterns of interorganizational relations in the terms applied to previous interfaces.

Dynamics of representatives' interaction.   Representatives to organization interfaces may actually be organizational subunits or departments rather than individuals. In this section I do not deal explicitly with the differences between subunit and individual representatives, but where subunits are the primary representatives it may be helpful to analyze their characteristics and interests apart from those of their individual members. The focus here is on the patterns of immediate perception, communication, and action that produce outcomes of too much, too little, or productive conflict among organization representatives.

Conflict among organizations sometimes escalates into bitter antagonisms and *interorganizational warfare.* Issues at organization interfaces can threaten the autonomy and survival of one or both parties, so disagreements may pack a lot of weight. Classic examples include warfare between Standard Oil and its competitors, or struggles between unions and management prior to federal regulation of industrial competition and collective bargaining. Warfare between relatively equal organizations can exhaust the parties and create a variety of destructive consequences for third parties. The city of Jamestown, New York, for example, faced serious community decline in terms of jobs and economic health, partly in consequence of continuing conflicts between unions and managements of local plants (Trist, 1979). The history of conflict produced negative stereotypes of each other in plant and union organizational representatives, and—worse still—negative perceptions among outsiders of the area as a location for new plants. Organization representatives found it difficult to talk to each other without fighting, and so communications declined between periodic wars at the bargaining table. Coercive influence tactics and nit-picking about contractual provisions made it impossible for organizations to adapt to changing market, technological, or political trends. Plants in the area were leaving or going out of business, and no replacements for lost jobs or resources were being discovered. The community decline was partly caused and considerably complicated by interorganizational warfare between unions and managements.

Too little conflict between organizational representatives can be linked to suppression of differences in *interorganizational collusion,* that compromises the autonomy of one or both parties. Such relations amount to an unintended merger of organizations that obscures differences important to them or to contextual parties. The American Medical Association for years acted as a regulator of marketing by pharmaceutical corporations: It evaluated drugs, limited brand-name advertising in its journals, published physician guides to drugs, and debunked industry marketing practices in editorials. But the AMA abandoned that role in the early fifties: It opened its journals to brand-name advertising; it reduced testing standards for new drugs; it ceased publishing its drug guide and left the field to an industry publication. The consequences of this shift were positive for both organizational parties: The AMA received greatly increased advertising income from the pharmaceutical companies, who had a much freer hand in marketing their products in return (Hirsch, 1975). But in the longer term, the change also undercut services to consumers, encouraged closer federal regulation, and promoted consumer suspicion of both the manufacturers and the medical profession.

Too little conflict between organizations can also be associated with withdrawal from differences to *interorganizational isolation,* in which organizational parties preserve a false sense of organizational independence. Organizations can fail to recognize interdependencies, avoid interaction that would produce disagreement, and reduce engagement that would help them recognize and manage common problems. In the city of Urban Heights, for example, organizations interested in changing patterns of home ownership—realtors, mortgage lenders, residents, municipal officials—pursued their activities in isolation from each other. Realtors sought to expand housing sales, and many engaged in forms of racial "steering" that tended to segregate new black residents. Local mortgage lenders recognized the potential for residential decay and devaluation and began to limit their investments in some racially integrated areas and to seek mortgages in more stable communities. Residents and municipal official remained largely unaware of real estate market pressures promoting residential deterioration and resegregation, though many realized that a neighboring city had recently suffered major problems of "white flight." Realtors, banks, citizen organizations, and the municipal government would all be hurt by the declines in housing stock and residential resegregation encouraged by their mutual isolation, but the parties remained unaware of, or unwilling to address, potentially conflictful issues (Gricar and Brown, 1981).

Productive conflict at organization interfaces, in contrast, may take the form of either bargaining or problem-solving. *Interorganizational bargaining* involves the representatives' recognition of both conflicting and common interests, but focuses on issues in which one organization's gain is perceived to be tied to another's loss. Representatives recognize their differences, communicate information in guarded and selective terms, and act to control each other's options without escalating past shared limits. Hirsch (1975) contrasts relations between broadcasters and record companies with those between AMA and pharmaceutical companies. Record companies sought to co-opt broadcasters for marketing purposes, but broadcasters faced severe competition from TV and were forced to encourage innovative new record producers and artists to tap new markets. The resulting interorganizational bargaining produced scandals around illegal influence tactics (e.g., "payola" to disc jockeys and broadcasters), increased variety of musical offerings to consumers, more record companies in the industry, and profits for record companies lower than those for pharmaceutical companies.

Interorganizational problem-solving, in contrast, brings together organizational representatives in circumstances dominated by issues in which common interests are perceived as more important than conflicting interests. Problem-solving involves perceptions of similarities and common concern, relatively open exchange of information, and search and selection of alternatives that benefit both parties. For example, Walton (1967) describes informal monthly meetings among agency representatives concerned with activities in a foreign country. The meetings were convened by a Foreign Service officer concerned with the country, who encouraged position presentations from representatives, dissent and exploration of alternatives, and continuing dialogue about different agency perspectives. Discussions reduced the negative perceptions of agencies held by representatives, expanded the flow of information among them, and created personal links that enhanced interagency coordination and information-sharing in the future.

Dynamics of organization interface development.   Figure 7.1 portrays patterns of interface development associated with conflict dynamics among organizational representatives. Over time, patterns of interaction and interface definition and organization tend to reinforce each other.

Interface development is often associated with interorganizational warfare (A). Conflict escalation among organizational representatives (small circles) is associated with organizations that are highly mobilized to fight (triangles) and with an underorganized interface (dotted boundary). Representatives' actions produce escalating conflict (divergent arrows) that further mobilizes the organizations and further disorganizes the interface. Negotiations between union and management representatives in Jamestown tended to produce strikes, lockouts, and other actions that produced a climate and process for future fighting. Interorganizational warfare tends to undercut interface organization and so prepare the way for future escalation.

Too little conflict at organization interfaces can be in the form of interorganizational collusion (B). Overorganized interfaces (solid boundary) constrain the expression and exploration of differences (truncated arrows) to the point of eroding the autonomy of one or both organizations. The American Medical Association ceased to be a regulator of pharmaceutical marketing as it became more dependent on their advertising revenue. Interfaces that tightly organize interaction between organizations may so constrain the exploration of organizational differ-

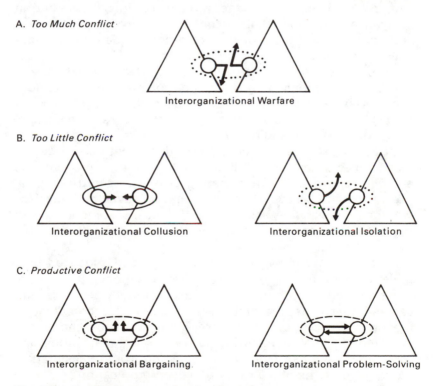

Fig. 7.1. *Conflict at organization interfaces.*

ences that they can no longer pursue separate interests or respond to changing conditions.

Too little conflict can also take the form of interorganizational isolation (B). Interorganizational isolation is associated with an underorganized interface (dotted boundary) that permits organizational representatives to withdraw from differences (arrows away) into a false sense of organizational independence. Representatives of Urban Heights residents, realtors, bankers, and government were not pressed by any shared interface organization to explore or negotiate their different interests and perspectives, so patterns of resettlement and residential maintenance undermined the generally shared community goals of stability and racial integration. Underorganized interfaces permit avoidance of tensions that, in the long run, reinforce interface underorganization and problems of interdependence that might have been averted by more engagement.

Productive conflict at organization interfaces is in the forms of interorganizational bargaining and problem-solving (C). Both patterns involve moderately organized interfaces (dashed boundaries) that control inputs and outputs and limit representatives' interactions. Bargaining relations may be antagonistic and confrontive, since the issues focus on conflicting interests, but representatives accept shared limits that encourage compromise and control escalation (negotiating arrows). Record company executives and broadcasters, for example, developed interface relations in which they achieved compromises (sometimes with the aid of under-the-table payments) that remained influenceable by consumers.

Interorganizational problem-solving, also associated with moderately-organized interfaces, is relatively open to information sharing (long arrows) that produces mutually beneficial outcomes. Agency representatives in the country coordination meetings all benefited from increased information and understanding of the other agencies perspectives and activities, and their interface organization developed norms and rules that encouraged patterns of relatively open communication.

ORGANIZATION INTERFACES AT THE GHETTO DEVELOPMENT CORPORATION

Problems at organization interfaces are illustrated in the case of the Ghetto Development Corporation's relations with the federal government, its local community, and the metropolitan Establishment.

The Ghetto Development Corporation is a federally funded community development corporation, in a large city in the industrial belt of the Northeast. The Corporation has been in operation for almost ten years.

Northeastern City was one of the early centers of United States industrialization, and heavy industry remains an important element of its financial base. But the city has been declining in both population and popularity as an industrial center for some time. Over the years residents who could afford to move to the suburbs have done so. The central core of the city has deteriorated, and the inner city is now populated by lower income groups. The eastern half of the city is populated almost exclusively by blacks; the western half has poor whites, Appalachians, Puerto Ricans, and a variety of other ethnic groups.

In the late sixties rioting erupted in the black ghettoes of Northeastern City, drawing national attention to conditions there. Soon afterwards the Ghetto Development Corporation was funded as part of a nationwide experiment in promoting economic development and improving living conditions in disadvantaged areas. The Corporation was expected to promote improved housing and to foster business ventures to provide services previously unavailable to local residents.

Northeastern City was shocked by the riots. The Corporation's first two presidents were both charismatic black personalities, who were able to win the support of ghetto community residents. Many ghetto residents had been mobilized by the riots and their aftermath to turn their community around. The presidents were also able to establish cordial, if guarded, relations with the city's business and political leadership, who were also interested in improving ghetto conditions.

Over the next decade the Corporation sponsored a variety of development projects, including a shopping mall and supermarket, a small manufacturing business, several fast-food franchises, housing construction and rehabilitation projects, a property management service, and a "handyman" service. These projects offered jobs to community residents and provided previously unavailable services to the community, but few of them became independently profitable. The Corporation continued to rely on the federal Community Services Administration (CSA) for funds to promote new ventures, underwrite administrative costs, and subsidize uneconomic projects. CSA, on the other hand, was pleased with the Corporation's record for creating new jobs; in the early seventies the Corporation was frequently cited in CSA reports as among the most successful of the thirty-odd community development corporations it funded.

By the mid-seventies conditions had changed. CSA, prodded by the Nixon administration, began to emphasize "the bottom line" in place of providing new services and jobs to ghetto residents. CSA wanted financially viable projects that could stand without continuing subsidies, and few Corporation projects met this standard. A new President of the Corporation was appointed, chosen in part for his competence in financial matters—he had originally been the Corporation's controller.

The organization and enthusiasm of ghetto residents dwindled as the seventies marched on without visible improvements in the community. Some effective organizers found jobs that allowed them to move out of the area. Others gave up in frustration. Almost a third of the community's population moved in the course of the decade, taking irreplaceable skills and energy with them. The community was no longer able to mount the mass demonstrations with which they had supported the Corporation in its early years.

Northeastern City had also declined over the decade. Ghetto outmigration and deterioration of the sixties had spread throughout the city during the seventies. Some politicians and business people retreated from investing resources in deteriorated ghetto areas, arguing that it was "too late" for those areas and limited resources should be invested in areas that might still be "saved."

Links between the Corporation and other organizations had evolved as well. Corporation influence at City Hall, strong during the tenure of a black mayor in the sixties, eroded during the reigns of his white ethnic successors. The Corporation President was not comfortable with "politicking," and had neither widespread contacts nor easy relations with political leaders and business people. Some members of the business community were disappointed by their early contacts with the Corporation, for its management style differed from that of large corporations. Interpersonal frictions between Corporation staff and representatives of Establishment institutions led to misunderstandings, antagonism, and mistrust — some on racial grounds. By the middle seventies Corporation members had relatively little contact with either political or business leadership of the city.

Fragmentation in the ghetto community hampered Corporation efforts to identify sources of community support. By law the Corporation's Board was composed of 90 percent local residents. But few local residents held management, financial, or legal expertise and contacts needed for Corporation policy development, and the three outsiders on the Board could seldom influence the twenty-seven community members. The latter spent much of the Board meetings in bickering and vendettas with old community opponents, further eroding the Board's ability to make decisions.

Tensions within the Corporation also hindered its effectiveness. Conflict between the President and his Directors took up much time and energy. The staff was entangled in the endless job of rewriting proposals for the year-by-year funding cycle. Positions for street workers had been cut from the budget, so little work with community members was possible.

In 1976 the Corporation faced a crisis. On the basis of an unsatisfactory site visit, CSA rejected the Corporation's proposal for refunding. They called on the President to resolve personnel problems, to clarify Corporation priorities, and to arrange training to make the Board more effective. Without refunding by the administration, the Corporation could not survive.

This case can be examined from the perspectives of organization interface elements and dynamics.

Interface Elements at Ghetto Development Corporation

The *parties* in this case include the Ghetto Development Corporation itself, the Community Services Administration, the Establishment of Northeastern City, and the ghetto community. The interests and characteristics of these parties varied considerably at any given point, and they also shifted over time. The Corporation, for example, was committed to improving the lot of people in the ghetto, and its staff was often antagonistic to others who did not share this commitment. Over the years the Corporation's internal characteristics shifted from charismatic leadership and idealistic staff commitments in the late sixties to more bureaucratic management and some staff cynicism in the mid-seventies. The initial cohesion of a group committed to a shared vision of social change and social justice was at least partially replaced by more formally structured roles and the skepticism of experience.

The Community Services Administration was concerned with preserving its own funding base by encouraging Corporation activities approved by Congress and the executive branch. Priorities in Washington had shifted from providing more ghetto jobs and services to creating economically viable ventures, so

CSA standards for evaluating Corporation performance also changed. Personnel shifts and policy changes also promoted attention to financial control and reduced emphasis on social experimentation.

The business and political Establishment in Northeastern City had been shocked by the riots, and joined in the idealistic crusade to "do something" about conditions in the ghetto. But continuing decay in the city as a whole brought similar physical deterioration and population declines to many other areas of the city in the seventies. The business community remained well-organized and well-financed, but the combination of project failures in the ghetto and growing problems in other areas reduced their interest in and commitment to ghetto problems.

The ghetto community was galvanized into widespread mobilization and social action efforts during the sixties. Great expectations for improvement were fostered by the attention of outsiders and local organizations, but those expectations did not last. Community organizations declined in membership and effectiveness as leaders moved and the difficulties of lasting social change became apparent. Those who got jobs moved out as soon as they could, leaving behind a community even less able to organize itself. Bickering among leaders who remained increased as the available resources declined. The community as a whole became less organized and less able to pursue common objectives over the decade.

Representatives of different parties reflected changes in party interest and organization. The new President of the Corporation was better prepared to manage a bureaucratic organization than his predecessors, but less comfortable in "politicking" and "wheeling and dealing" with the Establishment and the ghetto community. Some of his staff were comfortable and skilled at work with the Establishment; others were angered by the lack of Establishment attention to ghetto problems and sometimes vented that anger on Establishment representatives; the "administrative assistants" on the payroll to maintain contact with "the street" in the early days had been cut from the budget, and few remaining staff members were comfortable with community residents on the Board or elsewhere. CSA representatives had become concerned with financial control and suspicious of Corporation use of funds, and so were more likely to adopt investigative and coercive tactics. Representatives of the Establishment were often skeptical about the possibility of doing anything effective in the ghetto, and they were less inclined to take initiatives or to respond favorably to Corporation initiatives. Even large institutions located within the ghetto (e.g., educational institutions, hospitals, manufacturing firms) tended to avoid contact with Corporation representatives. As the community lapsed back into disorganization, it became increasingly difficult to identify representatives who could speak for organized community groups. Board elections often selected representatives of small community subgroups, who would vigorously represent subgroup interests rather than larger community concerns in Board meetings. Community elections seldom produced Directors with managerial, financial, or political skills and connections that would promote Corporation contact with the Establishment or CSA, or even large sectors of the community.

Organization *interfaces* are critical to the Corporation because it was constituted to link together the federal government, the local Establishment, and the ghetto community to foster economic development and better services in the ghetto. Its success depended on Corporation ability to create effective linkages with those organizations or groups.

The organization interface between the Corporation and CSA, for example, was clearly defined and tightly organized. The Corporation depended on CSA for funds, and CSA depended on the Corporation (among others) to justify its continued existence and appropriations. Corporation staff, particularly the President, felt greatly confined by formal requirements for reporting and funding proposals, so much so that little time or energy was left over for other activities. The financial failure of some Corporation projects inspired CSA skepticism about Corporation effectiveness, and well-publicized federal budget cuts encouraged Corporation paranoia about CSA's intentions. Corporation autonomy was severely limited by tight CSA regulation of funds and documentation. Relations with CSA often resulted in suppression of conflict, at least from the Corporation's perspective.

Relations with the local business Establishment, in contrast, were poorly defined and underorganized. The Corporation no longer had close relationships with many business organizations or even institutions (e.g., hospitals, plants, schools) within the ghetto area. Although relations with the business community offered clear benefits to the Corporation, it was less clear how business would benefit, given the track record of past ventures in the ghetto. Personal contact and "politicking" to define common interests and organize linkages was difficult for many Corporation staff; sometimes initial contacts resulted in antagonism rather than cooperation. Relations with the business Establishment were more characterized by withdrawal and avoidance than by constructive engagement and confrontations.

Social disorganization in the ghetto community made it difficult to identify community representatives. Board meetings brought together Corporation staff and community residents elected to the Board. But community Directors often saw Board meetings as opportunities to pursue personal interests or vendettas rather than represent broad community interests. Few community Directors had experience and skills for formulating Corporation policies. The Board included representatives of many small community groups, but it lacked the organization provided by common goals, shared expectations and expertise, or accepted formal procedures for managing its business. In consequence, Board meetings often became microcosms of the fragmentation and loose organization common in the ghetto, and so permitted conflict escalation among Board members or between them and Corporate staff.

Contextual factors of various kinds affected Corporation interfaces with other organizations. Relations with Community Services Administration, for example, were shaped by changing federal priorities under Nixon to increase emphasis on profit-making ventures in the ghetto areas, and by widespread disillusionment with the efficacy of government intervention to deal with social problems. These trends pressed the Corporation to reorient its programs to new objectives, some of which were ideologically offensive to its staff. Relations with the Northeastern City Establishment were affected by the decline of the city as a whole, and by Establishment disappointment with early efforts to aid the ghetto. These trends promoted skepticism in the business community about ghetto ventures, and encouraged investing limited resources in less deteriorated areas. Within the ghetto community, factors like high levels of unemployment, increasing crime, and rapid outmigration of employed residents undermined community mobilization to influence the Corporation or other parties. The resulting community disorganization undermined the profitability of ongoing Corporation ventures and nearly paralyzed the Corporation's Board.

Interface Dynamics at Ghetto Development Corporation

Interaction between CSA and Corporation representatives was frequent, charged, and explicitly focused on survival. If the Corporation could not satisfy CSA, it would be defunded. But the pattern of behavior had a self-reinforcing quality. The more Corporation staff members concentrated on writing elaborate proposals and seeking ways to keep CSA happy in the short term, the less time and energy they had for developing new ventures with the local Establishment, improving old ventures, or developing community support. The Corporation feared to challenge CSA, lest its support be withdrawn, and so was trapped in a cycle that limited its autonomy to experiment with new development strategies.

Interaction between Corporation staff and the business community, in contrast, was sporadic; it produced either too much or too little conflict. The Corporation's largely black staff was intolerant of perceived white business indifference to ghetto problems. There were angry exchanges between Corporation staff and business representatives. But more common was the withdrawal from potential conflict by representatives of both parties.

Interaction between Corporation staff and the community was also sporadic. Most staff members lived outside the community and had little casual contact with community members.

Board meetings provided an interface where staff and community representatives regularly disagreed. Corporation staff saw the Board members as incompetent to make policy, oriented to their own interests, and obstructive to decisions needed by the Corporation; Board members mistrusted staff intentions and competence, and believed they manipulated the Board for their own ends. Since Board meetings required the parties to remain in contact to make decisions, escalating conflict over critical decisions was quite common.

The Ghetto Development Corporation had been funded to link together federal government funding, Northeastern City Establishment resources, and ghetto community residents to promote economic development and increased services in the ghetto—to create, in short, a series of organization interfaces with the Corporation at their center. The Corporation was initially quite successful in this task, but changes in the external context altered the dynamics of *interface development* in recent years. Changes in CSA and the federal context encouraged the development of interface overorganization and the loss of much Corporation autonomy. Fear of defunding led Corporation staff into interorganizational collusion with CSA that undermined Corporation capacities to actively develop linkages with local organizations, and that lack of local support fed back to increase its dependence on CSA.

The interfaces with the local Establishment and the ghetto community, in contrast, had become vaguely defined and loosely organized as a consequence of changes in parties and context. The Corporation suffered from interorganizational isolation from the City Establishment, in part because of its focus on CSA and in part because of trends that distracted Establishment attention from the ghetto. The underorganized interface with the ghetto community, on the other hand, permitted interorganizational warfare in Board meetings, as representatives of community groups fought with each other or with Corporation staff—and so paralyzed the Board's ability to formulate policy for the Corporation. What were effective linkages with external organizations in the late sixties were much less effective in the changed conditions of the seventies.

MANAGING CONFLICT AT THE GHETTO DEVELOPMENT CORPORATION

Responses to problems facing the Ghetto Development Corporation can be analyzed as efforts to manage conflict at organization interfaces.

> *The crisis at the Ghetto Development Corporation took the form of a Community Services Administration threat to defund the organization unless it immediately complied with several demands. CSA wanted a substantially rewritten funding proposal, immediate action on senior staff who did not meet performance standards, and training to improve Board capacity to make effective decisions.*

> *The Corporation President agreed that several staff members had not performed to expectations, and he finally fired two senior members of the Economic Development Division. This decision satisfied CSA, but left the Corporation without staff for developing new joint ventures with the business community. The President decided to hire replacements only when he could find individuals who would be more effective in making contacts with local business people. In the interim, he used external consultants to search for joint venture opportunities. The search for a replacement took more than a year, but the new Director of Economic Development rapidly created improved links to the business community when he finally took office.*

> *Creating a more effective Board was more difficult. Board training, again using outside consultants, was arranged, but many of the most powerful (and some of the most disruptive) Board members did not attend. But events in the Board pursued a logic of their own. In an unexpected coup d'etat in the spring of 1977, the old slate of officers was summarily turned out in the annual election. The old Chairman, a veteran of the early days of the Corporation, was replaced by a relative newcomer. The new Chairman and the President viewed each other with considerable suspicion. But it gradually became clear that the new Chairman was better able to*

handle disruption within the Board than his predecessor. The Board did not become a positive link to the ghetto community, but it ceased to be a constant roadblock to all policy decisions.

The President also used consultants from a nearby university to discuss long-term objectives and strategy for the Corporation. He invited those consultants to diagnose the Corporation, and several consultant teams examined internal and external aspects of the organization. Some consultants interviewed Corporation staff; others collected data from organizations in the larger context (CSA, local business people, government officials, community representatives, Board members, and large institutions in the ghetto community such as schools and hospitals). The resulting internal and external diagnoses were discussed with the President and Corporation staff.

These discussions reframed staff perspectives on the Corporation. Much internal conflict was traced to external pressures imposed by conflicting external constituencies. Staff members recognized the need for diverse skills and attributes to work effectively within different constituencies ("a dashiki for the ghetto, a CPA for CSA, and a three-piece suit for the Establishment"). Indeed, attributes that increased credibility with the business community might decrease it in the ghetto ("It's hard to wear a dashiki over your three-piece suit."). So differences in skills and interests made conflict among individuals within the Corporation likely and even necessary.

Reconceiving the Corporation as an interface among three environmental constituencies helped explain external relations as well as internal conflicts. This perspective helped shape the new funding proposal submitted to CSA. Emphasis was placed on expanding activities (e.g., Housing Division projects) that enjoyed relatively good linkages to the community and the business Establishment. The combination of staff changes, Board training, strategy reformulation in the new proposal, and successful sale of several losing ventures persuaded CSA that "the start of a new day" was at hand. The Corporation was refunded for twenty months rather than the customary twelve.

In the following months the President actively sought to improve and expand links to other organizations. He personally accepted invitations to participate in citywide meetings and educational programs, trying to develop his own skills at "politicking." He accepted positions on the Boards of several city institutions, offered in part because of his new visibility. The Corporation sought to diversify its funding base by tapping community block grant funds and city government resources. The Corporation also launched new programs that would generate community support, such as an effort to build new single-family dwellings in the ghetto for families who would remain in the community if they could find adequate housing. As of 1978 the Corporation was once again in the good graces of CSA, and developing links to other critical organizations in its complicated environment.

These events can be analyzed as conflict management activities at organization interfaces between the Corporation and CSA, between the Corporation and the local Establishment, and between the Corporation and the ghetto community.

The Corporation and Community Services Administration

The interface with CSA posed the most immediate problem and the most direct threat to the Corporation's survival; the Corporation was overwhelmingly dependent on CSA and its loss of autonomy impaired its immediate effectiveness at other interfaces as well as its chances for continued existence. Reestablishing some degree of independence involved changing both internal characteristics and external links of the Corporation.

Changes within the Corporation were partly a response to direct CSA demands: Symbolically important personnel changes in the Economic Development Division and training for the Board were explicitly requested by CSA. But the President postponed hiring replacements until he could attract individuals who would be more effective in work with the local Establishment. Discussions of future strategy and organizational diagnosis also encouraged redefining organizational objectives, interests, and internal dynamics. Corporation staff reoriented their understanding of the Corporation's mission around bringing together the constituencies of Establishment, ghetto community, and CSA. They recognized that conflict among staff members might be evidence of commitment and effectiveness rather than incompetence—since close ties with constituencies in conflict could be expected to bring those conflicts into staff relations. This recognition made available considerable staff energy that had been lost in internal feuding.

These internal changes contributed to loosening the organization interface with CSA. The rewritten funding proposal presented a Corporation role and strategy in which tight supervision by CSA distracted Corporation staff from important work at other interfaces. CSA's decision to fund the Corporation for a longer-than-usual period in effect relaxed CSA control over day-to-day staff activity. The new proposal also emphasized the expanding role of the Corporation's Housing Division, a subunit with linkages in business and ghetto communities that made it more able to resist CSA pressure. Dependence on CSA was also reduced by initial successes in generating alternative funding sources, so that the Corporation was not totally tied to CSA as a sole financial supporter.

The crisis with CSA also led Corporation staff, particularly the President, to make more use of third parties and to recompose several interfaces in ways that promoted credibility with CSA. Consultants were used to develop new joint ventures; other consultants trained the Board; still others helped diagnose the situation and plan for the future. In many ways the organization interface between CSA and the Corporation was adrift on tides running in the larger society; the reorientation of the federal bureaucracy away from social service projects in favor of profit-making ventures reflected a societywide conservative trend. But that trend offered resources to organizations that could effectively respond: Community development corporations able to start profit-making ventures had been deluged with attention and resources. Forces and trends in the larger context offered both threats and opportunities to the Corporation.

Actions in response to CSA requests and the rewritten proposal were the most immediate Corporation responses to the crisis. But those actions in some degree redefined the issues and alternatives in contention by demonstrating Corporation commitment to performance in CSA's terms and by shifting attention to new alternatives for performance improvement. Firing incompetent staff members and selling unprofitable ventures were important symbolic acts in the eyes of CSA. The decision to refund the Corporation for an unusually long period appears to be a CSA grant of increased autonomy and resources to pursue the "new day."

The combination of activities reduced the overorganization of the CSA-Corporation interface to permit more Corporation autonomy and attention to other interfaces.

The Corporation and the Business Establishment

The interface between the Corporation and local business had become weakly defined and loosely organized over the years. Relatively few linkages remained, contributing to problems with CSA, since joint profit-making ventures could not be developed without such contacts.

The reorientation of Corporation strategy drew attention to business links as a critical resource. The new business development Director was more skilled at working with business people. The President's increased visibility in the community and his efforts at more "politicking" also contributed to building relationships and expanding communication with the Establishment. Since CSA required less attention under the new funding arrangement, more Corporation time and energy could be devoted to developing joint projects with business people. Citywide recognition of the problems of urban decay and racial tensions predisposed business people and institutional administrators to attend to new initiatives from the Corporation, even though they had become skeptical about social change projects in general. The combination of changes created more resources for representing the Corporation to the Establishment, more initiatives from the President and the Business Development staff, and expanded Establishment receptiveness—and so created potential for defining and organizing a variety of new interface linkages in the form of joint ventures.

The Corporation and the Ghetto

Although the new regime in the Board was able to prevent community feuds from paralyzing Board decision making, the Board did not become much more active as an interface between the Corporation and the ghetto community. In part this reflects the deterioration of the community itself. When the Corporation was founded, the community was mobilized by riots and community activists to speak with a united voice, and some representatives spoke for large blocks of active supporters. But continued outmigration had eroded community organization and leadership. Board members no longer represented large groups, if they represented any organization at all. Loose Board organization permitted flare-ups of intense conflict among representatives of small minorities, but representatives often avoided serious debate of issues relevant to the community as a whole. Changes within the Corporation staff and within the Board leadership could not compensate for the community disorganization reflected in its representation at the interface.

Figure 7.2 represents changes in the three organization interfaces of the Ghetto Development Corporation over this period. At the point of the crisis (A), the interface with CSA was overorganized and compromised Corporation autonomy and flexibility, while the interfaces with the Establishment and the ghetto community were underorganized and characterized by withdrawal at the former and withdrawal and periodic escalations at the latter. Efforts to manage these interfaces eventually changed this picture (B): The interface between CSA and the Corporation permitted more autonomy to the latter; a better-defined and organized interface between the Corporation and the business community permitted more communication; the Board as an interface between ghetto community and Corporation was less subject to escalation and obstruction.

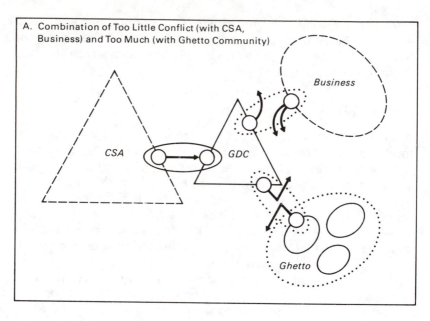

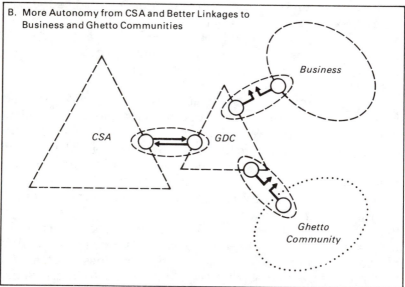

Fig. 7.2. *Organization interfaces at Ghetto Development Corporation.*

MANAGING CONFLICT AT ORGANIZATION INTERFACES

This section focuses more generally on strategies for managing conflict at organization interfaces. Some strategies focus on reducing conflict when organizations are engaged in interorganizational warfare; other strategies promote productive engagement in place of interorganizational isolation or collusion. This section offers options for conflict managers, but no effort is made to examine exhaustively all the strategies available.

Reducing Interorganizational Conflict

At organization interfaces, as at other interfaces, conflict management strategies may focus on the dynamics of immediate representative interaction, or on the long-term development of interface definition and organization.

Changing representatives' interaction: three strategies.   Intervention can focus on altering the patterns of perception, communication, and action between organizational representatives that produce excessive conflict at the interface.

Strategy 1. *Alter representatives' perceptions.* Intervention can alter stereotypes or clarify the importance of interdependencies, and so alter information-processing of boundary-spanning roles and individuals (Miles, 1980). Events that produce better understanding of the interests and perspectives of the other organization, or that clarify organizational interdependencies, can reduce conflict. The Mayor of Jamestown, for example, brought together senior representatives of local government, unions, and businesses to examine differences that promoted community decline (Trist, 1979). Educative interventions may help representatives understand the dynamics of interorganizational warfare, and so enable them to control unwanted escalations. As Jamestown union officers and plant managers understood their situation and the available options, they began to develop alternative approaches to handling their differences.

Strategy 2. *Alter representatives' communications.* Interventions can change the representing and scanning/monitoring functions of organization representatives (Miles, 1980). Creating new opportunities for communication, and ensuring that the communications exchanged are credible, can reduce conflict. The Mayor of Jamestown increased the quantity and quality of communications among contending parties by bringing representatives together and mediating between them. Representative roles and departments can also be better equipped to represent their constituencies or to take in new information. The participation of plant and union leaders in the Jamestown Committee meetings provided important resources for communications among the parties. Representatives' discussions of factors that restrict or distort interorganizational communications can also improve relations. The emergence of a new vision of potential labor-management relations in Jamestown, and concepts of how to promote those relations, provided an important alternative to the patterns in existence.

Strategy 3. *Alter representatives' actions.* Interventions can reframe issues and alternatives or redirect representative tactics at the interface. These changes can alter the representing, protecting, and transacting functions of organizational boundary-spanners (Miles, 1980). The stakes at organization interfaces may be high: Organizational survival is often tied to transactions with other organizations, and issues that threaten the survival of one or both parties understandably may generate rigid positions and entrenched commitments. Interventions can separate out threats to organizational survival so they do not contaminate other more easily solved issues. Focusing on issues of community decline that affected all the parties in Jamestown permitted enough exploration of differences so the parties could eventually formulate issues and alternatives that offered benefit to both sides. Representative tactics at organization interfaces, as elsewhere, can contribute to reduced conflict: Explicit acceptance of organizational differences, clear expression of peaceful intentions, peaceful initiatives combined with self-defense against exploitation, and cogent formulations of common interests in reduced conflict are all examples. The Mayor of Jamestown and his colleagues were able to create an initial climate for reducing conflict with the focus on community decline, and recently developed tactics for launching cooperative labor-management experiments offered ways to promote better relations within participating plants.

Changing interface development: three strategies.   Interorganizational warfare is carried on in the context of underorganized and poorly defined interfaces. Interventions can affect interfaces through redefinition or reorganization of the interface itself, or by changing the parties or the larger context that interact with it.

Strategy 4. *Alter the organization interface.* Interventions can redefine the boundaries or composition of organization interfaces. Intervenors can formulate a common vision that brings parties together to preserve shared values, to accomplish common tasks, or to recognize geographical interdependence (e.g., Emery and Trist, 1965; Galbraith, 1977). Common interests permit the definition of interface boundaries around organizational coalitions whose members would ordinarily be in conflict: Joint ventures, cartels, and trade associations all link potential competitors for common goals (Thompson, 1967; Aiken and Hage, 1971; Pfeffer and Salancik, 1978). The Jamestown Labor-Management Committee, for example, brought together public officials, plant managers, and union officials for the common interest of preventing regional economic decline—and work on the common problem reduced other conflicts among them. Common interest in the economic health of their shared location created an external boundary around previously unconnected senior organizational representatives.

Redrawing boundaries can alter organization interface composition. Interorganizational warfare can be moderated and protest absorbed by including new representatives in the interface. The response of the Tennessee Valley Authority to local organizations provided the prototype of interorganizational co-optation: Protesting groups were invited to participate in decision making, and their representatives became defenders of resulting policies (Selznick, 1949). Some organizations systematically compose their Boards of Directors to establish interorganizational linkages: Pfeffer and Salancik (1978) found that the composition of hospital boards could be predicted from knowledge of the resources (e.g., funds, administrative resources) the hospitals needed from outside. Including third parties can also reduce conflict: The Mayor and external consultants played roles in managing the tensions between Jamestown union and management representatives. Transactions at interface boundaries can be closely regulated to reduce uncertainty and potential for conflict escalation. Boundaries can be closed to disruptive inputs and outputs, for example, by the development of interorganizational contracts whose provisions establish controls over the flow of information between the parties, or between parties and outsiders with respect to interface issues (e.g., Thompson, 1967; Pfeffer and Salancik, 1978). Controls over interaction within the interface can be tightened to reduce the potential for unintended escalations of conflict. Formal mechanisms can be instituted to regulate organizational representatives: Contracts between coal company suppliers and utility consumers regularly reduce future uncertainties by legally binding commitments, and joint venture agreements formally spell out party responsibilities to avoid future conflict. Shared norms can be evolved that define appropriate behavior and prevent excessive conflict: Steel industry "price leadership," for example, informally coordinates price changes that would not be legal if undertaken formally. Interface parties can also coordinate their activities through shared theories about the world: As the Jamestown Committee developed visions of organizational innovations to simultaneously increase worker productivity and satisfaction, cooperative initiatives between labor and management became more feasible. Such informal mechanisms are particularly appropriate when relatively few parties are involved and norms may be easily enforced; more formal mechanisms, such as a relatively centralized and powerful trade association, may be required to reduce conflict among large numbers of parties (Pfeffer and Salancik, 1978).

Strategy 5. *Alter one or both organizations.* Redefining organizational interests or altering their internal characteristics can reduce conflict among them. Redefining organizational missions and domains can reframe the importance of other organizations at organization interfaces. The conflict between federal regulatory agencies and tobacco companies, for example, may be abated by tobacco company decisions to diversify their product mix so they become less dependent on the controversial cigarette market. Strategic choices of location, technology, and mission by organizations can reduce conflict at organization interfaces (Child, 1972; Galbraith, 1977; Miles et al., 1978). It was precisely this sort of strategic choice *not* to invest in Jamestown that prompted the formation of the Labor-Management Committee.

Organizational parties can also adopt internal changes that reduce interface conflict. Critical outputs or inputs can be stockpiled or rationed to prevent uncertainty about critical resources (Thompson, 1967); departments can be created to manage problematic relations and given more power and resources if problems are difficult to resolve (Hickson et al., 1971). Boundary-spanning departments that deal with much conflict can be "loosely coupled" to the rest of the organization to buffer external uncertainties and dependencies (Weick, 1976): "Flak catching" departments were created by many public agencies to deal with angry community groups with a minimum of disturbance to the everyday workings of the agency. For more difficult conflicts, leadership involvement may be required. Leaders can commit their own energies and resources to managing important conflicts, as at Jamestown. Or leaders can be used as symbols to reduce challenges; Pfeffer and Salancik (1978) argue that symbolic firings of visible leaders may be used to defuse external pressure. Organizations can also recruit personnel from each other and so reduce stereotyping and improve communications (Evan, 1966).

Strategy 6. *Alter the context.* Contextual forces may be intimidatingly large and complex, but organizations are sometimes extremely successful at imposing their needs on the larger context. Strategic choices, for example, can dramatically redefine problematic contextual forces. Redefining organizational products or markets, for example, can reduce the stakes of interface conflict by changing organizational interdependencies with supplier or consumer organizations. Or moving into a different location can reduce conflicts: Many firms have recently abandoned plants in Northeast locations (e.g., Jamestown) for the sunny climes, weak unions, and municipal welcomes of the Sunbelt—revamping in a single stroke many different contextual forces.

The immediate contexts of organization interfaces vary greatly in constraints placed on interorganizational conflict. Some immediate contexts are highly organized and likely to restrict conflict: "Mandated cooperation" in the public sector, and highly concentrated industries in the private sector, restrict conflict escalation that threatens the interests of powerful third parties (Perrow, 1970). But in other contexts there is little contextual restriction on interorganizational warfare. Conflicts over money and power among social and public service organizations may be brutal (Benson, 1975), and interorganizational networks that bring together public and private organizations like the Jamestown Labor-Management Committee are relatively rare. Interventions that develop such linkages can be important mechanisms for managing future interorganizational tensions and interdependencies (Trist, 1977).

Conflict at organization interfaces can also be moderated by forces in the larger context whose impact is only indirect. Interventions can enlist public support for reduced conflict or reduce the legitimacy of some organizational positions. Big Oil advertising, for example, directs attention to their efforts to solve energy shortages, rather than to their profits. Lobbying activities with third parties can shape the legislative context of interface conflict: Big Oil pressures for deregulation may eventually produce profits big enough to simultaneously satisfy shareholders and finance new explorations. Early recognition of trends in the larger context may enable organizations to surf on the waves of social change. The Jamestown Committee benefited from funding and consultant resources interested in a test case of communitywide labor-management cooperation that would not have been available for less innovative projects.

Interventions for reducing conflict at organization interfaces are summarized in Table 7.1. This list is not exhaustive—new strategies for handling environmental pressures are being invented continually. But the list offers stimulation for conflict

TABLE 7.1

Reducing conflict at organization interfaces

Changing representatives' interaction

1. *Alter perceptions*

Improve representatives' information-processing:
- increase understanding of other positions
- recognize interdependencies

Educate representatives about:
- dynamics of interorganizational warfare
- their own contributions to those dynamics

2. *Alter communications*

Develop representatives' scanning/monitoring capacities:
- to gain more information
- to evaluate trustworthiness of information

Develop representation capacities:
- to communicate clearly positions of organization
- to match status and resources with other representatives

Communicate about blocks to interorganizational communication

3. *Alter actions*

Separate and manage organizational survival issues without contaminating less critical problems

Expand alternatives considered beyond entrenched positions in which stakes are prohibitive

Train or recruit representatives in de-escalation tactics:
- explicit recognition of legitimate differences
- low-risk initiatives toward peace
- express intentions clearly
- formulate long-term common interests
- tactics for managing escalatory events

Changing interface development

4. *Alter the organization interface*

Redefine interface boundaries:
- formulate compelling vision of interdependence and shared values, location, or resources
- create or strengthen boundaries around organizational representatives: joint ventures, consortia, cartels, trade and professional associations

TABLE 7.1 (continued)
Reducing conflict at organization interfaces

	• recompose interface to co-opt unrepresented organizations or include third party peacemakers Tighten interface organization: • close interface boundaries to external invasions or leaks that increase conflict • create formal procedures for regulating disputes • central interface authorities to handle conflict • rules for dealing with differences (e.g., contractual provisions) • negotiate norms and shared theories for informal coordination of activity
5. *Alter one or both organizations*	Redefines organizational interests by strategic choices: • new products, services, or markets • changed location or technology • diversification of suppliers or markets to reduce interdependence Redefine organizational characteristics: • boundary management activities: buffering, rationing, smoothing to reduce external challenges • create and empower boundary-spanning subunits • loosely couple boundary-spanning units for buffering • use organizational leaders as symbols of organizational commitment or change ("symbolic firings") • exchanges of personnel that debunk stereotypes
6. *Alter the larger context*	Invite moderating interventions from organized context: • appeal to sector (industry, social service) authorities, such as trade and professional associations • appeal to sector norms against warfare • appeal to interested third parties (e.g., government regulators)

TABLE 7.1   (continued)
Reducing conflict at organization interfaces

>   Tighten context organization for more
>   constraint:
>   • lobby for legislation or enforcement
>   • erect barriers to entry of new combatants
>   • public relations and image management
>   to reduce conflict
>   Use contextual developments to encourage
>   conflict-reducing innovations

---

managers who are developing ideas for dealing with their specific situations.

Promoting Interorganizational Conflict

Promoting productive conflict between organizations may be necessary when interorganizational collusion suppresses differences important to the organizations or the larger context, or when interorganizational isolation avoids these differences. Interventions considered in this section focus first on changing the dynamics of interaction among organizational representatives, and then on the patterns of organization interface development.

Changing representatives' interaction: three strategies.   Interventions can promote productive conflict among organizational representatives by altering perceptions, communications, or actions that support suppression or withdrawal.

Strategy 1. *Alter representatives' perceptions.* Interorganizational collusion can be reduced in some situations by new information and different interpretations of the situation. Interventions can bring to light unperceived differences, or debunk overemphasized similarities that suppress interorganizational conflict. The President of Ghetto Development Corporation examined his relations with the Community Services Administration and recognized both their conflicting interests and the collusive effects of his own discomfort with "politicking." Educating representatives about the dynamics of interorganizational collusion can allow more productive conflict because they can then choose not to participate. The Corporation President decided to build toward more independence from CSA when he recognized some of the long-term implications of further conflict suppression.

Interventions can reframe perceptions that support interorganizational isolation. Representatives of isolated organizations tend to emphasize differences and de-emphasize interdependencies, so it may be necessary to clarify the common interests and benefits of interorganizational debate. Productive debate about residential resegregation and community decline was initiated among Urban Heights realtors, lenders, citizens, and government officials by citizen representatives who foresaw the consequences of "redlining" some areas and financial "disinvestment" in the community. Their challenges to lenders raised the awareness of many other interested parties (Gricar and Brown, 1981).

Strategy 2. *Alter representatives' communications.* For problems of interorganizational collusion, interventions can expand the exchange of controversial information. Improving the capacity of representatives to accurately monitor relevant sources, or to present their own positions without glossing over differences, can promote productive exchange. The President of the Ghetto Development Corporation more actively presented his case for increased corporate independence from CSA as he became more aware of the debilitating impact of being too dependent: His presentation of the drain on corporate resources imposed by CSA's yearly refunding process gained the Corporation a longer cycle for the next year, and so freed personnel to work at other pressing interfaces.

Problems of interorganizational isolation, on the other hand, require interventions that expand communications in general between organizations that avoid exchanging information. Interventions that encourage contact, and reduce perceptions of each other as irrelevant or extremely different, promote engagement. The initial contacts between citizen representatives and mortgage lenders in Urban Heights were confrontations which threatened to escalate into interorganizational warfare. The City Manager as a powerful third party invited representatives to and chaired the meetings of the Committee on Residential Lending, so communications became less distorted and more productive. Interorganizational isolation may sometimes flip over into interorganizational warfare, and interventions to expand communications among isolated representatives must be carefully managed to promote productive rather than destructive conflict.

Strategy 3. *Alter representatives' actions.* Interventions to reduce interorganizational collusion can focus on the issues and alternatives in contention, or on the tactics by which representatives influence each other. The stakes of conflict are often obscured in interorganizational collusion: The costs of collusion and the importance of differences may have to be linked together to promote more debate. Decisions to fire incompetent Ghetto Development Corporation executives and to sell unprofitable Corporation ventures refocused attention on other issues and alternatives where mutually beneficial outcomes could be negotiated with CSA. Organizational representatives can be recruited or trained in tactics for shifting from suppression to constructive debate: recognizing suppressed differences, articulating differences constructively, initiating productive debate, and managing suppression tactics. For the President of the Ghetto Development Corporation, more productive conflict with CSA representatives involved learning to "politick"—to articulate new visions, to build relationships across conflicting perspectives, to recognize and accept pressures on CSA, and to preserve Corporation autonomy while demonstrating the value of that autonomy to CSA in its own terms.

Interorganizational isolation is often associated with failure to recognize issues and alternatives that link the organizations. Interventions can formulate issues and alternatives for representatives to discuss without avoiding important differences on one hand or exploding into warfare on the other. The Urban Heights City Manager, for example, initially guided the new Committee on Residential Lending away from issues confirming stereotypes of each other as intractable, to topics important enough to sustain continuing engagement without leading to blowups. After their success in initial discussions, representatives were better prepared to take on more difficult problems. Representatives can be trained or recruited for skill in tactics to end isolation: recognizing interdependencies, initiating contacts, managing efforts to withdraw, controlling escalation, and sustaining productive engagement in spite of differences. The Urban Heights City Manager played a crucial role in initiating interaction in the Committee: He controlled efforts of representatives to either withdraw from or escalate the conflict; he formulated discussable issues; and he provided a climate in which constructive debate could take place.

Changing interface development: three strategies. Productive interorganizational conflict can also be encouraged by intervening in the interplay of interface, organizations, and the larger context, all of which define and organize the interface. Interorganizational collusion is associated with overorganized interfaces; and interorganizational isolation is associated with underorganized interfaces, so they require different intervention strategies.

Strategy 4. *Alter the organization interface.* Interventions can redefine interface boundaries or revise its internal organization. Interorganizational collusion may require reducing the strength of interface definitions. Alternative goals or conflicts of interest at the interface can be emphasized or articulated, and boundaries can be redefined by competing criteria. Recognizing conflicting interests between the Ghetto Development Corporation and CSA, and clarifying the geographic boundaries that united Corporation, local Establishment, and ghetto community, helped to promote more debate between the Corporation and CSA. Interface composition can be altered to produce more debate: Researcher-consultants examined Corporation interfaces with external organizations and encouraged more challenge of CSA.

Interorganizational collusion can also be reduced by interventions that loosen interface organization. Interface boundaries can be opened to information or personnel that stimulate more debate, such as consultant diagnoses of the Corporation-CSA interface. Formal arrangements that organize interaction within the interface can be relaxed: The formal constraints on time that CSA held over the Corporation were relaxed in the new contract. Informal expectations can also be negotiated for more discretion. The President's "hard decisions" to terminate personnel and projects not up to CSA standards may have reassured CSA so that they were more willing to "give him his head" for the coming year. Reducing resources available to both parties can foster more debate: The notorious expense of "cost-plus" contracts stem in part from interorganizational collusion at the expense of other parties (e.g., the taxpayers).

Interorganizational isolation, in contrast, can benefit from interventions that create or strengthen weakly defined interface boundaries. Formulating common goals or visions, for instance, can define a new interface. The Urban Heights Committee on Residential Lending emerged from activities of citizen activists and the City Manager, who jointly articulated the economic and geographical interdependencies that brought the other parties to the interface. The diverse organizational representatives included in the Committee ensured different viewpoints, and the City Manager was a third party who could keep conflict from escalating beyond productive levels.

Interventions can tighten internal organization of interfaces loosened by interorganizational isolation. Closing excessively open boundaries can reduce the threats associated with open debate. The Committee on Residential Lending agreed to limit outside discussion of meetings, and decided against encouraging early media interest in the Committee. Formal rules and roles can be developed to control withdrawal or escalation. The City Manager was formally Chairman of the Committee, and he used explicit rules of procedure to run meetings and to control conflict. Informal norms can also constrain interaction. Formally defined subgroups of the Committee met regularly on special issues, and they developed informal norms and theories about responsibility (typically, outside the Committee membership) for problems. These informal expectations supported continuing engagement among diverse representatives (Gricar and Brown, 1981).

Strategy 5. *Alter one or both organizations.* Interventions can alter the parties to reduce interorganizational collusion. Organizations can redefine their interests at the interface by strategic choices that alter goals, markets, technologies, locations, or other organizational factors central to interface relations (Child, 1972; Miles et al., 1978). The decision to pay more attention to other interfaces by the Ghetto Development Corporation refocused organizational resources away from CSA and so enhanced the likelihood for short-term conflict. Strategic choices sometimes increase organizational interdependence: Divestiture or consolidation of organizational activities can increase the stakes of interorganizational exchanges at remaining interfaces by putting more organizational eggs into fewer baskets. Or such choices can eliminate organization interfaces entirely: Turning an "unintentional merger" into formal integration of organizations turns an organization interface into a department or level interface.

Other organizational changes can reshape organizational characteristics to reduce collusion. Boundary management activities used to reduce conflict, such as buffering, smoothing, and rationing, can be altered or discontinued to highlight differences and discontinuities at organization interfaces. The CSA threat to discontinue Ghetto Development Corporation funding dramatically terminated their collusion. Boundary-spanning units can be charged with confronting other organizations, and links between boundary-spanners and their constituencies may be "tightly coupled" for close control. Changes in organizational leadership can be used to symbolize new commitments to interface engagement, as in the personnel decisions at the Ghetto Development Corporation. Or recruitment policies can bring in new staff whose experiences promote more engagement, such as outsiders aware of collusion costs.

For interorganizational isolation, in contrast, strategic choices may be required that explicitly recognize external dependencies and require increased interaction. Organizational choice of goals, technologies, locations, and mix of suppliers and markets can be tailored to emphasize more engagement at critical interfaces (Ackoff, 1974). The City Manager of Urban Heights believed in the responsibility of the municipal government to bring together community groups and organizations to work out conflicts, and so conceived the Committee. His interest in "looking for trouble" made the previous passive stances of many community groups less tenable. Or diversification may reduce stakes at the interface and so allow more engagement on one hand, or complete separation and genuine independence on the other.

Changing organizational characteristics can also promote productive conflict among isolated organizations. The strategy of ignoring outside agencies, to manage boundaries (Pfeffer and Salancik, 1978), can be revised. Boundary-spanning subunits can more actively engage other organizations; organizational leaders can actively attend to external events; personnel can be recruited or "outplaced" to other organizations (Miles, 1980; Evan, 1966). Members of the Urban Heights Committee on Residential Lending were senior executives in their organizations. who became de facto boundary-spanners actively linked to organizations previously isolated from each other.

Strategy 6. *Alter the larger context*. Intervenors seldom seek to influence interorganizational collusion unless its consequences are obvious. Histories of problematic collusion encourage contextual organization and third party regulation: The Justice Department regulates interorganizational collusion that undermines market competition, and the Food and Drug Administration expanded its regulatory role after the pharmaceutical corporations co-opted the American Medical Association. The intervention of such third parties can be invited to promote debate between colluding organizations. More generally, interventions can focus on contextual forces that permit or encourage collusion: Legislation that prevents or hampers conflict can be revised; resource pools can be reduced; public relations activity can legitimate more conflict; normative standards can encourage diversity.

Problems of interorganizational isolation can be reduced by the intervention of third parties concerned with continuing engagement. The Urban Heights city government undertook this role vis-à-vis financial disinvestment and resegregation. The problems may be particularly difficult when relevant contextual forces are not organized. It may be necessary to create contextual organization forces by supporting legislation, establishing legal precedents, shaping public opinion, or otherwise influencing the larger context to promote productive conflict among organizations (e.g., Trist, 1977).

Table 7.2 summarizes interventions for promoting productive conflict between collusive or isolated organizations. These interventions, which are illustrative rather than exhaustive, are intended to stimulate ideas for intervention or combinations of interventions appropriate to the situation.

SUMMARY

Organization interfaces bring together organizations that depend on exchanges to survive and grow. Organizational parties may be equal or unequal, but they are typically quite vulnerable to forces in the larger context—which may be relatively unorganized in comparison to the contexts of other interfaces.

Organizations bring mixes of common and conflicting interests to their interfaces, and these mixes create potentials for too much, too little, or appropriate conflict. Too much conflict produces interorganizational warfare that debilitates one or both parties. Too little conflict may lead to interorganizational collusion, in which important differences are suppressed in a kind of "unintentional merger" that preserves harmony at the expense of the organizations or the context. Or too little conflict may be associated with interorganizational isolation, in which important interdependencies are ignored for a "false independence" harmful to the interests of parties or context. Productive conflicts, in contrast, bring organizations together for interorganizational bargaining, in which interaction over conflicting interests produces compromises based on recognition of underlying common concerns, or for interorganizational problem-solving, in which representatives explore differences as a prelude to discovering mutually beneficial solutions.

Conflict management interventions can reduce interorganizational conflict when there is too much, or promote it when

TABLE 7.2
Promoting conflict at organization interfaces

	INTERORGANIZATIONAL COLLUSION	INTERORGANIZATIONAL ISOLATION
Changing representatives' interaction		
1. *Alter perceptions*	Improve information-processing: • recognize unseen differences • debunk seen similarities Educate representatives to: • dynamics of collusion • own contributions	Improve information-processing: • recognize interdependence • debunk threats of interaction Educate representatives to: • dynamics of isolation • own contributions
2. *Alter communications*	Expand controversial information exchange: • expand scanning capacity • improve representing capacity Communicate about blocks to better communication	Expand general information exchange: • encourage contact that does not confirm stereotypes • promote credible exchanges Communicate about blocks and dangers of communication
3. *Alter actions*	Link together issues for debatable differences Focus on alternatives to continuing collusion Recruit/train representatives to: • recognize differences • initiate debate • counter suppression	Formulate issues to reveal costs of isolation, benefits of engagement Emphasize low-threat alternatives Recruit/train representatives to: • recognize interdependencies • initiate contacts • counter withdrawal or escalation

TABLE 7.2   (continued)
Promoting conflict at organization interfaces

	INTERORGANIZATIONAL COLLUSION	INTERORGANIZATIONAL ISOLATION
	• limit negotiation	• sustain productive interaction

Changing interface development

4. *Alter organization interface*	Redefine interface boundaries: • weaken boundaries by clarifying goal conflicts • emphasize cross-cutting boundary criteria • include representatives who ask hard questions	Redefine interface boundaries: • strengthen by emphasizing superordinate goals • emphasize converging boundary criteria • include representatives or third parties who control conflict
	Loosen interface organization: • open boundaries to controversial inputs and outputs • loosen formal rules, roles, and procedures • loosen informal norms, expectations, and theories to allow debate	Tighten interface organization: • close boundaries to irrelevant inputs and critical outputs • tighten formal rules, roles, and procedures to prevent withdrawal • negotiate informal norms, expectations, and theories to support engagement
5. *Alter one or both organizations*	Strategic choice for more conflicting interests: • tailor choice of goals, technol-	Strategic choice for more interest in engagement: • tailor choice of goals, technol-

TABLE 7.2   (continued)
Promoting conflict at organization interfaces

	INTERORGANIZATIONAL COLLUSION	INTERORGANIZATIONAL ISOLATION
	ogy, location for emphasizing differences	ogy, location for more interaction
	• divest, consolidate to increase stakes at interface	• diversify to reduce stakes at interface
	• formal merger to restructure interface	• formal separation to end interface
	Redefine organization:	Redefine organization:
	• alter buffer, smooth, and ration strategies to disrupt collusion	• alter buffer, smooth, and ration strategies to compel more interaction
	• charge boundary-spanners to challenge	• charge boundary-spanners to increase contact
	• tightly couple units for responsiveness	• tightly couple units to prevent withdrawal
	• leadership attention and succession for debate	• leadership attention and succession for engagement
	• personnel exchanges with outside to clarify differences	• personnel exchanges with other party to debunk fears
6. *Alter the larger context*	Invite intervention from organized context:	Invite intervention from organized context:
	• sector authority (trade association, funding agency) for debate	• sector authority encouragement of increased interaction

TABLE 7.2 (continued)
Promoting conflict at organization interfaces

INTERORGANIZATIONAL COLLUSION	INTERORGANIZATIONAL ISOLATION
• third party pressure for debate	• third party pressure for interaction
Alter less organized context:	Alter less organized context:
• legislation against collusion	• legislation for engagement
• reduce resource pools	• reduce threat of interaction
• public relations to legitimate conflict	• public relations to legitimate engagement
• encourage pro-conflict sector norms	• encourage pro-engagement sector norms

there is too little. Interventions can interrupt the patterns of representatives' immediate behavior by altering their stereotyped perceptions, distorted communications, or problematic actions. Or interventions can alter the interplay of organization interface, organizational parties, or the larger context to redefine and reorganize the interface within which representatives interact. Or interventions can affect both levels of analysis, simultaneously or sequentially.

How do organization interfaces differ from interfaces considered in previous chapters? First, organization interfaces exist at a different level of analysis from the department, level, and culture interfaces described in earlier chapters. Organization interfaces bring together organizations, not subunits, and the issues are correspondingly more complex. Second, since the stakes at organization interfaces often involve organizational survival, very senior executives may become involved. Many of the examples considered in the chapter (e.g., the Urban Heights Committee on Residential Lending, the Jamestown Area Labor-Management Committee, the Ghetto Community Development Corporation) involved contacts among chief executives. Third, contextual forces have impacts on organization interfaces that are extremely varied and difficult to predict. Relatively loose contextual organization and low third party interest, for instance, put responsibility for managing interorganizational relations squarely on the parties. At other interfaces with tightly organized contexts, organizational parties become as subject to contextual control as organizational departments. Contextual impact is difficult to predict without understanding the specific interface in detail. Finally, organization interfaces and contextual forces may be particularly vulnerable to each other. Expanding dependence and uncertainty in the larger context challenges organizational autonomy and effectiveness; increased organizational attention to managing contexts threatens to subordinate those contexts—particularly relatively unorganized contexts—to narrow organizational interests. Other parties may be harmed or galvanized by events at organization interfaces. Consumers of pills had little protection against the combination of the pharmaceutical companies and the AMA until the government stepped in. As interorganizational linkages increase in the face of growing interdependence and environmental uncertainty, it becomes increasingly important to manage organization interfaces, and the last to respond to this challenge will suffer consequences for their tardiness.

Complex Interfaces

8

The last four chapters have dealt with "simple" interfaces—simple in that the interfaces were defined by issues limited in concept rather than by complex amalgams of differences. This approach to interfaces produces a set of conceptual lenses that can be applied *separately* to problems at organizational interfaces. A problem may be analyzed from several perspectives: as a department interface concerned with task issues, as a level interface concerned with power issues, as a culture interface concerned with tensions from the larger society, or as an organization interface concerned with organizational missions and survival.

But most interfaces in organizations, on close inspection, do not appear simple. On the contrary, conflict between departments often involves links to other organizations or the distribution of power, as well as shared tasks. Maintenance and Production at the Riverview Chemical Works were concerned about market pressures, Corporate Headquarters surveillance, and their own relative influence, as well as getting the job done. Or conflict among levels may be compounded by cultural differences. The Old Guard and the New Hires in the South Side Hospital Laboratory were at odds over both the distribution of power and racial differences. Managing conflict at organizational interfaces often requires understanding simple interfaces and their *interaction* when conflicts involve several different issues.

This chapter concerns complex interfaces at which two or more simple interfaces interact. The next section reviews and briefly compares the simple interfaces presented in the last four chapters. The second section examines complex interfaces created by the interaction of two or more simple interfaces, and suggests rules of thumb for analyzing them. Cases described in previous chapters will be used to illustrate these rules of thumb. The third section describes interventions at complex interfaces, illustrates those interventions by reference to earlier cases, and suggests rules of thumb for intervening at complex interfaces. The last section summarizes the chapter.

SIMPLE INTERFACES: A REVIEW

Department interfaces, level interfaces, culture interfaces, and organization interfaces have been discussed at some length in the last four chapters. At the risk of dragging readers over well-plowed ground, this section reviews and compares those interfaces as a prelude to considering their combination in complex interfaces.

Simple Interfaces

Department interfaces bring together subunits that must interact to accomplish organizational tasks. The Maintenance and Production Departments at Riverview Chemical Works, for example, had to coordinate their activities to achieve safe, high-volume, low-cost production. Effective coordination of such interdependent but different departments is associated with moderate levels of conflict in bargaining or problem-solving interactions among representatives. Too much conflict undercuts coordination with destructive departmental competition; too little conflict undermines effectiveness with avoidance of important differences or collusion to preserve harmony at the expense of performance. Departments and their interfaces are defined by organizational task requirements, and are influenced by interventions couched in task-relevant terms. The parties are embedded in a common organizational context that is attentive to their joint effectiveness, so visible problems at their interface may attract intervention by common hierarchical superiors.

Level interfaces link parties granted different degrees of formal power by the organization, but whose cooperation is necessary to accomplish organizational goals. The distribution of formal power, and the informal ability of upper and lower parties to influence each other, are central issues at the interface. Questions about the relative strengths of workers and management at the College City Transit Authority, for example, underlay their negotiation of substantive issues. Appropriate conflict between upper and lower parties involves mutual acceptance of power differences and recognition of legitimate rights and duties for both parties, to permit negotiated or facilitative leadership. The dynamics of unequal conflict can produce rapid and covert changes toward too much or too little conflict. Power struggles among parties can produce sabotage, warfare, and wholesale disruption of their interdependence. Or upper party dominance may be matched with lower party apathy to produce spiraling oppression. Or abdication by both parties may produce drift, rather than coherent action at their interface. Extreme restrictions on information exchange and explosive changes may develop at level interfaces as a consequence of upper party ignorance and lower party fear. The parties are embedded in a common organizational context, but lower party suspicion of organizational bias for upper parties may undermine hierarchical influence at the interface and encourage lower party search for allies from the outside. Interventions at level interfaces must deal with power differences among the parties, balancing information and influence asymmetries, and formulating legitimate relations in the teeth of highly volatile relations.

Culture interfaces exist where representatives of culturally different parties share organizational interdependence. Cultural differences may be based on subgroups in the larger society (e.g., men and women, blacks and whites) or the meeting of several societies (e.g., Americans, Japanese, Indians). The parties are brought together by organizational arrangements, but their cultural differences, rooted in their experience outside the organization, influence their interaction. The conflict between the Old Guard and the New Hires in the South Side Hospital Laboratory, for example, centered on white discrimination against minorities, particularly blacks. Cross-cultural relations can generate productive conflict, for party differences in perspective and resources may be constructively utilized through multicultural bargaining or problem-solving. But cultural differences can also produce problems, particularly when the differences are not clearly recognized. Too much cross-cultural conflict is associated with misunderstanding, bias, discrimination, and cultural polarization. Too little conflict may cause representatives to withdraw into cultural isolation, so they fail to understand or use their differences constructively. Or representatives may suppress their differences to enforce cultural homogeneity. Cultural differences are rooted in the larger social context rather than in organizationally controlled distinctions, so culture interfaces are often dispersed throughout organizations that remain unaware of their importance and unsophisticated about their management. Cultural differences may be unrecognized but still evoke strong feelings, so that events trivial to one party have important symbolic meaning to others. Conflict at culture interfaces calls on organizations to manage problems from the larger social context as they emerge in organizational microcosm.

Organization interfaces operate at a different level of analysis. They bring together whole organizations (rather than organizational subunits) that must interact to survive and achieve their missions. Organizational parties wish to reduce critical uncertainties and to ensure the flow of critical resources at organization interfaces. The Ghetto Development Corporation and the Community Services Administration, for example, were concerned with the flow of financial resources and the development of viable economic projects in the ghetto. Productive conflict among organizations is associated with interorganizational bargaining and problem-solving to reduce uncertainties, without drastically compromising organizational autonomy and flexibility. Too much conflict at organization interfaces generates interorganizational warfare that increases uncertainty and retards the flow of critical resources among them. Too little conflict can produce interorganizational collusion and "unintended mergers" that reduce the autonomy of the parties, or interorganizational isolation in a sense of "false independence" that encourages parties to avoid critical interdependencies. The stakes of conflict at organization interfaces are high; organizational survival and growth depend on relations with other organizations. The immediate context of organizations varies from tightly to loosely organized. Conflict among some organizations is externally controlled by powerful third parties, but the regulation of conflict among others depends largely on the organizations themselves or on forces from the larger context.

Comparing Simple Interfaces

Perhaps the most obvious difference among these four interfaces is the distinction between interfaces *within* organizations and interfaces *between* them. Department, level, and culture interfaces bring together parties within a common organizational context. Organization interfaces, in contrast, bring together organizations in a larger context. Although task, power, and cultural differences can exist between organizations as well as between smaller units, the focus here, for the sake of simplicity, is on interfaces that involve smaller subunits. In general, organizations provide more tightly organized contexts for department, level, or culture interfaces than industries, communities, societies, or other contexts provide for organization interfaces. Larger contexts sometimes exert considerable regulatory impact on organizations and their interfaces, but they seldom provide the level of legitimate and widely accepted assumptions common in a shared organization.

Comparing interface elements. Interfaces in organizations typically emerge to deal with issues growing out of organizationally defined interdependencies, since the parties are brought together by the organization. Without these interdependencies, parties could withdraw at the first sign of difficulty without paying any price in the long run. Concern over organizational tasks dominates department interfaces, but is subordinate to both concern with distribution of power at level interfaces and concern with cultural differences at culture interfaces. Conflict is likely over task differences, but issues of power inequalities and cross-cultural misunderstandings are often more emotionally charged and more likely to produce severe conflict problems.

Parties to different simple interfaces have different interests and internal characteristics. Departments are defined by task specializations; levels are defined by formal power allocation; cultural parties are defined by membership in subgroups of the larger society. The quality of member commitments may vary accordingly; involvement in a task group has a flavor different from investment in an upper or lower party, and both differ from membership in a culture. Generally departments tend to mobilize at the same pace. Upper and lower parties often mobilize asymmetrically, so that one party is more mobilized than the other at a given time. Cultural parties are typically dispersed throughout organizations, mobilizing only in the face of serious and widely visible problems.

Representatives at different simple interfaces may be diverse in role and personal characteristics. Representatives at department interfaces are often selected for task competencies, and their roles are defined by explicit choices of party and organization. Representatives of upper parties may differ greatly from their lower party counterparts, both in terms of personal characteristics and in terms of organizational legitimation. Representatives at culture interfaces often emerge without explicit choices by either organization or parties, and their roles may be self-defined rather than planned or legitimated by their parties.

Contextual forces also vary across different interfaces. The organizational context moderates problems at department interfaces and protects departments from the impacts of the larger context. But organizational contexts may be suspect at level interfaces, and lower parties in particular often seek aid from the larger context. And organizational contexts may be insensitive to cultural differences, whose definition and sensitive issues are rooted in the larger society.

Comparing interface dynamics.   The dynamics of conflict *escalation* involve cycles of representatives' negative stereotypes, distorted communications, and coercive tactics within a loosely organized and defined interface. Attention from the organizational context often moderates conflict escalation over task-related issues between departments. But the organizational context is a less credible moderator of tensions between levels, where upper and lower party differences, and severe restrictions on information exchange permit explosive power struggles. Escalations at culture interfaces are complicated by cultural misunderstandings and emotional reactions, relatively dispersed and unorganized parties, and special vulnerability to external events. Too much conflict is more likely and more problematic at level and culture interfaces than at department interfaces.

The dynamics of conflict *suppression* involve denials of difference, censored communications, and suppression tactics in the context of an overorganized interface. Interdepartmental suppression is often moderated by concern for performance in the organizational hierarchy. Power differences can produce increasing asymmetry and oppression of lower parties by dominant upper parties. Suppression of cultural differences may deny realities of the larger context for cultural homogenization or institutional discrimination. Too little conflict denies important differences, and may be associated with extreme reactions, particularly at level and culture interfaces.

Too little conflict may also be rooted in *withdrawal* linked to cycles of perceived mutual threat, reduced communications, and avoidance tactics within an underorganized interface. Withdrawal by interdependent departments again may be moderated by hierarchical attention. Differences in formal power can produce abdication by upper parties and apathy among lower parties. Avoiding cultural differences promotes cultural isolation and ignorance. Interfaces that are too loosely organized to prevent withdrawal are also poorly organized to control conflict, so withdrawal—particularly at level and culture interfaces—can be rapidly transformed into conflict escalation.

Table 8.1 summarizes these comparisons of the four simple interfaces. This summary provides a basis for considering combination of simple interfaces into complex interfaces.

TABLE 8.1
Comparisons of simple interfaces

	DEPARTMENT INTERFACE	LEVEL INTERFACE	CULTURE INTERFACE	ORGANIZATION INTERFACE
Interface elements:				
● Interface	Defined by task interdependence	Defined by task interdependence; formal power differences	Defined by task interdependence; societal cultures	Defined by organizational interdependence; survival and mission
● Parties	Defined by special tasks; mobilization symmetrical	Defined by formal power; mobilization asymmetrical	Defined by external cultures; dispersed mobilization	Defined by missions; mobilization varies
● Representatives	Defined by organization; task competencies	Defined by organization (upper) or constituency (lower)	Defined by self-selection and external culture	Defined by organization and outside challenges
● Context	Organization context (superiors) moderates problems	Organization context suspect; external allies sought	Organization context unaware; external cultures critical	Immediate context varies in influence; much interaction with larger context

Interface dynamics:

• Escalation	Escalation moderated by organization hierarchy and task interdependence	Power struggles intensified by asymmetries of power and organization	Cultural polarization based on emotional misunderstanding and bias	Interorganizational warfare combines multiple threats
• Suppression	Suppression moderated by shared organization and task	Dominance and oppression increased by increasing asymmetries	Homogenization devalues cultural differences	Interorganizational collusion threatens autonomy and flexibility
• Withdrawal	Withdrawal moderated by hierarchy and task interdependence	Abdication and apathy fueled by mutual fear and ignorance	Cultural isolation emphasizes unbridgeable differences	Interorganizational isolation creates false sense of independence

ANALYZING COMPLEX INTERFACES

This section focuses first on possible varieties of complex interfaces, and then suggests rules of thumb for analyzing complex interfaces.

Varieties of Complex Interfaces

To begin, let us focus on interfaces within an organization. There are four possible combinations of simple department, level, and culture interfaces: departments and levels, departments and cultures, levels and cultures, or all three at once.

Department/level interfaces combine task specializations and formal power differences, creating potentials for interdepartmental power struggles, dominance, or abdication. Interaction between Maintenance mechanics and Production managers, or between Production operators and Maintenance managers, at Riverview Chemical Works are examples. The top row (A) of Figure 8.1 illustrates problems of too much or too little conflict at department/level interfaces. Note that such interfaces may be afflicted by asymmetrical party mobilizations (dotted and solid party boundaries in center triangle), interface underorganization (left and right triangles) or asymmetrical organization (center triangle), involvement of external contextual forces, and representative interaction dynamics (arrows) characteristic of level interfaces.

Department/culture interfaces combine task specializations with cultural differences. Relations among male mechanics and female bus drivers within the Transit Workers Union, or between black personnel staff and white operations managers within the College City Transit Authority, are examples of such complex interfaces. The middle row (B) of Figure 8.1 portrays conflict problems that emerge at department/culture interfaces, such as department/culture polarization, homogeneity, or isolation. At such interfaces departmental relations are vulnerable to party mobilization based on external cultures, involvement of other parts of the organization as a consequence of culture party dispersion, influence of external cultural forces, and emotionally charged dynamics (arrows) that involve the personal identities of cultural representatives.

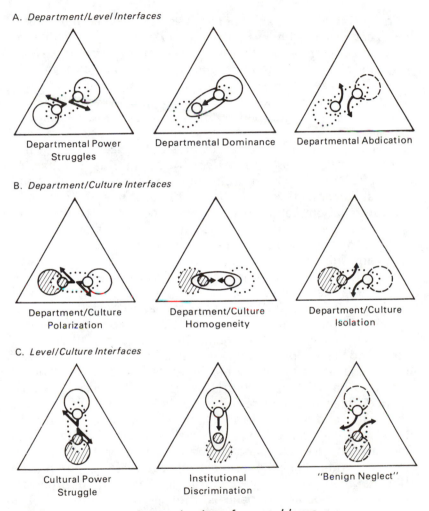

Fig. 8.1. *Varieties of complex interface problems.*

Level/culture interfaces bring together power differences and cultural differences. The white supervisors and the black technicians in the South Side Hospital Laboratory, for example, confronted each other across racial and formal power gulfs. The third row (C) of Figure 8.1 depicts conflict problems at level/culture interfaces, including cultural power struggles, institutional discrimination, and "benign neglect." Level/culture interfaces can produce intense party mobilization as a consequence of mutual threat and culturally based misunderstanding (left triangle), underorganized (left and right triangles) or asymmetrically organized (center triangle) interfaces, invited and uninvited influence from contextual forces, and dynamics that involve emotionally charged differences and covert escalations (arrows).

Finally, at some interfaces all three differences converge in a *department/level/culture interface.* At South Side Hospital, for example, low-status black lab technicians of the Old Guard had interests incompatible with those of high-status white doctors concerned about Laboratory performance. Although direct engagement between those parties was not common, the possibilities of misunderstanding at department/level/culture interfaces are high. Problems at such interfaces that combine all three simple interfaces are probably uncommon in organizations, given organizational control over personnel assignment. They may be more common, however, in the larger societal context.

Still further complexity may be introduced by linking organization interfaces to within-organization interfaces. Culture interfaces and level interfaces, for example, are particularly likely to encourage participation by parties outside the organizational context. The addition of cultural and level differences to department differences can undermine the organizational context as a third party, and so open the door to outsiders. When organization interfaces become linked to internal conflicts, the stakes can increase drastically. Expanding conflict between Old Guard and New Hires involved the larger organization (e.g., South Side Hospital management, the union local) and external organizations (e.g., regulatory agencies, the parent corporation). The involvement of outside organizations may move from the inside out or from the outside in. Conflict began inside the South Side Hospital Laboratory and gradually expanded to include external organizations. At the Ghetto Development Corporation, in contrast, larger society tensions entered the organization through organization interfaces to create conflict among staff members linked to different constituencies. In both cases, however, conflict problems that involved external organizations raised the stakes for managers.

The discussion of complex interfaces so far assumes that the simple interfaces combine in complex interfaces defined by multiple differences. Department, level, and culture differences are assumed in Figure 8.1 to be *correlated,* so that they all converge to define the same issues, parties, and interfaces. Correlated differences created well-articulated issues, easily identifiable parties, obviously necessary interfaces, and representatives who speak for constituencies bounded by multiple criteria. Correlated conflicts of interest create the potential for extreme escalation (e.g., Coser, 1956; Blau, 1974; Alderfer, 1976), and correlated suppression or withdrawal patterns may also be expected to create extremes as well. Relations between the Old Guard and the New Hires at South Side Hospital are illustrative: Cultural differences (black vs. white) and level differences (workers vs. management) converged to produce well-defined and highly charged issues, strongly mobilized parties, the involvement of external organizations allied with the parties, and escalating conflict between party leaders as clearly defined representatives. Figure 8.2 portrays the South Side Hospital Laboratory as simple interfaces correlated to form a complex interface (B). Note how arrows linking the parties converge at the underorganized Old Guard/New Hire interface.

But multiple interfaces do not always converge so closely on the same parties, interface, and issues. Interfaces may be complex in the sense of being affected by several *crosscutting* simple interfaces. Simple interfaces may operate to suppress or to transform each other's effects. At the Riverview Chemical Works, for example, issues between Production and Maintenance were frequently muddied by tensions between labor and management in both departments. Department mobilization was hampered by intense labor and management mobilization in both departments for level interface conflict. Contextual pressure on management from upper management and corporate headquarters, and on workers from the local and international unions focused attention on level differences, not department differences. So problems between departments were subordinated to tensions between levels. Figure 8.2 depicts department and level interfaces at the Riverview Chemical Works as a crosscut complex interface (A). The arrows portraying possible points of conflict in this diagram cut across rather than reinforce each other. Such

A. Crosscut Interface:
Production and Maintenance
at Riverview Chemical Works

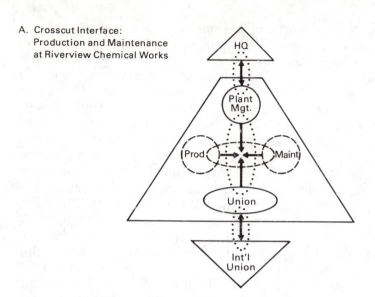

B. Correlated Interface:
Old Guard and New Hires at
South Side Hospital
Laboratory

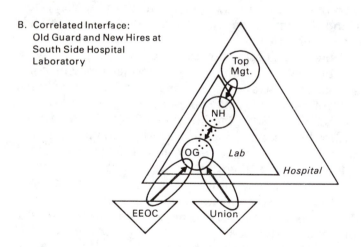

Fig. 8.2. *Correlated and crosscut complex interfaces.*

crosscut interfaces exhibit poorly articulated or even contradictory issues, parties fragmented by inconsistent loyalties, confused interface definition and organization, few or inconsistent contextual interventions. Behavioral dynamics at such interfaces may be episodic or inconsistent, and withdrawal may be particularly common since the parties have other problems that require attention. The Production and Maintenance Departments at Riverview Chemical Works devoted more attention to their department interface only after tensions between management and labor had been reduced.

Analysis Rules of Thumb for Complex Interfaces

The rules of thumb presented here are intended to be heuristics for understanding complex interfaces. They propose tactics for diagnosis applicable to many situations rather than specific guides for each type of complex interface.

   1. *Identify problems and relevant simple interfaces.* Problems take many forms at complex interfaces. Crosscut interfaces produce multiple or contradictory problems, and parties can debate, suppress, or avoid issues that combine tasks, power, or cultural differences in chaotic interactions. At the Riverview Chemical Works, Maintenance and Production representatives debated task responsibilities and performance as well as labor-management relations. Problems could be identified that were relevant to at least two interfaces—department and level—although those problems were not closely connected. Fragmentation of the issues is characteristic of crosscut complex interfaces.

   On the other hand, multiple interfaces can produce over-determined problems of too much or too little conflict, by coalescing issues based in multiple differences. At the South Side Hospital Laboratory, for example, the conflict between the Old Guard and the New Hires initially involved issues related to level and culture differences, and eventually involved organization interfaces as well. Level, culture, and organization differences converged to define a few highly charged issues, in contrast to the many, low-energy issues at the Maintenance/ Production interface.

Thus complex interfaces can produce problems that focus multiple differences into single issues, as at the South Side Hospital Laboratory. Or they can produce a welter of partially contradictory problems, as at the Riverview Chemical Works. Identifying the problem at correlated interfaces may be easier than untangling the simple interfaces that contribute to it. Identifying a primary problem may be more difficult at crosscut interfaces though relevant interfaces may be more visible. In both cases, identifying problems and relevant simple interfaces is an important step toward understanding the situation.

2. *Analyze interactions among simple interfaces.* Interactions among simple interfaces can reinforce or dampen their impacts on representatives' behavior. Complex interfaces that correlate differences can be expected to produce more serious problems of too much or too little conflict. At the South Side Hospital, conflict escalations between the Old Guard and the New Hires grew out of the convergence of culture and level differences. As the conflict continued, external agencies (top management, the local union, external regulators) became supporters of one side or the other. Disputes that might have been handled by the internal grievance system, had they been limited to level differences, became subject to intervention by external agencies because of their racial and religious discrimination overtones. Culture and level differences converged, and so encouraged extremes of party mobilization, interface disorganization, external intervention, and conflict escalation.

When simple interfaces cut across each other, on the other hand, tensions may be reduced at the interface. Level interfaces between workers and management at the Riverview Chemical Works cut across the Production/Maintenance interface. Maintenance and Production workers cooperated to deal with management, and Maintenance and Production managers joined together to cope with the union. Conflict at the Maintenance/Production interface remained relatively mild. Crosscutting interfaces at the Riverview Chemical Works tended to suppress conflict between Maintenance and Production.

Untangling the interaction between simple interfaces can reveal a continuum of complex interface correlations, ranging from completely *correlated* on one pole to completely *crosscut* on the other. Correlated simple interfaces reinforce problems of too much or too little conflict. Extremes of destructive competition, power struggles, or cultural misunderstandings may be expected when parties differ on several correlated dimensions. Extremes of collusion, oppression, or cultural homogeneity may be expected from converging simple interfaces that suppress differences. Extremes of avoidance, abdication, and cultural isolation are likely at interfaces that either correlate withdrawal patterns from several simple interfaces, or that crosscut differences and so distract attention from particular problems. Teasing apart interactions among simple interfaces is central to understanding problems at complex interfaces.

3. *Identify elements and dynamics for change leverage.* Some interface elements (interfaces, parties, representatives, contexts) and some interface dynamics (cycles of representative interaction, patterns of interface development) offer particularly good leverage for conflict management at complex interfaces. How can such critical elements or dynamics be identified? Leverage points for intervention depend on the facts of specific cases, but general guidelines for analyzing those cases direct attention to clues from crosscut or correlated complex interfaces.

Complex interfaces crosscut by multiple differences generate confusion. Fragmented issues, multiple parties, myriad contextual forces, vaguely defined interfaces, and contradictory dynamics compete for analytic attention. Two alternative, potentially contradictory, guidelines can focus analysis in the midst of chaos:

1. Focus on the critical interface and related crosscutting factors.
2. Focus on crosscutting sources of the dominant perceived problem.

The first guideline focuses attention on one interface, and relates other events and forces to understanding elements and dynamics of that interface. This approach offers a conceptual center in the midst of a chaotic whirlwind. It has the advantage of allowing conflict managers to focus on issues they believe important without constant buffeting by the latest and most pressing concerns, but it has the corresponding disadvantage of mobilizing little support if the others involved do not see the same issues as important. At Riverview Chemical Works, for example, this approach would focus on Production-Maintenance Department relations even though most people in the organization were obsessed with labor-management problems.

The second guideline centers attention on concerns of representatives and parties, and analyzes interface elements and dynamics that influence these concerns. This approach follows the energy of people involved. It has the advantage of keeping the analysis relevant to participants in events, though it may subject the analysis to the twists and turns of day-to-day change and confusion. Focusing on the sources of pain in the Riverview Chemical Works would center attention on labor-management relations rather than on the Production-Maintenance interface.

At correlated interfaces the difficulty may be untangling the contributions of different simple interfaces to choose leverage points at which to intervene. Separating the contributions of different facets of a correlated interface is easier if analysts focus on explaining specifics.

1. Analyze correlated precursors of specific interface events.
2. Analyze correlated precursors of interface definition and organization.

Focusing on behavior and events at interfaces directs attention to the representatives' perceptions, communications, and actions that precede problems. Relations between the Old Guard and the New Hires in the South Side Hospital Laboratory, for example, grew from initially noncontroversial decisions to hire new people into major confrontations over abuses of power and racial discrimination. The evolution of individual perceptions and actions that led to confrontations offers clues to elements and dynamics that might be influenced. This approach has the advantage of clarifying participants' perspectives on problems, but it is also vulnerable to participants' distortions of events and stereotypes of each other.

Examining the interface involves attention to the mobilization of parties, the role of contextual forces, and the history of complex interface definition and organization. Analyzing the joint pattern and present levels of party mobilization can produce clues about the impacts of different interface factors. The rapid mobilization of the Old Guard around discrimination issues, for example, shifted Laboratory interface problems from suppression to escalation of conflict. Analyzing contextual history can identify areas for intervention leverage. Past contact between National Health Care and the EEOC had important implications for later relations between the Old Guard and the New Hires. The development of interface definition and organization can also reveal complex interface dynamics. Culture interfaces within the South Side Hospital, for example, provided little precedent or support for dealing with conflicts, so Laboratory tensions produced too little conflict across cultures initially and too much later on. Analysis of interface development offers a larger perspective on issues and events, but it may also seem far removed from the flesh-and-blood realities of events to participants.

4. *Recycle the diagnosis.* The first three rules of thumb move from identifying problems and simple interfaces, to examining their interaction, to identifying leverage points for intervention. The final rule of thumb emphasizes the dynamics of complex interfaces.

Elements of complex interfaces are interdependent, so over time changes in one element will affect others. Change at correlated interfaces may be very rapid, as covert forces produce swift and difficult-to-predict escalation or suppression of conflict. From the perspective of outsiders, for example, the change from little to extreme conflict in the Laboratory at South Side Hospital was very rapid, though the buildup of tension was visible to the Old Guard long before any overt confrontations. The reduction of conflict after the intervention of upper management was almost equally swift. Rapid change at complex interfaces may require continual diagnosis to avoid surprises.

Conflicts curtail the flow of information between and about the parties, so initial diagnoses are often incomplete or distorted.

Multiple cycles of diagnosis and intervention may be required for conflict managers to understand the situation adequately. Alderfer and Brown (1975), for example, found their initial diagnoses of school discipline problems in terms of student relationships led to ineffectual intervention; only after further diagnosis revealed the impact of student-faculty relations on student-student relations could effective interventions be designed.

The diagnostic process itself is often an intervention into interface relations. Discussion of interface problems can provoke new behavior by representatives, even when intervention is not intended. Maintenance managers at the Riverview Chemical Works proposed work with Production after recognizing unproductive conflict within their own department. They made the connection to the department interface as a consequence of diagnosing internal relations.

Recycling the diagnostic process, in short, provides new perspectives generated by change efforts, picks up unintended changes, and can in itself promote representatives' attention to and action on problems. At complex interfaces, recycling diagnoses allows conflict managers to gain fuller understanding of entangled differences which can mean the difference between effective and ineffective intervention.

CHANGING COMPLEX INTERFACES

Changing complex interfaces is often a complex process. This section considers intervention categories relevant to interfaces and suggests rules of thumb for intervenors.

Varieties of Complex Interface Intervention

Several different intervention strategies may be appropriate at complex interfaces, depending on the situation. Three approaches are considered here: (1) simple interface interventions, (2) simple interface interventions designed to promote complex interface changes over time, and (3) complex integrations of simple interface interventions to promote immediate changes at complex interfaces.

Simple interface interventions apply strategies from preceding chapters to problems at complex interfaces. The use of simple interface interventions is appropriate (1) when conflict managers do not recognize the complex nature of the interface, or (2) when complex interface problems are dominated by simple differences. At the Riverview Chemical Works, conflict managers initially focused on the union-management interface as a dominant conflict problem; it was only after success at the union-management interface that Maintenance-Production problems gained more recognition and attention. So changing the level interface at the Works—a simple interface strategy—indirectly called more attention to the department interface, where conflict had been suppressed by the crosscutting level interface.

Simple interface interventions to promote complex change employ interventions from previous chapters in conjunction with complex interface analysis for long-term conflict management. Long-term strategies are appropriate when managers foresee future problems at complex interfaces, and have the time to make simple changes now that will forestall major problems later. Changes in representatives, parties, interfaces, or contextual forces today can forestall the convergence of several simple interface problems whose management would require complex interventions in the future. Had the managers at South Side Hospital foreseen the convergence of level and culture differences in the Laboratory, they could have prevented major problems by minor changes at the level interface (e.g., training and promoting Old Guard members to supervisory roles) or at the culture interface (e.g., hiring minority supervisors). The combination of advance planning and simple interventions can be used to avoid difficult problems posed by correlated interfaces, or to deal sequentially with problems posed by crosscut interfaces.

Complex integrations of simple interface interventions may be required for promoting immediate change when multiple issues and correlated differences combine to define difficult-to-resolve problems. Initially the level-culture interface at the South Side Hospital Laboratory suppressed conflict through a combination of supervisory behavior and institutional discrimination. More open conflict was catalyzed by representatives' initiatives (e.g., personal attacks), appeals to external regulatory agencies, and the balance between managerial power and fear of adverse publicity. These events "evened the odds" between Old Guard and New Hires, and drew managerial attention to Old Guard concerns at the price of considerable disruption. Too little conflict in the Laboratory was almost instantly succeeded by too much, and simple interface interventions were no longer enough to deal with the interacting issues and differences that underlay the conflict. Consultant interventions that dealt with task and power issues without enough attention to culture differences failed. Eventually interventions that included symbolic recognition of cultural discrimination by top management, organizational commitment to improving opportunities for minorities, senior management attention to developing performance standards with Laboratory staff, and senior management participation in performance appraisal combined to provide a package responsive to many facets of the complex interface. Substantial changes for the organization as a whole and specific alterations in Laboratory management were needed to reduce conflict in the Laboratory.

At complex interfaces, as elsewhere, "An ounce of prevention is worth a pound of cure." Simple interface interventions solve problems posed by complex but crosscut interfaces and reveal the existence of previously unrecognized complexities. Simple interface interventions can also be utilized to prevent problems at complex interfaces. But complex interfaces with correlated differences may require combinations of interventions that deal simultaneously with many different problems.

Intervention Rules of Thumb for Complex Interfaces

These rules of thumb are general guides for planning and implementing interventions at complex interfaces rather than detailed instructions. Specific plans must be based on particular situations and combinations of interfaces.

1. *Match intervenors' resources to complex interface diagnoses.* The resources of conflict managers must be appropriate to the situation if interventions are to have a reasonable chance of improving complex interfaces. Conflict managers must establish a minimally credible relationship with the parties, and their knowledge, skills, and influence resources must be relevant to interface problems.

The credibility of conflict managers is related to their organizational positions and personal characteristics. Representatives or members of primary parties may have more credibility within their party than outside it, and so be most effective at intervening to reshape party interests and characteristics. Third parties, such as organizational superiors or outside mediators, may be credible with both parties and so better positioned to influence interfaces directly. The credibility of conflict managers may be substantially enhanced if they are perceived to have skills or characteristics relevant to the multiple issues posed at complex interfaces: Recognized technical expertise in both specialties is an important asset to "integrators" at departmental interfaces (Lawrence and Lorsch, 1967), multicultural awareness and composition of intervenor teams may be critical at culture interfaces (Alderfer et al., 1980), and an independent power base may be critical for conflict managers at level interfaces (Gillers, 1980). Credibility at complex interfaces depends on many attributes of conflict managers.

Conflict managers may also require special resources to understand and influence the situation. Department interfaces may require technical expertise from both departments to understand the issues and promote appropriate changes; level interfaces may require sufficient power in intervenors to balance relations between parties and to limit escalation or suppression of conflict; culture interfaces may require intervenors' understanding of both cultures and cross-cultural communication skills to manage misunderstandings and strong feelings at the interface. Complex interfaces, whether correlated or crosscut, need combinations of information, skills, and knowledge in conflict managers that fit their particular mixes of problems and differences.

Conflict managers whose resources do not match their diagnoses have several options. Often the best, but not always the most feasible, is to find more relevant resources. Another option is to choose not to intervene, particularly if unsuccessful interventions are likely to make the situation worse. A third option is to go ahead and intervene without some relevant resources, paying close attention to problems predictable from the resource-diagnosis mismatch. The consultants at the South Side Hospital Laboratory, for example, recognized and tried to increase consultant resources appropriate for intervening at a racially polarized interface—but the recognition came too late to be of much use. Recognizing mismatches at least sensitizes conflict managers to potential problems before they become unmanageable.

2. *Plan to change interface convergence.* Correlated interfaces are particularly vulnerable to escalation and suppression of conflict and generate issues sharply defined by the convergence of multiple differences. Crosscut interfaces, in contrast, are plagued by withdrawal and the proliferation of confused and contradictory issues based in divergent interfaces. In either case, productive conflict at complex interfaces may be catalyzed by interventions that realign simple interfaces to decrease convergence at correlated interfaces, or to increase convergence at crosscut interfaces.

Realigning correlated interfaces involves redefining some simple interfaces to cut across others. To return to the example of the South Side Hospital Laboratory, the convergence of culture and level differences at the Old Guard/New Hire interface could have been reduced by promoting Old Guard members or recruiting minority supervisors and so recomposing the parties. Or inflammatory contextual pressures could have been reduced by top management support for Old Guard positions and union understanding of New Hire dilemmas. In the long run, management did support the Old Guard by accepting external findings of discrimination, by acting to reduce institutional discrimination, and by providing more management presence in the Laboratory. Intervening to realign converging differences that define a correlated interface can reduce potentials for multiply determined conflict escalation or suppression.

Realigning crosscut interfaces requires redefining simple interfaces so that they are *more* correlated. When party energies and resources are diffused into unrelated or contradictory problems, increased convergence of simple interfaces can focus problems and make more resources available for their management. Resources of the Ghetto Development Corporation were redirected to interfaces with the Establishment and the ghetto community by focusing Corporation and Community Services Administration attention on those interfaces. The reformulation of Corporation strategy emphasized the interdependence of CSA, business, and community interfaces if the Corporation were to succeed, and raised the stakes of interaction at the latter two. Realigning crosscut interfaces can formulate issues more clearly and focus resources for managing them.

   3. *Alter critical elements or dynamics.* What elements are critical is always to some extent an empirical question—there is no substitute for diagnosing complex interfaces to illuminate representatives' actions, party attributes, contextual forces, or interface characteristics that are suitable targets for intervention. But there are theoretical reasons for choosing to alter some aspects of complex interfaces before others.

   At crosscut complex interfaces, multiple differences produce a chaotic variety of competing parties, interfaces, and issues. This variety offers opportunities for dealing with simple interfaces and issues that influence each other sequentially, rather than struggling with multiply determined problems fostered by convergence of several differences. Two guidelines are worth considering:

1. Alter elements and dynamics critical to focal interface divergence.
2. Alter elements and dynamics critical to parties and representatives.

   The first guideline involves change to alter targets that are central in intervenors' diagnoses of the complex interface. This approach puts the diagnosis at the center of intervention activity. The consultants' concern with relations at the Riverview Production-Maintenance interface predated the managers' concern (because of attention to labor-management relations). Work began within the parties to clarify party understanding of interface issues as a prelude to bringing representatives together at an interface not yet recognized as critical. Diagnostic understanding of the situation permits coordinated and conceptually coherent interventions to promote convergence of crosscutting interfaces, but those interventions may encounter resistance from parties and representatives who do not share the diagnosis.

The second guideline emphasizes changing interface elements and dynamics regarded as critical by participants. This approach relies on the concerns of parties and representatives to give direction to intervention efforts. Management interventions at Riverview Chemical Works focused on improving labor-management relations without much attention to the department interface. Guiding interventions by participants' concerns has the advantage of mobilizing representative and party energies for change, but it can also focus interventions at points where they are less effective in producing long-term convergence.

The two guidelines are not necessarily contradictory. They supplement each other when conflict managers' diagnoses are understood and accepted as valid by interface representatives and parties. Declining tensions between Riverview Chemical Works labor and management resulted in consultant and party agreement about the importance of department interface changes and the development of joint activities to produce these changes.

Correlated complex interfaces offer different challenges, for converging differences reinforce definitions of parties, interfaces, and issues to promote escalation or suppression of conflict. Interventions often must deal simultaneously with multiple differences. Relevant guidelines for correlated interface intervention include:

1. Alter convergent representative interaction patterns.
2. Alter interface, party, and context developments that increase interface correlation.

Correlated interfaces are vulnerable to multiply determined escalation or suppression of conflict, particularly when power and culture differences are involved. Interventions can decrease the convergence of representatives' perceptions, communications, and actions and so considerably reduce correlated interface problems. Patterns of conflict suppression in the South Side Hospital Laboratory were undercut by increasingly alienated and militant Old Guard perceptions and actions with respect to New Hires. Management's willingness to settle resulting lawsuits out of court recognized—at least symbolically—the justice of Old Guard grievances, and so set the stage for reducing correlated perceptions, communications, and actions on both sides. Interventions that untangle the correlated differences that have an impact on representatives' perceptions, communications, and actions can encourage more productive conflict among them.

The second guideline emphasizes interventions to alter the interplay of interfaces, parties, and contextual factors around correlated differences. Untangling attributes of correlated interface definition and organization, for example, involves dealing with some issues before others. Since culture and level differences often produce more serious problems of interface definition and organization, interventions to balance power asymmetries or to clarify cultural misunderstandings may be needed prior to interventions to resolve task problems associated with department interfaces. Issues between Old Guard and New Hires, for example, were difficult to discuss before regulatory agency support for the Old Guard balanced power differences between the parties.

Party mobilization at complex interfaces is often asymmetrical. Lower parties and upper parties often feel threatened and mobilize at different times, and then surprise each other. Cultural party mobilization is difficult when party members are dispersed throughout the organization, and sudden mobilizations may spring from events significant to one party but not the other. Surprise challenges from newly mobilized parties can touch off escalation or suppression. Interventions that coordinate party mobilization can reduce surprises and encourage effective voice at complex interfaces. Correlated level and culture differences sometimes produce unmobilized parties that are hard-to-resist targets for suppression. Strong leaders and mobilizing events can alter lower party passivity at such interfaces, as the emergence of the militant Old Guard at the South Side Hospital Laboratory dramatically illustrates.

Finally, correlated interfaces are often invaded by external forces, given lower party interest in recruiting external allies and the affiliations between cultural parties and external groups. Managing complex interfaces requires special attention to shaping contextual interventions to reduce convergence of multiple differences. At least three contextual interventions influenced events between Old Guard and New Hires: Regulatory agencies adjusted the power balance within the Laboratory by supporting the Old Guard, outside consultants clarified problems and signaled top management concern, and upper management altered organizational policies to reduce institutional discrimination and to modify abuses of power in the Laboratory. External interventions catalyzed change in multiply determined escalation.

4. *Follow up initial interventions to support changes.* Interface problems are rooted in an ongoing stream of forces and events. That stream may not be diverted by one or even several interventions. Continued monitoring and support by conflict managers is often required, particularly at complex interfaces, to prevent return to old or rapid progression to new problems.

At crosscut interfaces, conflict management activities can solve problems at some interfaces only to produce new difficulties—sometimes unexpected problems at previously unrecognized interfaces. Conflict managers must deal with new problems as they emerge, as well as cope with pressures that reproduce old issues. At the Riverview Chemical Works, as has been pointed out, successful interventions at the labor-management interface preceded the emergence of new problems between Production and Maintenance. Initial interventions at the Production-Maintenance interface set off a series of activities—from team-building within the parties to interface meetings at various levels to structural redesign of the organization—that built on previous work. Sequences of interventions at crosscut interfaces can be used to handle conflict problems whose characteristics become clearer as change activity and rediagnosis proceed.

At correlated interfaces, conflict management activities often face conservative forces that cancel out initial interventions, or rapid changes that produce new problems. At overorganized interfaces that suppress conflict, countervailing forces that cancel out initial interventions are common. Early challenges to institutional racism at the South Side Hospital, for example, culminated in Hospital agreement to substantial organizational changes—which were never implemented. Overorganized interfaces often require raising issues again and continually chipping away at factors that maintain problems. On the other hand, interventions at underorganized complex interfaces can have large short-term effects but never create sufficient organization to prevent future escalation or withdrawal. Once the overorganized interface within the Laboratory was blown apart by the Old Guard/New Hire conflict, each new event provided another occasion for further escalation. Resolving specific disputes did not resolve the more generalized tensions until longer-term attention was guaranteed by new structures and upper management involvement.

Problems at complex interfaces require continuing attention. Interventions can be damped out by systemic reactions that return the interface to its original state, or they can set in motion dynamics that pose new opportunities and problems. Conflict management requires ongoing diagnosis and action, not "quick fixes."

Figure 8.3 summarizes the rules of thumb for analyzing and managing conflict at complex interfaces articulated in the last two sections. The central column lists the general rules of thumb. The column on the left lists the steps appropriate to analysis and intervention at crosscut interfaces, when the rules of thumb suggested are specific to such interfaces. The column on the right lists rules of thumb specific to correlated interfaces. The solid arrows indicate the linear progression of steps that would be appropriate to a logical and orderly world that responds predictably to careful planning. The dashed arrows reflect the importance of continuing to analyze and intervene, particularly since

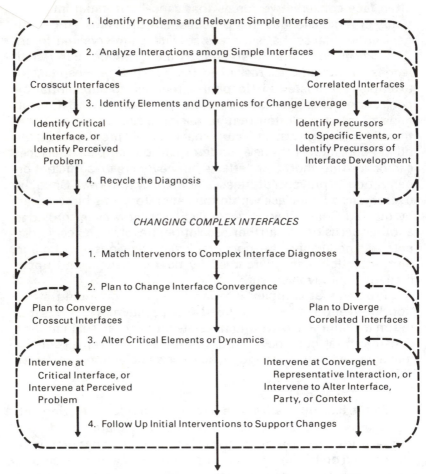

Fig. 8.3. *Conflict management at complex interfaces: a flow chart.*

events at interfaces frequently do not seem to follow the orderly sequences envisioned in intervenors' plans.

SUMMARY

In this chapter I have reviewed simple interfaces based on department, level, culture, and organization differences, and then discussed briefly the complications posed by their combination in various forms of complex interfaces. The chapter is focused particularly on differences within organizations and I consider organization interfaces primarily as they influence combinations of department, level, and culture interfaces.

Analysis of complex interfaces involves examining the interactions among simple interfaces. Simple interfaces can combine in myriad ways, notably along a dimension anchored by completely correlated interfaces at one pole and completely crosscut interfaces at the other. Correlated interfaces converge multiple differences to define the same parties, issues, and interfaces; crosscut interfaces define multiple issues, parties, contexts, and interfaces on the basis of uncorrelated differences. Correlated interfaces often display extremes of conflict escalation or suppression; crosscut interfaces are more vulnerable to avoidance and withdrawal. Rules of thumb for analyzing complex interfaces include (1) identifying relevant simple interfaces, (2) analyzing their interactions, (3) identifying critical elements, and (4) recycling diagnostic activity to track new developments.

Interventions for complex interfaces range from altering simple interfaces, to altering simple interfaces for long-term impacts on complex interfaces, to combinations of simple interface interventions designed to change several aspects of correlated interfaces simultaneously. Rules of thumb for intervening at complex interfaces include (1) matching intervenors' resources to interface diagnoses, (2) planning to change interface convergence, (3) altering critical elements and dynamics, and (4) following up interventions to manage countervailing forces or emergent problems.

Complex interfaces are difficult to analyze and still more difficult to reliably influence. But they are common sources of intractable conflict problems in organizations, and so demand close attention by conflict managers.

Interventions and Intervenors

9

This final chapter focuses on intervention, and particularly on choosing interventions and intervenors likely to be effective for different interface problems. It is a review of earlier chapters and provides general recommendations for conflict managers planning interventions.

First the case studies discussed in earlier chapters are reviewed, focusing on the intervenors and their interventions. The following section examines intervention options described in Chapter 3 as they influenced events in the cases. The third section considers positions from which conflict managers may intervene, and the merits of different intervenors for different conflict problems. The fourth section links the analysis of preceding sections in general rules of thumb for intervention planning. In the final section I summarize the chapter, and comment on the future of interfaces and conflict management.

INTERVENING AT INTERFACES: A REVIEW

Four cases of interface conflict have been discussed in some detail as illustrations of simple and complex interfaces. This section reviews these cases to emphasize the interventions of different individuals and groups that influenced events at the interfaces.

Chapter 4 describes the *department interface* between Production and Maintenance at the Riverview Chemical Works, where interdepartmental bickering and withdrawal contributed to increased costs and plant safety problems. Initial interventions encouraged new perceptions of the interface: External consultants raised questions about conflict, and improvements in labor-management relations had the side effect of raising awareness of interdepartmental bickering. Team-building workshops, which brought external consultants and department members together to examine work relations internal to departments, focused attention on interdepartment relations. As a consequence, external consultants met with managers from both departments to diagnose interdepartment relations and to plan changes. Subsequently, third parties from within the Works met for similar purposes with mechanics and operators. These meetings improved communications and reduced bickering between the parties, but outside contextual pressures from market demand and corporate requirements increased problems at the interface. Works management, internal consultants, and the parties concerned jointly developed a team management structure that integrated most of the Maintenance staff into Production departments.

The *level interface* between workers and management at the College City Transit Authority was described in Chapter 5. Support from the larger context for a Quality of Work Committee helped create a viable level interface. Federal funds provided resources for the Committee, and external consultants offered training and process consultation that reframed perceptions and redirected the behavior of work and management representatives. Committee representatives developed their own organization, evolved mutual trust, and undertook cooperative projects that astonished their colleagues. The Committee eventually took a third party role to recruit an external consultant for a prenegotiations workshop for union and management bargaining committees. The workshop encouraged new perceptions and expanded communications at the collective bargaining interface, and encouraged representatives to negotiate formal ground rules to govern their coming negotiations. In these negotiations the parties experimented with innovative approaches to bargaining, such as using consultants to learn more about the bargaining process and structural rearrangements to explore complex issues in subgroups. Under pressure from their constituencies, representatives deadlocked and tested each other's strength in a short work stoppage, but a proposed settlement by a state-appointed fact finder was quickly accepted.

In Chapter 6 tensions between the Old Guard and the New Hires at the South Side Hospital illustrated *culture interfaces*. Although conflict between majority and minority groups in the hospital had always been suppressed, tensions between the Old Guard and the New Hires in the Laboratory escalated rapidly in a series of "insubordinations" and "abuses of power" by their representatives. The Old Guard's success in enlisting contextual support from regulatory agencies combined with the failure of top management to implement previous agreements to reduce power differences in the Laboratory and set the stage for open conflict. External consultants sought to improve communications and solve specific problems in a series of meetings, but opposition from a union representative blew apart the fragile truce between the parties. Old Guard challenges to consultant credibility resulted in the introduction of a minority consultant, but the expanded consultant team only reproduced in microcosm the same conflict that plagued the Laboratory. Ultimately, organizationwide changes to reduce institutional discrimination combined with active upper management participation in Laboratory affairs to reduce Laboratory tensions.

Finally, Chapter 7 described relations at several *organization interfaces* of the Ghetto Development Corporation. Challenges from the Community Services Administration representatives forced the Corporation staff to examine their mission and their interfaces with CSA, the local ghetto community, and the city Establishment. The Corporation engaged consultants to help reformulate its strategy and structure, resulting in reframed perspectives on the corporate mission. It also reallocated resources to upgrade the staff and to provide for more external consultants. New behavior by President and staff generated more connections with the local business community. At about the same time new Board officers training for all Board members by outside consultants encouraged better links to the ghetto community. The Corporation redefined its mission and became more aware of its external dependencies. In addition, more emphasis was placed on the role of the Housing Division, and innovative proposals for new ventures were presented to CSA. The new negotiations with CSA produced a longer-than-usual funding cycle and new perceptions of the Corporation in Washington.

Table 9.1 summarizes interventions and intervenors in the four cases. Actions taken by different intervenors are listed in rough chronological order for each interface. In parentheses after each action are descriptions of their primary impacts, whether on behavior, perceptions, resources, or underlying structures. These interventions and intervenors are the focus of attention in the next two sections.

TABLE 9.1

Interventions and intervenors in cases

Department Interface: Riverview Chemical Production and Maintenance Departments

Outside consultants direct attention to department interface (perceptions)

Consultants and departments do internal team-building (behavior, perceptions)

Consultants and department managers meet to discuss interface (behavior, perceptions)

Operators, mechanics, and internal consultants meet to discuss joint work (behavior, perceptions)

Assistant work manager, internal consultants, department representatives discuss team management redesign (perceptions, resources)

Organizational implements team management design (resources, structures)

Level Interfaces: College City Transit Authority Management and Workers

Quality of Work Committee Interface:

   Contractual agreement to have a joint Quality of Work Committee (resources, structure)

   External federal government funds to support Committee (resources)

TABLE 9.1   (continued)
Interventions and intervenors in cases

External consultants train and assist Committee members to
manage initial conflicts (behavior, perceptions)
Representatives develop trust, ground rules, cooperative projects (behavior, perceptions, structure)
Collective Bargaining Interface:
Quality of Work Committee suggest prenegotiations workshop
(behavior, perceptions)
External consultant and representatives share information and
negotiate ground rules for collective bargaining in workshop
(perceptions, structure)
Representatives negotiate by new ground rules and invent
new bargaining procedures and structures (behavior,
structures)
Upper management and rank and file join strength-testing
strike (perceptions)
State fact finder offers jointly acceptable compromise position
(behavior, perceptions)

Culture Interface: South Side Hospital Laboratory Old Guard and New Hires

Representatives are insubordinate and coercive (behavior,
resources)
Old Guard representatives file grievances and external lawsuits
(behavior)
External regulatory agencies settle suit with management out of
court (behavior, resources)
External consultants hold information-sharing meetings with
parties (perceptions)
Union representatives challenge joint meeting (behavior,
perceptions)
External consultants seek to build credibility with Old Guard
(behavior, perceptions)
Upper management revises organizational policies relevant to
minorities (perceptions, structures)
Immediate superior works with Laboratory staff to develop
and implement unbiased performance appraisal process (perceptions, structure)

*Organization Interfaces: Ghetto Development Corporation and Its
Environment*

With Community Services Administration:
President and external consultants discuss future strategy
(perceptions)

TABLE 9.1   (continued)
Interventions and intervenors in cases

President complies with CSA demands about staff, Board, re-
port (behavior)
External consultants diagnose and discuss internal and exter-
nal challenges with organization (perceptions)
President and staff reformulate priorities and roles (resources,
structure)
President and CSA representatives negotiate longer funding
cycle (perceptions, resources)
With the ghetto community:
External consultants train Board members (perceptions)
Board elections bring new officers to power (resources)
President negotiates improved relations with new Board
Chairman (behavior, perceptions)
New proposal emphasizes Housing Division's good relations
with community (resources)
With the city Establishment:
Interim consultant and new Business Development Director
improve Corporation credibility (perceptions)
Increased President visibility and "politicking" with Estab-
lishment (behavior, perceptions)
New Corporate emphasis on diversified funding from new
sources (behavior, resources)

INTERVENTIONS

How can conflict managers choose among the array of interventions discussed in previous chapters? In this section we reexamine the intervention strategies described in Chapter 3 in terms of
the four cases and how they can be used in different situations.

In Chapter 3 conflict management interventions fell into four
categories: (1) redirecting behavior, (2) reframing perceptions,
(3) reallocating resources, and (4) realigning underlying structures. All four strategies were used in all four cases, albeit some
more than others.

Interventions to *redirect behavior* include redefining issues,
raising alternative solutions, altering patterns of communication

between the parties, or revising the immediate behavior of representatives. Efforts to redefine the issues were quite common in these cases: Interdepartmental discussions at the Riverview Chemical Works redefined issues that produced conflict, and meetings of the College City Transit Authority Quality of Work Committee shifted attention to concerns quite different from their initial bones of contention. New alternatives emerged in several cases: The Transit Authority prenegotiations workshop led to new ideas from both sides, and the Ghetto Development Corporation proposed a new conception of its mission to the Community Services Administration. Communications patterns between Riverview Chemical Production and Maintenance Departments and between Ghetto Development Corporation and the city Establishment were all altered by interventions. The tactics of the representatives changed substantially in several cases: South Side Hospital management adopted a conciliatory stance to the Laboratory Old Guard, and the Riverview Chemical Maintenance Department proposed a new initiative to their Production Department. Behavior redirecting interventions were relatively common (see Table 9.1).

Redirecting behavior has several advantages. It immediately influences patterns of interaction among the representatives by redefining the issues and alternatives, by altering communications, or by changing tactics. As a result, successful intervention can have a rapid impact on problematic conflict. The major requirements are the skills and imagination of the intervenor; behavior redirection can be relatively inexpensive when these resources are available. Well-chosen behavior changes can interrupt cycles of representative interaction, and so lead to positive changes that greatly outweigh the costs of the intervention. Interventions to redirect behavior are particularly effective when the interface and the context limit conflict problems, as at department interfaces. On the other hand, unskilled or poorly timed intervention can reinforce problematic cycles of interaction and make a bad situation worse. When structural characteristics of the interface and the larger context promote problems between representatives, as at cultural and level interfaces, focusing on interface behavior can divert attention from more fundamental problems. Even successful interventions that redirect behavior in the short term can be washed out in the long run if structural factors do not complement new patterns of interaction among representatives.

Interventions to *reframe perspectives* include reformulating party interests, altering unrealistic stereotypes, changing perspectives on the situation, and educating parties about the dynamics of conflict. Discussions between Riverview Chemical Production and Maintenance representatives, for example, reemphasized their common interests. The appointment of a new Business Development Director improved the Ghetto Development Corporation's credibility in the local business community, and altered negative stereotypes about the competence of its staff. Discussions at the Maintenance-Production interface at Riverview Chemical Works improved understanding in both departments about situational pressures on each. By participating in the prenegotiations workshop at the Transit Authority, union and management bargaining committees learned about the dynamics of escalating conflict and their own contributions to it.

Interventions to reframe perspectives depend on how new information is used and interpreted, if they are to change participants' interests, stereotypes, and understanding of the situation and its dynamics. Such information is often available at relatively low cost. Changing perspectives is a particularly powerful intervention when unrealistic stereotypes have strong emotional overtones, such as stereotypes associated with symbolic issues at culture interfaces, or stereotypes of upper and lower parties at level interfaces.

Reframing perspectives can influence the interaction among representatives or the interplay of parties, context, and interface. Consequently, this kind of intervention can be used for short-term impacts or longer-term changes in interface definition and organization. It was the most commonly used intervention (see Table 9.1).

But interventions that reframe perspectives can be undermined by cycles of behavior and communication that are inconsistent with new perceptions. New perceptions that are not complemented by changed behavior and communication do not last.

Changed perspectives can also be undercut by unchanging pressures from parties and the larger context.

Interventions to *reallocate resources* change the character of the interdependence among the parties, or alter the resources available for managing conflict. When Community Services Administration reporting requirements were relaxed for the Ghetto Development Corporation, for example, more resources became available at the Establishment and ghetto community interfaces. In the South Side Hospital Laboratory, Old Guard and New Hire representatives, upper management, union leaders, external consultants, and many party members all committed much time and energy to managing conflict at the culture interface.

Resource reallocations can influence the representatives' interactions relatively rapidly, or the development of the interface over the long term. Resource reallocation intervention requires resources, so an intervenor's control over relevant resources is prerequisite to the intervention. Resource reallocations are often relatively expensive and relatively visible to the rest of the organization. Changing resource allocations can have a powerful impact when the resources are linked to issues of importance. Resources for task accomplishment are central at department interfaces; resources relevant to power differences are critical at level interfaces; resources related to culturally symbolic issues are crucial at culture interfaces.

Finally, interventions to *realign underlying structural forces* include redefining boundaries, altering their permeability, revising formal rules and procedures, renegotiating informal norms and values, and refocusing organizational incentives that influence conflict. The organizationwide shift to team management at the Riverview Chemical Works, for example, redefined departmental boundaries to encourage interaction and conflict lower down in the organization. The creation of a Quality of Work Committee at the Transit Authority encouraged more permeable boundaries around management and worker levels. The development of new performance appraisal standards and procedures at the South Side Hospital created tighter interface organization and more incentives for joint work. The Transit Authority prenegotiations workshop encouraged shared informal norms and understandings to regulate future conflicts between bargaining committees. Structural realignment was the least frequently employed intervention strategy (see Table 9.1).

Realigning structural forces alters interface definition and organization by influencing the interplay of interface, parties, and context. The impact of structural change is often not immediately obvious, but emerges instead over the long run. Structural changes require that intervenors possess the formal authority and the informal influence to alter boundaries, rules, norms, and reward systems. Changes in such fundamental underlying factors is typically expensive, in terms of both the effort involved in producing the change and the organizational disruption that occurs as a consequence. Underlying structures constrain and guide events at the interface, and new structures can complement interventions to interrupt representative interaction dynamics. Structural changes are particularly appropriate when forces from the organizational and larger contexts exacerbate interface problems, as at level interfaces and culture interfaces.

Table 9.2 summarizes some important intervention characteristics. These are approximations rather than specific guidelines. Conflict managers can use the table to assess the costs and gains of intervention, keeping their specific situation in mind.

INTERVENORS

Who can intervene to manage conflict at problematic interfaces? Table 9.1 lists many actors who contributed to managing conflict in the cases, inevitably an incomplete catalogue of the people who influenced events. But interest in outcomes of conflict at interfaces is not always linked to positions or resources for effective intervention. Much attention has been paid in the conflict management literature to the roles of third party intervenors (e.g., Young, 1967; Walton, 1967, 1969; Laue and Cormick, 1978; Goldman, 1980). Actually, conflict managers may intervene from many positions, providing they are aware of the potentials and limitations created by their skills and roles.

The influence of would-be conflict managers depends largely on their access to relevant individuals and groups, on their information about the conflict, on their credibility with intervention targets, and on their resources for undertaking interventions. *Access* to individuals and groups and *information* about
the conflict depend on the position of the manager: The role of
representative, for example, often provides access to and information about other representatives that is not available to external allies. Their *credibility* with intervention targets depends on
perceived interests and past track records: Conflict managers
with interests vested in the "other side," or with histories of
partisan activity are less influential than managers who are on
"our side" or who are neutral. Finally, a conflict manager's *resources* for intervening may be more or less congruent with the
interventions chosen: Redirecting behavior requires behavioral
skills and imagination that can be used to redefine issues and
alternatives, improve communications, or alter tactics; reframing perspectives involves persuasive use of new information and
interpretations; reallocating resources requires control over resources relevant to interface issues; realigning structures depends on formal or informal influence to change parameters
underlying the interface. Conflict managers in different positions
differ in information, access, credibility, and resources for intervening. Seven alternative positions for intervenors are considered here: (1) representatives, (2) party leaders, (3) party members, (4) hierarchical superiors, (5) organizational third parties,
(6) external allies, and (7) external third parties.

Representatives often alter the course of interface conflict,
usually by altering their interactions or by changing their own
parties. The initiative of Maintenance managers for a joint meeting with Production managers, for example, set the stage for
better relations between them. Parties at the Transit Authority
were reassured by each other's willingness to participate in a
prenegotiations workshop, and representatives' restraint in discussions of sensitive issues permitted them to negotiate mutually agreeable ground rules. More active "politicking" by the
Ghetto Development Corporation President improved relations

TABLE 9.2
Intervention characteristics

INTERVENTION	TARGET DYNAMICS	RESOURCES REQUIRED	ADVANTAGES/ DISADVANTAGES
Redirect behavior ● issues ● alternatives ● communications ● tactics	Representative interaction (quick impact)	Skills Imagination (low cost)	With good timing can interrupt cycles of problematic interaction Effective when interface and context moderate conflict problems (e.g., at department interfaces) Vulnerable to continuing cycles and structural pressures
Reframe perspectives ● interests ● stereotypes ● situations ● dynamics	Representative interaction (quick impact) Interface development (slower impact)	Information Interpretations Persuasion skills (low cost)	Can alter highly charged perspectives (e.g., at level, culture interfaces) Complements other interventions Vulnerable to continuing cycles and structural pressures

Reallocate resources • interdependence • conflict management resources	Representative interaction (quick impact) Interface development (slower impact)	Resource control (moderate cost)	Can match resources to central issues (e.g., task, power, culture issues) Creates press for long-term solutions Relatively visible and expensive
Realign structural forces • boundaries • permeability • rules, procedures • norms, values • incentives	Interface development (slower impact)	Formal, informal influence (moderate to high cost)	Complements changes in interaction dynamics by altering long-term pressures (e.g., at level, culture interfaces) Creates press for long-term solutions Expensive and disruptive to other parts of system

at several organization interfaces. Actions and initiatives by interface representatives can directly alter patterns of representative interaction, and change the development of interface organization and definition as well.

Representatives have excellent access to and information about themselves and other representatives, and usually they also have good access to and information about their own parties. Their credibility rests on interests and past behavior perceived by others: Representatives may have to trade off credibility with their parties for credibility with other representatives, particularly if there is much conflict. Representatives caught between their party and other representatives can lose their influence with both. The representative role allows direct impact on interface events to representatives with appropriate skills and information, but potential conflicts of interest at the interface can erode that advantage.

Party leaders have opportunities for influencing party perspectives, party resource allocations, and party structural arrangements. They can also influence representatives' actions. Party leaders' willingness to experiment with the prenegotiations workshop at the Transit Authority made that event possible, and signaled that representatives who reduced conflict would have party support. The Ghetto Development Corporation President reorganized its mission, personnel, and resources and so altered pressures for interaction at organization interfaces.

Party leaders can have access to their representatives and to the organizational context as well as to their parties. They are typically less informed than representatives about the conflict, but more able to influence parties and organizational contexts. At important interfaces party leaders often double as representatives. The President of the Ghetto Development Corporation combined representative and leader roles to build better relations at organization interfaces. The credibility of party leaders depends on party interests and past behavior. The leaders of dispersed and undefined groups, such as unmobilized cultural parties, may have difficulty controlling their representatives or influencing the organizational context.

Party members can also, in some circumstances, influence events at the interfaces. The rank and file of the Transit Workers Union pressed its leadership to test the strength of management, and so encouraged a symbolic work stoppage, even though negotiations had been unexpectedly productive. It is doubtful that Old Guard members would have accepted a rapprochement between Ms. Grey and Ms. Williams, even if the two leaders had been willing to bury the hatchet.

Party members' positions offer access to other party members and to their representatives, though their information about conflict problems is likely to be more restricted than that of the party leaders. Their credibility with intervention targets depends on their party history and party perceptions of their interests. Party member influence is largely based on their personal characteristics and their informal role in the party; they are more often influential in parties that are highly mobilized for power struggles or cultural polarizations.

Hierarchical superiors can intervene to alter interface problems that impact organizational concerns. The Assistant Works Manager at the Riverview Chemical Works, for example, was the primary architect of the organizational redesign of the Production-Maintenance interface. Top management settlement of Old Guard lawsuits, and subsequent organizationwide changes to reduce institutional discrimination, were important prerequisites to interventions by upper level managers within the South Side Hospital Laboratory.

Hierarchical superiors are organizationally positioned for access to both representatives, both parties, the interface itself, the organizational context, and sometimes the larger context as well. But the rank that grants them legitimate access to events at the interface can simultaneously undercut the quality of information they receive: They are, after all, subject to the restriction of information characteristic of level interfaces. The credibility of hierarchical superiors depends on their past activity and perceived interests: Superiors often have good credibility at department interfaces but serious credibility problems at level interfaces, where they are seen to be aligned with the upper party.

Superiors have the formal authority to reallocate resources or realign underlying structures. But formal authority that appears biased in favor of culturally or hierarchically dominant parties can worsen problems at complex interfaces.

In some situations *organizational third parties* are effective forces for conflict management. Much attention has recently been paid to "integrator" roles and departments that help manage differences between departments (Lawrence and Lorsch, 1967; Galbraith, 1973), and similar experiments have been launched to deal with level and cultural differences (Alderfer, 1977a). The internal consultants at the Riverview Chemical Works played an important role in meetings between operators and mechanics, and the Quality of Work Committee sponsored the prenegotiations workshop between bargaining committees at the Transit Authority.

Organizational third parties can have access to both representatives, the interface, the parties, and the organizational context. Organizational third parties without formal authority over representatives or parties can gain information denied to superiors. Their credibility depends on their information and expertise, their interest in mutually satisfactory solutions, and their resistance to co-optation by either side. Neutral organizational position, links to resources and authority, and personal skills in managing conflict are all important resources for organizational third parties.

Sometimes, *external allies* are critical to altering the course of interface events. "Activists" mobilize party resources, and "advocates" represent them in negotiations (Laue and Cormick, 1978). The Old Guard would have had less leverage over the New Hires without support from external regulatory agencies and support from minority clienteles of the South Side Hospital. The Ghetto Development Corporation learned about organization interfaces and reformulated its mission with help from volunteer consultants committed to its work in the ghetto community.

External allies have access to allied parties and their representatives, and sometimes they influence the larger context as well. But their information about the situation is limited by their one-sided access, and their credibility with other parties to the interface is severely limited by their commitments and perceived interests. External allies offer information and support resources that can be important when interface odds are unevenly balanced within the organization: The Old Guard would have had difficulty in being heard without the support of the regulatory agency and the union in the South Side Hospital.

Finally, *external third parties* can play an important role at interfaces. "Third party peacemakers" (Walton, 1967, 1969) facilitate improved interaction processes; "researchers" provide valid information to both sides, "enforcers" enable joint obedience to rules, and "mediators" encourage effective negotiations (Laue and Cormick, 1978). External consultants drew attention to the Production-Maintenance interface at Riverview Chemical Works and helped manage initial interface meetings. External resources helped create and train the Quality of Work Committee and managed the prenegotiations workshop at the Transit Authority.

External third parties can gain access to both representatives, both parties, the interface, the organizational context, and even external forces. Their information about the situation, depending on how wide their access, may range from very restricted to very broad. The credibility of external third parties also depends on history and perceived interests, so bringing in such parties must be delicately handled to preserve their credibility. Joint control of payment by the interested parties, for example, is a common strategy for preserving third party credibility. Third parties from outside can bring resources—skills, information, influence with organizational and external contexts—tailored to the problems, though the costs of recruiting such specialized conflict managers may be high.

Table 9.3 summarizes the characteristics of different intervenors in terms of access, information, credibility, and resources. This table is illustrative rather than conclusive. It indicates general issues to be considered in choosing intervenors, but there is no substitute for analyzing specific cases to decide what intervenors are appropriate.

INTERVENORS AND INTERVENTIONS

How may the intervenors and interventions discussed in the two preceding sections be combined? Can the bewildering complex-

TABLE 9.3
Intervenor characteristics

INTERVENOR	INFORMATION ABOUT CONFLICT	ACCESS TO TARGETS	CREDIBILITY BASES	RESOURCES FOR INTERVENING
Representatives	High	Self Other representative Own party Interface	Perceived interests Past behavior	Personal skills Informal influence Information
Party leaders	Moderate	Own representative Own party Organizational context	Party interests Past party behavior	Authority within party Influence outside by party mobilization and importance
Party members	Low to moderate	Own representative Own party	Past history in party Interests in party	Party role Personal skills

Hierarchical superiors	Moderate to low	Both representatives Both parties Interface Organizational context Larger context	Past actions in organization Hierarchical interests at interface	Organizational authority and resources
Organizational third parties	Moderate to high	Both representatives Interface Organizational context	Expertise Interest in joint resolutions Past behavior	Information and perspective Organizational legitimacy
External allies	Low to moderate	Own representative Own party Larger context	Interests in party Past commitments	Support and resources
External third parties	Low to high	Both representatives Both parties Interface Organizational context Larger context	Expertise Outside reputation Common control by both sides	Information and access Professional skills External legitimacy

ity of intervenors, interventions, and interface elements and
dynamics be reduced?

Choosing Intervenors and Interventions

Table 9.4 presents choices of intervenors and interventions for
different targets. The conflict manager positions discussed in the
previous section are arrayed across the top of the table, and
intervention types and potential targets are listed vertically.
Within the cells of the resulting table, signs indicate the likelihood of success of intervenor-intervention combinations for different targets. When intervenor positions and characteristics
suggest they possess *both* access/credibility *and* required resources, a plus sign appears in the cell. When intervenors have
either access/credibility *or* resources, but not both, a question
mark appears. Finally, when intervenors have *neither* access/
credibility *nor* intervention resources, a minus sign appears.
Conflict managers who find minuses or question marks in their
cells are not automatically foreclosed from intervening. But the
table is intended to shift the burden of proof: Conflict managers
should examine carefully the fit between their access/credibility,
their intervention resources, and the situation if the table labels
their proposed combination with a minus or a question mark.

Examining Table 9.4 by columns allows us to compare different intervenors. The table suggests that intervenors in different
positions can differ widely in the likelihood of their success.
There are *no* intervenors who show pluses in all cells; hierarchical superiors and external third parties show no minus signs.
Organizational third parties and representatives show relatively
few minus signs but many question marks. Party leaders, external allies, and particularly party members, have limited potential
as intervenors. More importantly, however, *any* of these intervenors can intervene effectively if they choose carefully among
possible interventions and intervention targets. The Transit
Workers rank and file, for example, influenced events by encouraging their representatives to adopt tough bargaining tactics, even though their positions as party members offered restricted intervention access and resources.

Analyzing Table 9.4 by rows permits comparison across interventions. Interventions to influence representatives' interaction may be undertaken from many different positions, though it is easier to influence one's own representative than one of the other side. The table also suggests that fewer intervenors are likely to influence interface development dynamics by changing parties, interfaces, and contexts. Only hierarchical superiors, external third parties, and organizational third parties show positive signs for intervening in interface development. The shift to team management at the Riverview Chemical Works, for example, involved hierarchical superiors and organizational third parties, and probably could not have been undertaken without the formal and informal influence represented by that combination.

More generally, Table 9.4 suggests that no intervenors or interventions are universally appropriate. Hierarchical superiors—the most widely appropriate intervenors—often do not have the information needed to reframe perspectives, in part because of the very formal authority that allows them to reallocate resources or realign formal structures. The choice of intervention and intervenor requires attention to the characteristics of both in specific situations.

Intervening: Some Rules of Thumb

Conflict managers can focus on the immediate dynamics of representative interaction, or on the longer-term patterns of interface development, or on both. Given limited resources, most managers seek to influence one target at a time:

1. Choose target dynamics on the basis of (1) their centrality to conflict problems and (2) the risks and benefits of intervention.

For some problems the immediate patterns of representative behavior are central; for others the development of interface definition and organization is critical. When the interface is weakly defined or underorganized, for example, interventions that promote interface development may be prerequisite to changing representative interaction. Efforts to control conflict between the Old Guard and the New Hires at the South Side

TABLE 9.4
Choosing interventions and intervenors

INTERVENTIONS		INTERVENORS						
TYPE:	TARGET:	Representative	Party leader	Party member	Hierarchical superior	Organizational third party	External ally	External third party
A. Representative interaction								
Redirect behavior	Own representative	+	+	+	+	+	+	+
	Other representative	?	–	–	+	+	–	+
Reframe perceptions	Own representative	+	+	+	?	+	+	+
	Other representative	?	?	–	?	+	–	+
Reallocate resources	Own representative	+	+	?	+	?	+	?
	Other representative	?	–	–	+	?	?	?
B. Interface development								
Reframe perceptions	Own party	+	+	+	?	?	+	+
	Other party	?	?	–	?	?	–	+
	Interface	+	?	–	?	+	?	+
	Organizational context	?	+	–	+	+	?	+
	Larger context	–	–	–	?	?	?	?

Reallocate resources	Own party	?	+	?	+	?	+	+
	Other party	?	–	?	+	–	–	–
	Interface	?	–	?	+	–	?	+
	Organizational context	?	–	?	+	–	?	?
	Larger context	?	?	–	?	–	–	–
Realign structures	Own party	?	+	?	+	?	+	?
	Other party	?	–	?	+	–	–	–
	Interface	?	–	?	+	–	–	+
	Organizational context	?	–	?	+	–	?	?
	Larger context	?	?	–	?	–	–	–

+ = both access and resources
? = either access or resources
– = neither access nor resources

Hospital, for example, succeeded only after progress was made toward contextual and organizational constraints on escalatory dynamics between representatives. On the other hand, where there is minimal interface definition and organization, intervention can effectively change patterns of representatives' interaction directly. The interface definition and organization provided by the Transit Authority Quality of Work Committee set the stage for promoting new patterns of interaction between bargaining representatives. The choice between interface development and interaction dynamics as the intervention target depends in part on their contributions to problems.

The risks and benefits of the two are quite different. Interrupting patterns of representatives' interaction can produce rapid changes at low cost. The Transit Authority workshop dramatically improved the representatives' relations and negotiations for small investments of time and resources. Ineffective interventions in representatives' relations can waste resources, promote representatives' resistance to future change, or even deteriorate relations. The collapse of the consultants' efforts to change behavior and perspectives in meetings between Laboratory Old Guard and New Hires, for example, made things worse instead of better.

Intervention in interface development, in contrast, can produce changes in party, context, or interface that promote long-term improvements with little need for continuing attention. Changed norms for bargaining and mutual recognition of strength improved labor-management relations at the Transit Authority. The risks of intervening in interface development include slow impacts on immediate events and comparatively high costs. Changing organizational policy on minorities in the South Side Hospital involved major organizational changes without immediately visible impacts on the warfare between Old Guard and New Hires.

Target dynamics are not mutually exclusive. Interventions focused at one level sometimes have immediate consequences at another. Changes in perceptions, communications, and tactics at the Transit Authority workshop were closely linked to changes in the climate and informal norms of the interface. Interventions at one level may interact with other levels over time. Relaxing Community Services Administration reporting requirements for the Ghetto Development Corporation encouraged more open dialogue and debate in subsequent meetings. But resource constraints often press conflict managers to focus on change at one level of analysis, and the choice of level should encourage the most impact for the least risk.

Once the target dynamic has been chosen, conflict managers must choose among possible intervenors and interventions. If the initial conflict manager does not have the qualities needed for successful intervention, teams of intervenors may be created:

2. Combine intervenors to develop access, credibility, and resources appropriate to target dynamics and interventions.

As suggested in Table 9.4, interface development and representatives' interaction may require different constellations of intervenors' resources, access, and credibility. Representatives can influence their parties and their own behavior, but altering cycles of behavior at the interface may require combinations of representatives or third party intervenors. Different interface forms may require different intervenor attributes: "integrators" between departments are more effective if they have task expertise respected by both sides (Lawrence and Lorsch, 1967); mediators between powerful officials and community members are more effective if they are independent of the government hierarchy (Gillers, 1980b); third parties at cultural interfaces have more credibility if they combine elements of both cultures (Alderfer et al., 1980). Combining intervenors for expanded credibility and resources may be vital to effective intervention. At Riverview Chemical Works, external consultants, department managers, and internal consultants were all involved in interface meetings that improved information exchange and problem-solving. The organizational restructuring of team management involved the Assistant Works Manager, internal consultants, and a variety of department representatives in planning and implementing activity, and so used multiple credibilities and resources.

In some situations combinations of intervenors challenge each other. Old Guard questions about personal and institutional discrimination in the South Side Hospital Laboratory would have been muted without support from regulatory agencies and the union. As these intervenors negotiated with each other, they created constraints for resolving disputes within the Laboratory: Both Old Guard and New Hires, for example, recognized limits imposed by agreements between corporation and management regulatory agencies.

Third party intervenor combinations often display "parallel processes," in which events and feelings within third parties mirror dynamics at the itnerface (Alderfer et al., forthcoming). Intervenors who successfully manage those parallel processes can be more effective at the interface conflict management; intervenors who do not cope with parallel processes often repeat and reinforce the problems they seek to solve. The external consultants to the South Side Hospital, for example, recognized belatedly the importance of their own cultural homogeneity but found increased diversity difficult to manage—and so undercut their own credibility and effectiveness.

Limitations on resources or on single intervention effectiveness can encourage combining interventions:

3. Combine interventions simultaneously or in sequence to fit the resources of intervenors and the demands of the situation.

Interventions can be combined in a simultaneous attack on multiple aspects of the problem, or in a series of related efforts that build incrementally on previous actions. *Sequential* combinations are appropriate when issues are not urgent (so conflict managers can afford gradual solutions), when problems are poorly understood (so conflict managers do not know what interventions are appropriate), or when resources are not available (so conflict managers are constrained to piecemeal solutions). The sequential attack on Production-Maintenance problems at the Riverview Chemical Works is a case in point: The sequence of interventions included meetings between Production and Maintenance managers, meetings between operators and mechanics, widespread participation in planning for team management, and eventual implementation of the new organization structure. The sequence first altered the dynamics of representatives' interaction, and then changed the development of the interface. New patterns of interaction among representatives provided the base for participatory planning to realign organizational structures.

Simultaneous combinations of interventions may be necessary when waiting is costly (so conflict managers cannot afford experimental initial steps), or when diagnosis suggests that piecemeal intervention will not be effective. At complex interfaces, like the Laboratory in the South Side Hospital for example, incremental interventions can exacerbate problems by failing to deal with enough aspects of the situation to be credible. The simultaneous combination of organizationwide changes to end institutional discrimination, active upper management presence in the Laboratory, and joint definition of new performance standards and appraisal procedures, all contributed to reducing conflict between the Old Guard and the New Hires eventually. But they changed *both* the patterns of representative interaction *and* the characteristics of the interface before relations improved.

Table 9.2 implies that different intervention combinations are appropriate to different dynamics. Interrupting interaction dynamics may require redirecting behavior, reframing perspectives, and reallocating resources; redefining and reorganizing interfaces may involve reframing perceptions, reallocating resources, and realigning structures of parties, contextual forces, and the interface. The point to be emphasized is: Combinations of interventions are often needed, either together or over time.

Finally, time and its effects are an important aspect of intervening into self-reinforcing dynamics:

4. Use the self-reinforcing quality of conflict dynamics to (1) interrupt patterns of representative interaction, (2) redefine and reorganize interface constraints, and (3) recalibrate interdependent representative interactions and interface developments.

Conflict dynamics tend to be self-reinforcing. This quality has two implications for intervention. On the one hand, self-reinforcing cycles often resist change: Even the most skilled interventions can be cancelled out by repetitive cycles of activity. Self-reinforcing cycles can produce forces to countervail change.

The Old Guard and the New Hires at the South Side Hospital Laboratory, for example, rapidly entangled the external consultants in their conflict dynamics, and so wiped out initially successful steps toward diagnosis of Laboratory problems. On the other hand, self-reinforcing cycles are only as strong as their weakest link. The right change at the right time can become part of the cycle, and self-reinforcement will elaborate the change. Recognition by both Transit Authority bargaining committees that their opponents had legitimate interests (instead of being malevolent fanatics committed to total war) paved the way for agreement on many issues, and those agreements set the stage for further cooperation. The changes themselves can become self-reinforcing, and rapidly alter conflict problems.

Careful intervenors can sometimes discern "cornerstones" of conflict whose removal or reorientation will have catalytic effects. Critical changes in representatives' perception, communication, or action can dramatically interrupt patterns of representative interaction. Interventions that reshape perspectives, resource allocations, or underlying structures can drastically reshape interface definition or organization. Altering the linkage between interface development and representative interaction may set off constructive self-reinforcing changes in both. The Quality of Work Committee at the Transit Authority was at once a more organized interface and a new pattern of labor-management interaction, and it catalyzed future changes at both levels. The self-reinforcing aspects of conflict dynamics can be utilized to produce major changes with small interventions.

Figure 9.1 integrates the rules of thumb suggested in this section into the general process of conflict management at organizational interfaces. The diagnostic phase of the process (described in general in Chapter 2 and in specific forms in Chapters 4, 5, 6, 7, and 8) emphasizes understanding interface elements and dynamics. The planning phase combines choosing to intervene (described in Chapter 3) with choosing target dynamics, combining intervenors, combining interventions, and utilizing conflict dynamics (discussed in this section). The intervention phase employs intervention strategies (discussed in general in Chapter 3 and in specific applications in Chapters 4, 5, 6, 7, and 8) to influence representatives' interactions or interface development. The outcomes of interventions and continuing interface events feed back to influence interface elements and intervention planning. Conflict management does not end, even though specific issues may be resolved.

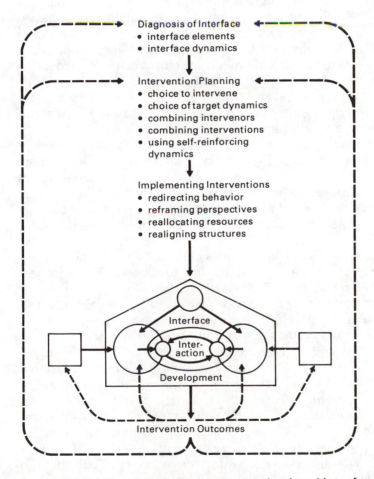

Fig. 9.1. *Conflict management at organizational interfaces.*

A FINAL NOTE

This chapter focuses on interventions, intervenors, and their combinations for managing conflict at organizational interfaces. The chapter began with a review of interventions and intervenors involved in the cases discussed in preceding chapters.

Interventions can alter the dynamics of representatives' interaction or redefine and reorganize interfaces. Interventions to redirect behavior, to reframe perspectives, or to reallocate resources can be employed to interrupt cycles of representative interaction. Interventions to reframe perspectives, to reallocate resources, or to realign underlying structures can be employed to alter the interplay of parties, context, and interface. These interventions vary in target and time of impact, in resource requirements, and in advantages and disadvantages, and they can be tailored to fit specific situations.

Intervenors come in several forms. Representatives, party leaders and members, organizational superiors or third parties, and allies or third parties from the external context can all intervene in interface conflict problems. Their effectiveness depends on their credibility and access to relevant elements, and on their skills, information, resources, and power for implementing different interventions.

Interventions and intervenors are often linked together, but not all combinations are equally likely to succeed. The final section of the chapter proposes rules of thumb for choosing target dynamics, combining intervenors, combining interventions, and making use of self-reinforcing dynamics at interfaces.

This book's focus on interfaces and conflict assumes that conflict problems at many different interfaces may be understood and managed on the basis of a simple integrative framework. The analysis brings together diverse lines of investigation—departmental relations, power inequalities, cross-cultural relations, interorganizational networks—that are not often joined. Some readers may not accept these claims for similarity across interfaces and organizations; or they may regard the differences between interfaces as more important than the similarities. Readers must judge for themselves whether this analysis is intellectually persuasive or pragmatically useful.

But organizational interfaces and the conflict problems within them will be an important part of our future. Technical specialization, power inequalities, cultural diversity, and organizational interdependence are continuing—often expanding—realities of life in complex societies. Managing differences creatively at the points where social units come together will continue to pose challenges. Inventors of innovative and effective responses to these challenges will be critical assets to their organizations—and to the larger societies in which they live.

References

Ackoff, R. *Redesigning the Future: A Systems Approach to Societal Problems.* New York: Wiley, 1974.

Adams, S. The structure and dynamics of behavior in organizational boundary roles. In M. Dunnette, *Handbook of Industrial and Organizational Psychology.* Chicago: Rand McNally, 1976, 1175–1199.

Aiken, M., and J. Hage. The organic organization and innovation. *Sociology* 5, 1971, 63–82.

Alderfer, C.P. Boundary relations and organizational diagnosis. In H. Meltzer and F.R. Wickert, *Humanizing Organizational Behavior.* Springfield, IL: Thomas, 1976.

Alderfer, C.P. Improving organizational communication through long-term intergroup intervention. *Journal of Applied Behavioral Science* 13, 1977a, 193–210.

Alderfer, C.P. Group and intergroup relations. In J.R. Hackman and J.L. Suttle, *Improving Life at Work: Behavioral Science Approaches to Organizational Change.* Santa Monica, CA: Goodyear, 1977b.

Alderfer, C.P. Consulting to underbounded systems. In C.P. Alderfer and C. Cooper, *Advances in Experiential Social Process,* Vol. 2. New York: Wiley, 1979.

Alderfer, C.P., C.J. Alderfer, L. Tucker, and R. Tucker. Diagnosing race relations in management. *Journal of Applied Behavioral Science* 16:2, 1980, 135–166.

Alderfer, C.P., and L.D. Brown. *Learning from Changing: Organizational Diagnosis and Development.* Beverly Hills, CA: Sage, 1975.

Alderfer, C.P., L.D. Brown, R.E. Kaplan, and K.K. Smith. *Group Relations and Organizational Diagnosis.* London: Wiley Interscience. Forthcoming.

Aldrich, H.E. *Organizations and Environments.* Englewood Cliffs, NJ: Prentice-Hall, 1979.

Aldrich, H., and J. Pfeffer. Environments of organizations. *Annual Review of Sociology* 2, 1976, 79–106.

Allport, G. *The Nature of Prejudice.* Reading, MA: Addison-Wesley, 1954.

Amir, Y. Contact hypothesis in ethnic relations. *Psychological Bulletin* 71:5, 1969, 319–342.

Amir, Y. The role of intergroup contact in change of prejudice and ethnic relations. In P. Katz, *Toward the Elimination of Racism.* New York: Pergamon Press, 1976, 245–308.

Argyris, C., and D. Schon. *Organizational Learning.* Reading, MA: Addison-Wesley, 1978.

Aronson, E. *The Jigsaw Classroom.* Beverly Hills, CA: Sage, 1978.

Ashmore, R.D., and F.K. DelBoca. Psychological approaches to understanding intergroup conflict. In P. Katz, *Toward the Elimination of Racism.* New York: Pergamon Press, 1976, 73–124.

Baker, F., and G. O'Brien. Intersystems relations and coordination of human service organizations. *American Journal of Public Health* 61, 1971, 130–137.

Bateson, G., D.D. Jackson, J. Haley, and J. Weakland. Toward a theory of schizophrenia. *Behavioral Science* 1, 1956, 251–264.

Beckhard, R. The confrontation meeting. *Harvard Business Review* 45, 1967, 149–155.

Beer, M. *Organizational Change and Development: A Systems View.* Santa Monica, CA: Goodyear, 1980.

Benson, J.K. The interorganizational network as a political economy. *Administrative Science Quarterly* 10, 1975, 229–249.

Berlew, D.A. Leadership and organizational excitement. In D.A. Kolb, I. Rubin, and J. McIntyre, *Organizational Psychology: A Book of Readings* (3rd ed.). Englewood Cliffs, NJ: Prentice-Hall, 1980.

Bion, W. *Experiences in Groups.* New York: Basic Books, 1959.

Birnbaum, M. The clarification group. In K.D. Benne, L. Bradford, J. Gibb, and R. Lippitt, *The Laboratory Method of Changing and Learning.* Palo Alto, CA: Science and Behavior Books, 1975, 341–364.

Blake, R., and J.S. Mouton. Reactions to intergroup competition under win-lose conditions. *Management Science* 4, 1961.

Blake, R.R., H.A. Shepard, and J.S. Mouton. *Managing Intergroup Conflict in Industry.* Ann Arbor: Foundation for Research on Human Behavior, 1964.

Blau, P.M. Parameters of social structure. *American Sociological Review* 39, 1974, 615–635.

Bowers, D., J.L. Franklin, and P.A. Pecorella. Matching problems, precursors, and interventions in OD: a systemic approach. *Journal of Applied Behavioral Science* 11, 1977, 391–409.

Braverman, H. *Labor and Monopoly Capitalism.* New York: Monthly Review Press, 1974.

Brown, L.D. Toward a theory of power and intergroup relations. In C.A. Cooper and C.P. Alderfer, *Advances in Experimental Social Processes,* Vol. 1. London: Wiley, 1978.

Brown, L.D. Managing conflict among groups. In D.A. Kolb, I.M. Rubin, and J.M. McIntyre, *Organizational Psychology: A Book of Readings.* Englewood Cliffs, NJ: Prentice-Hall, 1979.

Brown, L.D. Planned change in underorganized systems. In T.G. Cummings, *Systems Theory of Organization Development.* New York: Wiley, 1980.

Brown, L.D., J.D. Aram, and D.J. Bachner. Interorganizational information-sharing: a successful intervention that failed. *Journal of Applied Behavioral Science* 10, 1974, 533–554.

Burns, T., and G.M. Stalker. *The Management of Innovation.* London: Tavistock, 1961.

Callahan, R., and P. Salipante. Boundary spanning units: organizational implications for the management of innovation. *Human Resources Management* 2:18, 1979, 26–31.

Chalmers, W.E. *Racial Negotiations: Potentials and Limitations.* Ann Arbor: Institute for Labor and Industrial Relations, 1974.

Chesler, M.A. Contemporary sociological theories of racism. In P. Katz, *Toward the Elimination of Racism.* New York: Pergamon Press, 1976, 21–71.

Chesler, M., and J.E. Lohman. Changing schools through student advocacy. In R.A. Schmuck and M.B. Miles, *OD in Schools.* Palo Alto, CA: National Press, 1971, 185–211.

Child, J. Organizational structures, environment, and performance: the role of strategic choice. *Sociology* 6, 1972, 1–22.

Chin, R. The utility of system models and developmental models for practitioners. In W. Bennis, K. Benne, and R. Chin, *The Planning of Change* (1st ed.). New York: Holt, Rinehart and Winston, 1961, 201–214.

Clark, K.B., and M.P. Clark. The emergence of racial identification and preference in negro children. Reprinted in E.E. Maccoby, T.M. Newcomb, and E.L. Hartley, *Readings in Social Psychology* (3rd ed.). New York: Henry Holt, 1958.

Clegg, S. *The Theory of Power and Organization.* London: Routledge and Kegan Paul, 1979.

Coch, L., and J.R.P. French. Overcoming resistance to change. *Human Relations* 1, 1948, 512–532.

Collins, R.A. *Conflict Sociology.* New York: Academic Press, 1975.

Coser, L. *The Functions of Social Conflict.* New York: Free Press, 1956.

Crowfoot, J.E., and M.A. Chesler. Contemporary perspectives on planned social change: a comparison. *Journal of Applied Behavioral Science* 10, 1974, 278–303.

Davis, S., and P. Lawrence. *Matrix.* Reading, MA: Addison-Wesley, 1977.

Deutsch, M. *The Resolution of Conflict.* New Haven: Yale University Press, 1973.

Dill, W. Environment as an influence on managerial autonomy. *Administrative Science Quarterly* 2, 1958, 409–443.

Doob, L.W. *Resolving Conflict in Africa: The Fermeda Experiment.* New Haven: Yale University Press, 1970.

Doob, L.W., and W.J. Foltz. The Belfast workshop: an application of group techniques to a destructive conflict. *Journal of Conflict Resolution* 17, 1973, 489–512.

Doob, L.W., and W.J. Foltz. The impact of a workshop on grassroots leaders in Belfast. *Journal of Conflict Resolution* 18, 1974, 237–256.

Edwards, R. *Contested Terrain: The Transformation of the Workplace in the Twentieth Century.* New York: Basic Books, 1979.

Eiseman, J.W. Reconciling incompatible positions. *Journal of Applied Behavioral Science* 14, 1978, 133–150.

Emery, F., and E. Trist. The causal texture of organizational environments. *Human Relations* 18, 1965, 21–32.

Evan, W. The organization set: toward a theory of interorganizational relations. In J.D. Thompson, *Approaches to Organizational Design.* Pittsburgh: University of Pittsburgh Press, 1966.

Filley, A.C. *Interpersonal Conflict Resolution.* Glenview, IL: Scott, Foresman, 1975.

Fisher, R. Fractionating Conflict. *Daedalus,* (summer) 1964, 920–941.

Frank, A.G. *Dependent Accumulation and Underdevelopment.* New York: Monthly Review Press, 1979.

Friedlander, F., and S. Greenburg. The effect of job attitudes, training, and organization climate upon performance of the hard-core unemployed. *Journal of Applied Psychology* 55, 1971, 287–295.

Galbraith, J. *Designing Complex Organizations.* Reading, MA: Addison-Wesley, 1973.

Galbraith, J. *Organizational Design.* Reading, MA: Addison-Wesley, 1977.

Gamson, W. *The Strategy of Social Protest.* Homewood, IL: Dorsey, 1975.

Geertz, C. *The Interpretation of Culture.* New York: Basic Books, 1973.

Gillers, S. Dispute resolution in prison: the California experience. In R.B. Goldman, *Roundtable Justice.* Boulder, CO: Westview, 1980a, 21–38.

Gillers, S. New faces in the neighborhood: mediating the Forest Hills housing dispute. In R.B. Goldman, *Roundtable Justice.* Boulder, CO: Westview, 1980b, 59–86.

Glasl, F.F. The process of escalation of conflicts and roles of third parties. Paper presented to the International Conference on Industrial Relations and Conflict Management, Nijenrode, The Netherlands, June 1980.

Goldman, R.B. *Roundtable Justice: Case Studies in Conflict Resolution.* Boulder, CO: Westview, 1980.

Gricar, B., and L.D. Brown. Conflict, power, and organization in a changing community. *Human Relations,* 1981.

Guest, R. Quality of work life: learning from Tarrytown. *Harvard Business Review,* (July–August) 1979, 76–87.

Hall, E.T. *The Silent Language.* Greenwich, CT: Fawcett, 1959.

Hecksher, C. Worker participation and management control. *Journal of Social Reconstruction* 1:1, 1980, 77–102.

Heenan, D.A., and H.V. Perlmutter. *Multinational Organization Development.* Reading, MA: Addison-Wesley, 1979.

Heginbotham, S.J. *Cultures in Conflict: The Four Faces of Indian Bureaucracy.* New York: Columbia University Press, 1975.

Hickson, D.J., C.R. Hinings, C.R.A. Lee, R.E. Schneck, and J.M. Pennings. A strategic contingencies theory of intraorganizational power. *Administrative Science Quarterly* 16, 1971, 22–44.

Hirsch, P.M. Organizational effectiveness and the institutional environment. *Administrative Science Quarterly* 20, 1975, 327–344.

Janis, I. *Victims of Groupthink.* Boston: Houghton Mifflin, 1972.

Jones, E.W. What it's like to be a black manager. *Harvard Business Review,* (July–August) 1973, 108–116.

Kahn, R.L., D.M. Wolfe, R.P. Quinn, J.D. Snoek, and R.A. Rosenthal. *Organizational Stress.* New York: Wiley, 1964.

Kanter, R.M. Women in organizations: sex roles, group dynamics, and change strategies. In A. Sargent, *Beyond Sex Roles.* St. Paul: West, 1975.

Kanter, R.M. *Men and Women of the Corporation.* New York: Basic Books, 1976.

Kanter, R.M. Power failure in management circuits. *Harvard Business Review,* 1979, 65–75.

Katz, D., and R.L. Kahn. *The Social Psychology of Organizations* (2nd ed.). New York: Wiley, 1978.

Katz, R. Group longevity performance and the management of intragroup conflict. Paper presented to the International Conference on Industrial Relations and Conflict Management, Nijenrode, The Netherlands, June 1980.

Kipnis, D. Does power corrupt? *Journal of Personality and Social Psychology* 24:1, 1972, 33–41.

Klein, E.B., C.S. Thomas, and E.C. Bellis. When warring groups meet: the use of a group approach in police-black community relations. *Social Psychiatry* 6, 1971, 93–99.

Knowles, L.L., and K. Prewitt. *Institutional Racism in America.* Englewood Cliffs, NJ: Prentice-Hall, 1969.

Kochan, T.A., and L. Dyer. A model of organizational change in the context of union-management relations. *Journal of Applied Behavioral Science* 12:1, 1976, 59–78.

Kochan, T.A., G.P. Huber, and L.L. Cummings. Determinants of intraorganizational conflict in collective bargaining in the public sector. *Administrative Science Quarterly* 20:1, 1975, 10–23.

Kotter, J.P. Managing external dependence. *Academy of Management Review* 4, 1979, 87–92.

Laue, J., and G. Cormick. The ethics of intervention in community disputes. In G. Bermant, H.C. Kelman, and D.P. Warwick, *The Ethics of Social Intervention.* New York: Halsted Press, 1978, 205–244.

Laumann, E.P., J. Galaskiewicz, and P.V. Marsden. Community structure as inter-organizational linkages. *Annual Review of Sociology* 4, 1978, 455–484.

Lawler, E.E. *Pay and Organization Development.* Reading, MA: Addison-Wesley, 1980.

Lawrence, P.R., and J.W. Lorsch. *Organization and Environment.* Cambridge, MA: Harvard Business School, 1967.

Levi, A.M., and A. Benjamin. Focus and flexibility in a model of conflict resolution. *Journal of Conflict Resolution* 11, 1977, 405–425.

Lee, Hak-Chong. Lordstown plant of General Motors. Cambridge, MA: Harvard Business School Case Services, 1974.

Lindskold, S., and M.G. Collins. Inducing cooperation by groups and individuals: apply Osgood's GRIT strategy. *Journal of Conflict Resolution* 22, 1978, 679–690.

Lodge, G. *The New American Ideology.* New York: Knopf, 1975.

Lukes, S. *Power: A Radical View.* London: Macmillan, 1974.

Lundstedt, S. Personality determinants and assessment. *Journal of Social Issues,* (July) 1963, 3.

March, J. The business firm as a political coalition. *Journal of Politics* 24, 1962, 662–678.

McClelland, D. *Power: The Inner Experience.* New York: Irvington, 1975.

Mechanic, D. Sources of power of lower participants in complex organizations. *Administrative Science Quarterly* 7, 1962, 349–364.

Miles, R.E., C.C. Snow, A.D. Meyer, and H.J. Coleman. Organizational strategy, structure, and process. *Academy of Management Review,* (July) 1978, 546–562.

Miles, R.H. *Macro-Organizational Behavior.* Santa Monica, CA: Goodyear, 1980.

Miller, E., and A.K. Rice. *Systems of Organization.* London: Tavistock, 1967.

Mintzberg, H. *The Structuring of Organizations.* Englewood Cliffs, NJ: Prentice-Hall, 1979.

Mulder, M. Power distance reduction in practice. In G. Hofsteede and M.S. Kassem, *European Contributions to Organization Theory.* Assen/Amsterdam: Von Gorcum, 1976.

Nord, W. Developments in the study of power. In W. Nord, *Concepts and Controversy in Organizational Behavior* (2nd ed.). Pacific Palisades, CA: Goodyear, 1976, 437–450.

Osgood, C.E. *Graduated Reciprocation in Tension Reduction: A Key to Initiative in Foreign Policy.* Urbana, IL: Institute for Communications Research, University of Illinois, 1960.

Paige, J.M. *Agrarian Revolution.* New York: Free Press, 1975.

Perrow, C. Departmental power and perspective in industrial firms. In M. Zald, *Power in Organizations.* Nashville: Vanderbilt University Press, 1970, 58–59.

Pfeffer, J. *Organizational Design.* Northbrook, IL: AHM Publishing, 1978.

Pfeffer, J., and H. Leblebici. Executive recruitment and the development of interfirm organizations. *Administrative Science Quarterly* 18, 1973, 449–461.

Pfeffer, J., and P. Nowak. Joint ventures and interorganizational dependence. *Administrative Science Quarterly* 21, 1976, 398–418.

Pfeffer, J., and G. Salancik. *The External Control of Organizations.* Harper & Row, 1978.

Pondy, L.R. Organizational conflict: concepts and models. *Administrative Science Quarterly* 12:2, 1967, 296–320.

Robbins, S.P. *Managing Organizational Conflict: A Non-Traditional Approach.* Englewood Cliffs, NJ: Prentice-Hall, 1974.

Rosenhan, D.L. On being sane in insane places. *Science* 179, 1973, 250–258.

Rubin, J.Z., and B.R. Brown. *The Social Psychology of Bargaining and Negotiation.* New York: Academic Press, 1975.

Schein, E. *Organizational Psychology* (2nd ed.). Englewood Cliffs, NJ: Prentice-Hall, 1970.

Schelling, T.C. *The Strategy of Conflict.* London: Oxford University Press, 1960.

Schmidt, S., and T. Kochan. Conflict: toward conceptual clarity. *Administrative Science Quarterly* 17, 1972, 359–370.

Schon, D. *Beyond the Stable State.* New York: Random House, 1971.

Scott, W.G. *The Management of Conflict: Appeals Systems in Organizations.* Homewood, IL: Irwin-Dorsey, 1965.

Selznick, P. *TVA and the Grass Roots.* Berkeley, CA: University of California, 1949.

Sherif, M. Superordinate goals in the reduction of intergroup conflict. *American Journal of Sociology* 63, 1958, 349–358.

Sherif, M. *In Common Predicament.* Boston: Houghton Mifflin, 1966.

Sherwood, J.C., and J.C. Glidewell. Planned renegotiation: a norm-setting OD intervention. In W.G. Bennis, D.E. Berlew, E.H. Schein, and F.I. Steele, *Interpersonal Dynamics* (3rd ed.). Homewood, IL: Dorsey, 1973.

Smith, K.K. Behavioral consequences of hierarchical structure. Unpublished dissertation at Yale University, 1974.

Steele, F.I. *Physical Settings and Organizational Development.* Reading, MA: Addison-Wesley, 1973.

Stouffer, S.A., A.A. Lumsdaine, M.H. Lumsdaine, R. Williams, M.B. Smith, I.L. Janis, S.A. Star, and L.S. Cottrell. *The American Soldier,* Vol. 2. Princeton, NJ: Princeton University Press, 1949.

Strauss, G. Tactics of the lateral relationship: the purchasing agent. *Administrative Science Quarterly* 7, 1962, 161–186.

Sykes, A.J.M. A study in changing attitudes and stereotypes of industrial workers. In A.H. Rubenstein and C.J. Haberstroh, *Some Theories of Organization.* Homewood, IL: Irwin-Dorsey, 1966.

Tandon, R., and L.D. Brown. Organizational building for rural development: an experiment in India. *Journal of Applied Behavioral Science* 17:2, 1981, 172–189.

Terhune, K.W. The effects of personality in cooperation and conflict. In P. Swingle, *The Structure of Conflict.* New York: Academic Press, 1970.

Terreberry, S. The evolution of organizational environments. *Administrative Science Quarterly* 12, 1968, 590–613.

Thomas, J.M., and W.G. Bennis. *Management of Change and Conflict.* Harmondsworth, Middlesex: Penguin, 1972.

Thomas, K. Conflict and conflict management. In M.D. Dunnette, *Handbook of Industrial and Organizational Psychology.* Chicago: Rand McNally, 1976.

Thompson, J. *Organizations in Action.* New York: McGraw-Hill, 1967.

Tilly, C. *From Mobilization to Revolution.* Reading, MA: Addison-Wesley, 1978.

Triandis, H.C., and T.S. Malpass. Studies of black and white interaction in job settings. *Journal of Applied Social Psychology* 1, 1971, 101–117.

Trist, E. Organizational ecology. *Australian Journal of Management* 5, 1977, 161–175.

Trist, E. New directions of hope. *Human Futures* 2:3, 1979, 175–186.

Trist, E.L., G.W. Higgin, H. Murray, and A.B. Pollock. *Organizational Choice.* London: Tavistock, 1963.

Walton, R.E. Third party roles in interdepartmental conflict. *Industrial Relations* 7, 1967, 29–43.

Walton, R.E. *Interpersonal Peacemaking: Confrontations and Third Party Consultation.* Reading, MA: Addison-Wesley, 1969.

Walton, R.E., and J.M. Dutton. The management of interdepartmental conflict: a model and a review. *Administrative Science Quarterly* 14, 1969, 73–78.

Walton, R.E., J.M. Dutton, and H.G. Fitch. A study of conflict in the process, structure, and attitudes of lateral relationships. In C. Haberstroh and A. Rubenstein, *Some Theories of Organization.* Homewood, IL: Irwin, 1966.

Walton, R.E., and R.B. McKersie. *A Behavioral Theory of Labor Negotiations.* New York: McGraw-Hill, 1965.

Walton, R.E., and L. Schlesinger. Plant-level innovations: after a decade of experience. *Harvard Business Review,* (July/August) 1978, 88–98.

Wanous, J.P. *Organizational Entry: Recruitment, Selection, and Socialization of Newcomers.* Reading, MA: Addison-Wesley, 1980.

Warwick, D. *A Theory of Public Bureaucracy.* Cambridge, MA: Harvard University Press, 1975.

Watzlawick, P., J.H. Beavin, and D.D. Jackson. *Pragmatics of Human Communication: A Study of Interaction Patterns, Pathologies and Paradoxes.* New York: Norton, 1967.

Weick, K. Educational organizations as loosely coupled systems. *Administrative Science Quarterly* 21, 1976, 1–19.

Weissbach, T.A. Laboratory controlled studies of change of racial attitudes. In P. Katz, *Toward the Elimination of Racism.* New York: Pergamon Press, 1976, 157.

Young, O. *The Intermediaries: Third Parties in International Crises.* Princeton, NJ: Princeton University Press, 1967.

Zaltman, G., and R.B. Duncan. *Strategies for Planned Change.* New York: Wiley, 1977.

Zimbardo, P., C. Haney, W. Banks, and D. Jaffe. A Pirandellian prison: the mind is a formidable jailer. *New York Times Magazine* (April 8), 1973, 38–60.

Zwerdling, D. *Workplace Democracy.* New York: Harper & Row, 1980.

Name Index

Subject Index